EAST ANGLIAN ARCHAEOLOGY

Fen House

A Room, which one rude beam divides,
And naked rafters form the sloping sides;
Where the vile hands that bind the thatch are seen.
And lath and mud are all that lie between;
Save one dull pane, that, coarsely patched, gives way,
to the rude tempest, yet excludes the day.

... Ah! Hapless they who still remain,
Who still remain to hear the ocean roar,
Whose greedy waves devour the lessening shore,
Till some fierce tide, with more imperious sway,
Sweeps the low hut and all it holds away,
When the sad tenant weeps from door to door,
And begs protection from the poor.

(extracts from *The Village, Book I,* by George Crabbe, 1783)

Extraordinary Inundations of the Sea: Excavations at Market Mews, Wisbech, Cambridgeshire

by Mark Hinman and
Elizabeth Popescu

with contributions
by Steven Ashley, Nina Crummy, Julie Curl,
Chris Faine, Carole Fletcher, Charly French,
Lesley Hoyland, John Kington, Alison Locker,
Karen Milek, Catherine Mortimer, Adrian
Popescu, Andrew Rogerson, Duncan Schlee, Paul
Spoerry and Patricia E.J. Wiltshire

illustrations by
Jon Cane, Carlos Silva and Sue Holden

East Anglian Archaeology
Report No.142, 2012

Oxford Archaeology East

EAST ANGLIAN ARCHAEOLOGY
REPORT NO.142

Published by
Oxford Archaeology East
15 Trafalgar Way
Bar Hill
Cambridgeshire CB23 8SQ

in conjunction with
ALGAO East
www.algao.org.uk/cttees/regions

Set in Times New Roman by Jenny Glazebrook using Corel Ventura™
Printed by Henry Ling Ltd, The Dorset Press

East Anglian Archaeology was established in 1975 by the Scole Committee for Archaeology in
East Anglia. The scope of the series expanded to include all six eastern counties and
responsibility for publication was transferred in 2002 to the Association of Local Government
Archaeological Officers, East of England (ALGAO East).

For details of *East Anglian Archaeology*, see last page

Cover:
Image from *A true report of certaine wonderfull ouerflowings of waters, now lately in
Summerset-shire, Norfolke, and other places in England ...*, 1607 (Copyright British Library
Board. All Rights Reserved. Shelfmark 1103.e.58)

Contents

List of Plates

List of Figures

List of Tables

List of Contributors

Steven Ashley
Norfolk Landscape Archaeology

Jon Cane
Freelance illustrator

Nina Crummy
Freelance Small Finds specialist

Julie Curl
Faunal remains specialist, NAU Archaeology

Chris Faine
Finds Supervisor/Specialist, Oxford Archaeology East

Carole Fletcher
Finds Supervisor/Specialist, Oxford Archaeology East

Charly French
Dept of Archaeology, University of Cambridge

Mark Hinman
Formerly Project Manager, Oxford Archaeology East

Sue Holden
Freelance illustrator

Lesley Hoyland
Formerly Cambridgeshire County Council

John Kington
Climatic Research Unit, University of East Anglia, Norwich

Alison Locker
Freelance fishbone specialist

Karen Milek
Dept of Archaeology, University of Cambridge

Catherine Mortimer
Archaeological Consultant

Adrian Popescu
Senior Assistant Keeper, Dept of Coins and Medals, Fitzwilliam Museum, Cambridge

Elizabeth Popescu
Post-Excavation and Publications Manager, Oxford Archaeology East

Andrew Rogerson
Norfolk Landscape Archaeology

Duncan Schlee
Project Manager, Dyfed Archaeology

Carlos Silva
Formerly illustrator, CAM ARC

Paul Spoerry
Regional Manager, Oxford Archaeology East

Patricia E.J. Wiltshire
Institute of Archaeology, University College London

Acknowledgements

The authors would like to thank Wisbech Retail Ltd/ Bilsdale Properties for providing the initial funding and support for this investigation and Garnett Netherwood Architects for commissioning the work. The project was instigated through the production of a Brief for an Archaeological Investigation produced by Louise Austin, Archaeological Development Control Officer of Cambridgeshire County Council. The fieldwork project was directed by Mark Hinman and managed by Ben Robinson and Paul Spoerry. Mark Hinman managed the initial post-excavation analysis of the site, while the latter stages including preparation for publication were managed by Elizabeth Popescu. Thanks are extended to the evaluation/excavation teams who showed such a high degree of commitment during fieldwork: Oscar Aldred, Spencer Cooper, Steven Membery, Steve Ouditt and Wendy Wilson. In addition, Laura Thornton and Issa De Waal are thanked for their assistance with the evaluation stage.

Thanks are extended to each of the contributing specialists and illustrators. In addition, thanks are offered to Celia Honeycombe (conservation), and Vernon Phillpot (preliminary animal and bird bone report). Karen Milek and Charly French gratefully acknowledge the assistance of Julie Boast, who made the thin sections, Alex Powers-Jones and Arlene Rosen, who identified the phytoliths, and Alan Clapham, who identified the charred organic remains.

The authors would also like to thank Sarah Poppy (Cambridgeshire Historic Environment Record) for supplying relevant data so promptly and efficiently, as well as Quinton Carroll for providing a draft of the Extensive Urban Survey for Wisbech. They are also indebted to Tom Lane (Archaeological Project Services),

James Rackham (Environmental Archaeological Consultancy), Peter Rowsome (Museum of London Archaeology Service) and Alex Smith (Oxford Archaeology South) for providing information on relevant sites prior to publication. Robert Bell, Assistant Curator at the Wisbech and Fenland Museum, kindly provided useful details of the town's maps and records. Thanks are also extended to Alan Vince and Quita Mould for information relating to metalworking and associated issues and to Ken Hamilton (Norfolk Landscape Archaeology) for various references relating to medieval Perth.

Finally, thanks are offered to Jenny Glazebrook (East Anglian Archaeology) for managing this volume so efficiently through the publication process.

Abbreviations

CHER	Cambridgeshire Historic Environment Record	HEDI	Sible Hedingham (Essex) Fine ware
Corp. Rec.	Corporation Records	LANG	Langerwehe stoneware
FH	Matthew Paris, *Flores Historiarum*	LINCS	Lincolnshire (possibly Toynton ware)
	(Luard 1890)	LMR	Late medieval reduced ware
MP, Ch Maj	Matthew Paris, *Monachi Sancti Albani*	LMT	Late Medieval Transitional ware
	Chronica majora (Luard 1872-83)	MEL	Medieval Ely ware
SF	Small Find	OLIVE	Spanish olive jar
		OSW	Orange Sandy ware (Glapthorn Kiln)
Pottery Fabrics		SCAR	Scarborough ware
BOND	Bourne D ware	SSHW	Sandy Shelly ware
CSTN	Cistercian ware	TUDB	Tudor Brown ware
DUTR	Dutch redware	TUDG	Tudor Green ware
EMW	Early Medieval ware	UGBB	Unglazed Grimston or Blackborough End ware
ESMIC	Essex Micaceous redware	UNK	Unknown
GRIM	Grimston ware		

Summary

This publication describes a relatively small scale excavation, the size of which belies its significance. Incredibly, this is the first properly documented archaeological excavation in the core of Wisbech — an historic town long suspected to have preserved interesting medieval deposits. It fills a gaping void in previous knowledge of the character and quality of the archaeological remains in the town and represents an important first step in redressing the regional imbalance in published medieval port sequences, such as those of King's Lynn and Great Yarmouth.

The excavation took place in 1996 at the junction of Market Mews and Little Church Street (TF 4630 0969) and was conducted by Cambridgeshire County Council's Archaeological Field Unit, CAM ARC (now Oxford Archaeology East). The site lies within the confines of the New Market, to the north of the Norman castle. An impressive sequence of deeply stratified medieval to early post-medieval deposits was revealed, demonstrating at

least thirteen building phases, the earliest of which dates to the 13th century. One structure contained evidence for *in-situ* metalworking during the mid 14th to mid 15th century. The buildings were each sealed by fine silts deposited during episodic flooding which can be broadly linked to documented climatic conditions of the period. Detailed recording was achieved through micromorphological analysis and the use of high resolution thin sections.

While the alternate sequence of occupation and flooding found at Wisbech is broadly comparable to deposits in other regional port towns, it is almost without parallel in terms of its completeness, depth and state of preservation. A wealth of organic remains and subtle features are present, of types that survive in very few other locations in East Anglia. The discovery of this important archaeological resource highlights the requirement for consideration of its future management.

Résumé

Cette publication décrit des fouilles importantes malgré leur taille relativement modeste. Aussi incroyable que cela puisse paraître, il s'agit de la première fouille archéologique convenablement documentée qui ait été menée dans le centre de Wisbech, ville historique dont on pensait depuis longtemps qu'elle contenait des dépôts médiévaux intéressants. Cette étude complète les connaissances concernant la nature et la qualité des vestiges archéologiques de la ville. Elle constitue une étape importante qui permet de compenser le déséquilibre régional dans la série de publications sur les ports médiévaux tels que King's Lynn et Great Yarmouth.

Les fouilles se sont déroulées en 1996 au carrefour de Market Mews et de Little Church Street (TF 4630 0969), sous la responsabilité du Cambridgeshire County Council Archaeological Field Unit, CAM ARC (actuellement Oxford Archaeology East). Le site se trouve dans les limites de New Market, au nord du château normand. Les fouilles ont révélé une succession impressionnante de dépôts correspondant à des strates bien définis comprises entre la période médiévale et le début de la période post-médiévale. Un minimum de treize phases de construction a été dégagé, la plus ancienne remontant au treizième siècle. L'une des structures contenait des preuves de travail du métal *in-situ* pendant une période comprise entre le milieu du quatorzième siècle et le milieu du quinzième. Chacun des bâtiments était enfermé dans des limons fins qui se sont déposés lors d'inondations épisodiques. Celles-étaient en général liées aux conditions climatiques de la période qui ont été documentées. Il a été possible d'obtenir des données détaillées grâce à une analyse micromorphologique et à l'utilisation de fines sections à haute résolution.

Tandis que l'autre succession d'occupations et d'inondations découvertes à Wisbech est très comparable aux dépôts présents dans d'autres villes portuaires régionales, le site de New Market est pour ainsi dire sans équivalent en termes d'exhaustivité, de profondeur et d'état de la préservation. On a ainsi découvert une grande quantité de vestiges organiques et d'éléments ténus correspondant à des types qui ont survécu dans très peu d'autres endroits de l'East Anglia. La découverte de ces importantes ressources archéologiques met en lumière la nécessité de prendre en compte la gestion future du site.

(Traduction: Didier Don)

Zusammenfassung

Diese Publikation beschreibt eine vergleichsweise kleine Ausgrabung, deren Bedeutung ihr Ausmaß jedoch bei weitem übersteigt. Bemerkenswerterweise ist dies die erste genau dokumentierte archäologische Grabung im Herzen von Wisbech, einer historischen Stadt, in der man schon lange interessante mittelalterliche Befunde vermutet hatte. Die Grabung füllt eine große Lücke im Wissen um die Beschaffenheit und Qualität der archäologischen Überreste in der Stadt. Darüber hinaus ist sie ein wichtiger erster Schritt zur Beseitigung des Ungleichgewichts, das beim veröffentlichten Material über die mittelalterlichen Hafenstädte der Region wie etwa King's Lynn und Great Yarmouth besteht.

Die 1996 an der Kreuzung von Market Mews und Little Church Street (TF 4630 0969) durchgeführte Ausgrabung wurde von CAM ARC (nunmehr Oxford Archaeology East) geleitet, der Feldabteilung für Archäologie des Cambridgeshire County Council. Das Grabungsgelände liegt innerhalb der Grenzen des New Market nördlich der normannischen Burg. Entdeckt wurde eine bemerkenswerte, mindestens dreizehn Bauphasen umfassende Schichtenfolge, die vom Mittelalter bis in die frühe Neuzeit reicht und bis ins 13. Jahrhundert zurückdatiert. Eine Struktur enthielt Hinweise auf Metallarbeiten, die von der Mitte des 14. bis zur Mitte des 15. Jahrhunderts anhielten. Die einzelnen Häuser waren von feinen Schluffablagerungen bedeckt, die auf sporadische Überschwemmungen zurückgingen und grob mit den dokumentierten klimatischen Verhältnissen der Zeit in Zusammenhang gebracht werden konnten. Durch mikromorphologische Analysen und die Verwendung hochauflösender Dünnschnitte war eine detaillierte Bestandsaufnahme möglich.

Die in Wisbech gefundene Wechselfolge von Besiedlung und Überschwemmungen deckt sich überwiegend mit den Schichten in anderen Hafenstädten der Region, hat jedoch, was ihre Vollständigkeit und Tiefe sowie ihren Erhaltungszustand angeht, kaum eine Parallele. Es gibt Befundtypen, die nur an sehr wenigen anderen Stellen in East Anglia erhalten sind, bestehend aus reichhaltigen organischen Überresten und einigen subtilen Merkmalen. Die Entdeckung dieser bedeutsamen archäologischen Ressource macht Überlegungen zu ihrem künftigen Management nötig.

(Übersetzung: Gerlinde Krug)

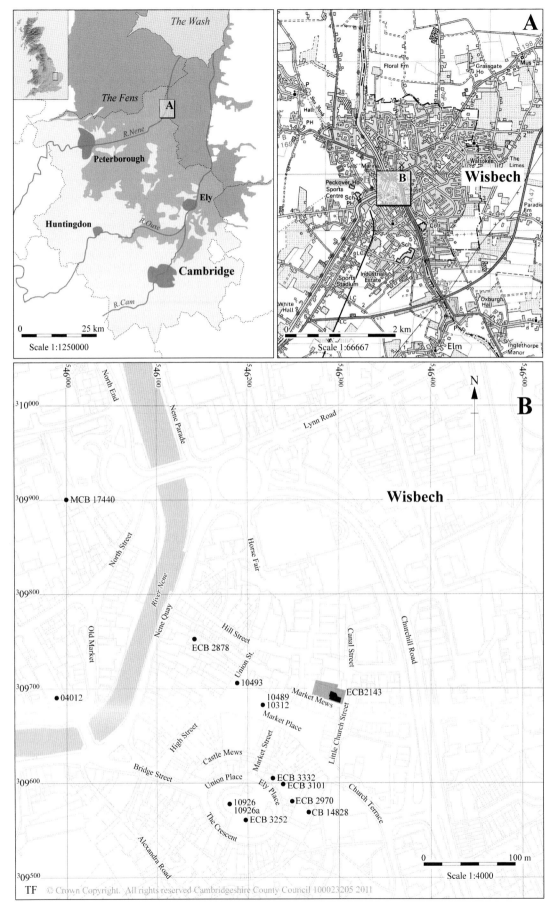

Figure 1 Site location, showing the development and excavation areas

Chapter 1. Introduction

I. General Introduction

Of all the important historic east coast ports, Wisbech has seen the least archaeological excavation. Given that it formed an interface between the medieval fens and the North Sea, its archaeological remains can be expected not only to reflect the development of the town itself, but also to demonstrate the effects of coastal trading and wider cultural contacts. The town's history is inextricably bound up with its position at the junction of the shifting outflows of two rivers — the Nene (Wysbeck) and the Ouse (Wellstream). Its low lying position, proximity to the sea and marked deterioration of the climate during the medieval and early post-medieval periods, combined to ensure that the town — as indeed the whole of the fenland — was the victim of frequent and severe flooding from both the rivers and the sea. Each episode of flooding carried enormous quantities of water-borne silts into the town, effectively burying phase upon phase of new development over the centuries. This project has served to highlight the incredible wealth of archaeological remains present within the development area. The results suggest that deeply stratified and exceptionally well preserved deposits relating to the development of Wisbech from its earliest Anglo-Saxon origins are likely to be present below much of the modern settlement.

II. Project Background
(Figs 1 and 2, Plates 1 and 2)

Between 19 and 27 June 1996 Cambridgeshire County Council's CAM ARC (now Oxford Archaeology East) carried out an archaeological evaluation at the junction of Market Mews and Little Church Street, Wisbech (TF 4630 0969; CHER 14619; Plate 1). The work was commissioned by Garnett Netherwood Architects on behalf of Wisbech Retail Ltd/Bilsdale Properties and was conducted within the terms of a brief set by the County Archaeology Office (Austin 1996). The development proposal for the evaluated area included the construction of an extension to the rear of two shop units.

During the course of the evaluation it became apparent that a considerable depth of medieval and early post-medieval stratigraphy survived over the whole of the development area. Since the construction programme for the new development was already set, any excavation had to be completed by 15 July 1996: a rapid response was therefore required. With a minimal delay it was possible to commence excavation of a portion of the development area on 2 July 1996 and to conclude the excavation on schedule. Initially the area of excavation covered $c.70\text{m}^2$ (Area 1, Plate 2a) giving a 14% sample of the total development area, although this was reduced to a 1.71% and 1.92% sample by area within Areas 2 and 3 respectively (Fig. 2, Plate 2b). The use of piling in the new buildings means that significant deposits, including the best preserved earlier elements of the stratigraphic

Plate 1 Little Church Street at the time of the excavation, looking south towards the Church of SS Peter and Paul. The excavation, bounded by fencing, appears to the right of the photograph

sequence, remain *in situ* although some damage will inevitably have resulted from the piling process.

Prior to this excavation, archaeological investigations within the town consisted of a single project conducted during 1991 to establish the presence, nature, date and state of preservation of archaeological deposits within the New Market in advance of pedestrianisation. Although the results of this fieldwork were inconclusive (below) an historical survey of the New Market area was undertaken which, with minor revisions, has been incorporated into the body of this report.

III. Geology, Topography and Meteorology

Geology and Topography
Wisbech lies approximately 64km north of Cambridge, some 16km from the current coastline of The Wash (Figs 1 and 33). The town was originally sited where the Wellstream joined the Wysbeck: the former was, in recent times, part of the Wisbech Canal which formed part of the

A

B

Plate 2 Working shots showing a) the excavation area (Area 1), looking east and b) one of the deeper trenches (Area 2), indicating the confined conditions

Figure 2 Detail of development and excavation areas. Scale 1:500

main outfall of the Great Ouse and is now part of the Nene (Fig. 3). Wisbech also lies on the crossing of the A47 King's Lynn to Peterborough and the A1101 Ely to Long Sutton routes. The former is a major arterial route from Leicester to Norwich, small sections of which follow an ancient east to west route across the coastal siltland parishes. The historic route through Wisbech itself is now the B198. The A1101 follows an historic course into Wisbech and through Outwell, along river banks.

Solid geology in the vicinity of Wisbech comprises Jurassic Ampthill clays, while pre-Flandrian gravels have been observed at below -15.0m OD (Waller 1994, 228). Settlement patterns, however, have been dictated by a complex and locally variable Flandrian sequence of marine transgressions, river channel (or roddon) formation, and reed swamp growth. These have led to the deposition of a thick accumulation of silts, clays and peats: peat growth has recently been dated to the Late Bronze Age near Wisbech, and may have continued into the Romano-British period in some places (Waller 1994, 250). The Flandrian deposits (those laid down since the last Ice Age) covering the Wisbech area consist of Terrington Beds comprising marine clays, silts and sands (British Geological Survey 1995), with most Roman and later activity occurring on an upper silt deposit. The silt area of the northern fenland is associated with complex environmental change over the past two millennia. A relatively high band of silt runs roughly east to west, from the estuary at King's Lynn to the Lincolnshire border, underlying Wisbech itself. The silt band on which

Wisbech stands has been subjected to repeated flooding. To its south lies the freshwater peat fen and to the north the waters of the Wash. The Nene estuary at Wisbech marks a salt water intrusion into the silt.

The current ground level, adjacent to the development site on the surface of Little Church Street, lies at approximately 7.00m OD. The lowest level reached during the excavations was c. 3.5 m OD, with augering to a depth of 2.5m OD. The benchmark on the Norman Church of SS Peter and Paul to the south is at 5.10m OD, well over a metre above the floor level within the church which provides an indication of 12th-century ground level. The low ground level immediately surrounding the church may result from both the scouring action of flood waters and successive attempts to dig the building out of flood deposits. Conversely, some areas of the town were evidently *raised* as a result of flooding, with new buildings being established above flood deposits (see Chapter 6). Various of the flood levels that affected Wisbech are recorded on the church tower.

Meteorological Background
With the decline in temperature levels associated with the so-called Little Ice Age, that began around 1250 and continued into the 17th century, there was an increase in the incidence of severe winters and a shortening — by about a month — of the growing season. In addition, during this same period, it appears that the main track of depressions over the eastern North Atlantic shifted further south. This effect, together with a rising sea level, explains

the increase in storminess and sea flooding recorded in the period around the North Sea. These conditions caused water bodies such as the Norfolk Broads in England and the Zuider Zee in Holland to be established. A great deal of land with many villages was also lost from the west coast of Denmark. Corresponding erosion on the eastern coast of England resulted in the loss of many coastal settlements including two great ports — Dunwich on the coast of Suffolk in 1326, which extended further east than it does today and Ravenspur or Ravensburgh in 1364, which stood on land east of Hull beyond the present Spurn Point. Fenland settlements around the Wash would also have been vulnerable to increased storminess and marine inundations during this period.

The devastating effects of abnormally high tides, lengthy wet periods and stormy weather were further exacerbated by intermittent periods of drought. During these periods the rivers had insufficient power to scour away the silts accumulating within their tidal channels so that they became shallow and incapable of dealing with either high tides or freshwater inundations.

Documentary Accounts of Severe Weather Episodes

A chronological list of severe weather events spanning the 14th to mid 16th centuries (compiled using data supplied from The Climatic Research Unit and various documentary sources) is included in Appendix 1: this records some 58 events between 1307 and 1500, the majority of which (42) were storms or floods. As noted above, in the most severe instances, towns were lost or badly damaged. In January 1362 one of the worst storms on record in south-eastern England occurred and was comparable in ferocity to the great storms of November 1703 and October 1987: its impact was so severe in England, the Netherlands and Northern Germany that it became known as the Grote Mandrenke (Great Drowning of Men). Many such severe weather events affected the eastern coast of England where, as the cover of this volume demonstrates (with a depiction of a flood in 1607 affecting Norfolk and other parts of Britain), flooding continued to be a regular event. As well as storms and floods, numerous wet summers or autumns were recorded (30 examples being noted in Appendix 1), often disrupting crop production and the harvest; most of those listed here occurred in the 14th century. A group of remarkable documents from Norfolk spanning c.1440 to 1504 — the Paston letters — provides vivid insights into the colder and wetter conditions of the time: 'mother, for God's sake take care that you make sure you take no cold on the way to Norwich, for it is the most perilous March that ever was seen by any man living' (letter of John Paston III to Margaret Paston, 8 March 1477; Virgoe 1989, 252).

Wisbech Castle was destroyed by flooding in 1236 and this flood may have been one of those recorded at the Market Mews site. The event was recorded by Matthew Paris who states in his *Flores Historiarum* (FH):

> But on the morrow of the blessed Martin (Nov. 12th) and throughout the octaves of the same, with the wind very strong, and accompanied with a rumble of thunder, the waves of the sea flooded in, transgressing their accustomed limits, so that in the confines of that same sea, and in the marsh, as at Wisbech and in similar places, small boats, herds, and also a great multitude of men perished (FH, vol. 2, 219; quoted in Hallam 1965, 127).

An additional description of this event is made in Paris' *Chronica Majora*:

> Then on the morrow of saint Martin and within the octaves of the same there burst forth suddenly at night extraordinary inundations of the sea, and a very strong wind was heard at the same time as unusually great waves of the sea. Especially in places by the sea, the wind tore up anchors and deprived the ports of their fleets, drowned a multitude of men, wiped out flocks of sheep and herds of cattle, ripped out trees by their roots, blew down houses and destroyed the beaches. And the sea rose up in waves for two days and the night between them — a thing unheard of; nor did it ebb and flow in the usual manner because of the onset of contrary winds, which are supposed to have held it up. Thereafter were seen the buried corpses of drowned people, lying in hollows made by the sea close to the beach, for at Wisbech, and in the neighbouring townships, thus next to the beach and sea side, an infinity of people perished, so that in one not particular populous township in one day a hundred bodies were given over to a grievous tomb (MP, Ch Maj, vol. 3, 379; quoted in Hallam 1965, 127).

It was during the 13th century that, as a result of a series of major floods, attention increasingly began to be directed to a systematic protection of the Fens by careful maintenance of the drains and embankments (see further discussion in Chapter 6). Following the diversion of the outfall of the Ouse from Wisbech to Lynn at some time during the late 13th century various attempts were made to return the river to its original course. An inquisition at Outwell in 1292, ordered the construction of three dams, in order to redirect a considerable body of the waters to their old outfall at Wisbech. The principal transactions for keeping up the drains and embankments, on which the habitableness and security of the Fens depended, centred on Wisbech, where the relevant Commissions were occasionally held at the castle. In 1329 Edward III 'being informed that the banks, ditches, and sewers about Wisebeche, Elme, and Welle, were broken and out of repair' issued a commission 'to inquire through whose default they became so ruinous, and who were the landholders thereabouts, or had safeguard by the said banks, and to distrain them for their repair according to the proportion of their lands' (Dugdale 1662, 299; quoted in Walker and Craddock 1849, 214). This was followed by a Session at Wisbech, whereby a remedy was proposed for protecting Wisbech, Elm, and Welle, by a causeway to be made at Congested Lake to Well Creek, 'and thence unto Marche Dyke, and that the Creek should be wholly stopped up, and that the said towns could not be preserved unless that were done' (Walker and Craddock 1849, 218).

As a result of these obstructions considerable flood damage was recorded in the local area which resulted in a series of legal proceedings. Finally in 1331 the Commission of Sewers decreed that 'the dam, so raised to the hurt of the king, and nuisance of all the persons before mentioned, and whatever else was of nuisance in this behalf, should be taken away' (Dugdale 1662, 306; quoted in Walker and Craddock 1849, 218). Although the dams were removed and the main outfall of the Ouse at Lynn was restored, these early actions (combined with widespread neglect following the dissolution of the monasteries) have repeatedly been blamed for later floods and related hardships.

Numerous accounts of the impact of such later flooding survive. 'In the winter of … [1334] … the sea was so outrageous, that it brake the banks in sundry places, drowned many cattle, and spoiled a great quantity of corn' (Dugdale 1662, 255; quoted in Walker and Craddock 1849, 105). The floods were so serious that an inquisition was held upon the state of the country, which recorded that Tilney (c.15km to the north-east of Wisbech) was overflowed with sea water for the space of seven days, by which the sown corn, and the winter corn and hay, and 'a hundred muttons, and sixty ewes, to the damage of £300, were destroyed. Within the compass of sixty years past one parish church with the parsonage, a manor house, twenty messuages, and a hundred acres of land were utterly lost' (Dugdale 1662, 255; quoted in Walker and Craddock 1849, 105). The king, on receiving details of the situation 'by which they represented their extraordinary losses by the before specified inundations; desiring that the assessment might not extend to any other of their goods and chattels than what they had remaining after these their disasters', made a considerable remission of taxes (Dugdale 1662, 255; quoted in Walker and Craddock 1849, 105).

In 1356 a survey of the manor of Wisbech mentions further flood damage, in some cases from upland waters (Pugh 1967, 244). The castle and manor house were valued at only £2 and there were many ruinous houses that would cost more to repair than they were worth.

In 1439 'The bank called Wisebeche Fenn-dyche was broken and decayed, and 4400 acres in Wisebeche, 4600 acres in Leverington, 1400 acres in Newton, and 2000 acres in Tyd, being thereby at that time overflowed and drowned' (Walker and Craddock 1849, 220). In October of the same year the area was hit by a great storm; 'Ely, Wisbech and all its neighbourhood was flooded some feet deep. The sea broke in between Wisbech and Walsoken'. Many towns and villages were flooded, including Hobhouse:

> This Hobhouse being an almshouse, and the water breaking down the walls of it, the wind blew the clothes off the bed of a poore man and his wife, who being cold, awaked and suddenly stepped out of his bed to reach up his clothes, and slipt up to the bellie in water, and then he thinking himself to be in danger (as he was indeed), and knowing the best way to escape the danger of the water, he took his wife on his neck and carried her away, and so were both saved. At the same time in Wisbech a tennis place and a bowling alley, walled about with brick worth £20 by the year to the owner, was quite destroyed by the water. (Holinshed 1577, 1213).

Furthermore at

> Mumby Chapell, the whole toune was lost, except three houses. A shippe was driven upon an house; the sailors, thinking they had bin upon a rocke, committed themselves to God: and three of the mariners lept out of the shippe, and chanced to take hold on the house toppe, and so saved themselves: and the wife of the same, lying in child bed, did climbe uppe into the toppe of the house and was also saved by the mariners, her husband and child being both drowned. (Walker and Craddock 1849, 221).

In 1571 the sea banks had been left to decay, and, during the delay necessary for obtaining an order for their repair from the court of sewers, a violent and unprecedented storm broke over the country, levelled the banks, and once again submerged the land, towns and villages under water. The value of the cattle destroyed was estimated at £20,000 in the villages around Wisbech, besides the quantity lost in the more remote places (Holinshed 1577, 1213). An account of two floods in 1613–14, which caused extensive flooding of Marshland and Wisbech, was formerly commemorated by an inscription in SS Peter and Paul's Church (Watson 1833, 138 and 139 fn). It was scrolled on three compartments of the east window, which is now walled up.

In 1680, Ralph Thoresby recorded the following account of another local phenomenon in his Diary:

> This morning before we left Wisbech, I had the sight of an Hygre or Eager, a most terrible flush of water, that came up the river with such violence that it sunk a coal vessel in the town, and such a terrible noise that all the dogs in it did snarl and bite at the rolling waves, as though they would swallow up the River, the sight of which (having never seen the like before) much affected me, each wave surmounting the other with extraordinary violence! (Watson 1833, 80).

The Hygre or Eager was a kind of tidal bore caused by obstructions to the incoming tide from poorly maintained or silted up channels resulting in the building of water pressure near the outfall of the river. The result could be as documented by Thoresby or more generalised flooding and was generally associated with high spring tides. It was recorded again in relation to the opening of the North Level main drain in the early 19th century. 'The tide, after its opening, flowed to an unprecedented height, and ebbed lower than had ever been known; whilst the constantly scouring force of the stream proved wonderfully advantageous to the river, by removing those precarious sands which in various parts used frequently to delay the free navigation. Nothing is perhaps more illustrative of the efficacious outfall gained by this work, than the circumstance of the Hygre having deserted the river on its opening in June 1830' (Walker and Craddock 1849, 29).

IV. Historical Background

Sources
(Plate 3)

Wisbech had eight guilds, the most significant of which was that of the Holy Trinity. All the property of the guilds on their final dissolution in 1549 fell into the King's possession and was used to found the Corporation of Wisbech: amongst the various historical and cartographic records pertaining to the town the most important are the Corporation Records. There are also records from the Commission of Sewers who held authority under the Common Law, but who received recognition in 1427 from a statute from Henry VI. Other records prior to the founding of the Corporation are the Ely Episcopal Registers and the fraternity proceedings of the Guild of the Holy Trinity (1379–1549). Later sources include the 'Committee of Works' (from 1771) and the Bedford Level Corporation (from 1772).

Most of the Corporation Records were referenced in the 19th century: Jackson made an index and short

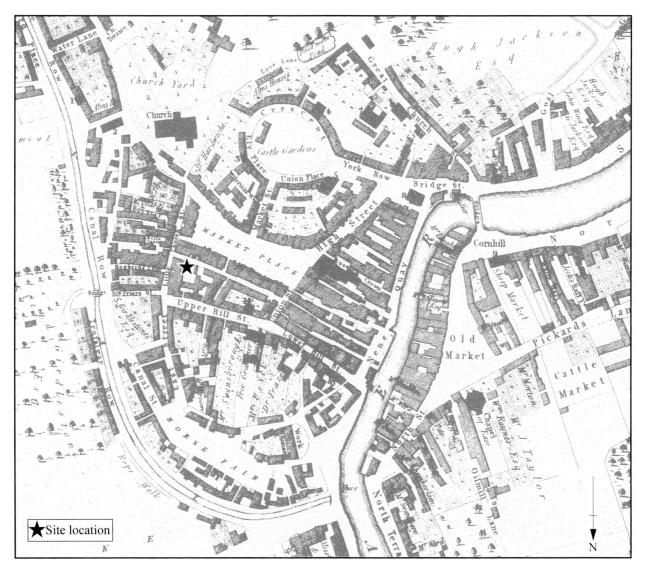

Plate 3 First survey of the whole town of Wisbech by J. Wood, 1830 (courtesy of the Wisbech and Fenland Museum)

descriptions of the records, and Watson catalogued the entries in Jackson's volumes (detailed in Section A of the bibliography). Histories written in the last century detail the main events of the town's history, transcripts of the records, and personal reminiscences.

There are no maps which show the entire town centre of Wisbech in any detail prior to 1830. A map of the late 18th or early 19th century of the castle (MIS/612:Wisbech Museum), gardens and premises indicates Market Street, and houses on the south side of Market Place and High Street. Church Lane is depicted with unmarked buildings to the west. Unfortunately there is no scale or title to the map. Another survey of the castle estates (Ref.408/ E6:CRO) is dated 1792 and is at a scale of 80 inches to the mile. This map is, however, less detailed than MIS/612 but illustrates the Custom House (later the Butter Market) and the entrance from Bridge Street to the High Street, although the Market Place is not shown.

The 1830 map by J. Wood (Plate 3) is the first surveyed plan of Wisbech. It locates properties in the High Street and Bridge Street by a numbered key: the Customs House, the Girls Charity School in Lower Hill Street, the Chapel in Upper Hill Street, and the Rose and Crown in the High

Street are all listed. One small square feature is marked in the Market Place.

A detailed map of the town (Wisbech Museum) was produced in 1853 under the auspices of the Public Health Act 1848. It was surveyed by R.H. Dobson at 44 feet to the inch. Inns and other properties in the Market Place, High Street, Bridge Street and Hill Street are named, and the Market Place is formally laid out with the locations of lamp-posts, sewer grates, pumps and pavements shown. The map is tinted to show land-use. A smaller scale version of this map is held in the Cambridge Record Office, and has revisions edited by C. Mumford in 1867. The sewers which traverse the Market Place on this map are reflected in the position of modern services.

Wisbech
by Elizabeth Popescu
(Fig. 3)
Wisbech's position on a low-lying peninsula formed by the confluence of the Rivers Nene and Ouse enabled it to function as a nodal point for both riverine and marine trade. Its name derives from the Wysbeck, now the main outflow of the River Nene; effectively meaning 'the stream or valley of the *Wisse*', either the Wissey or the

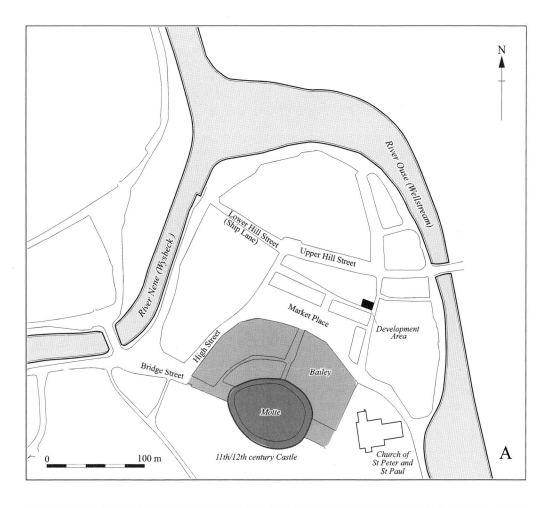

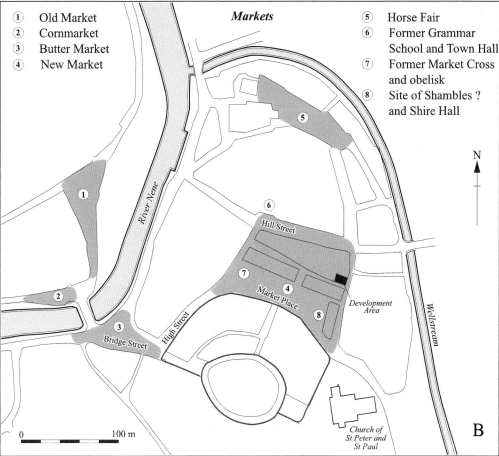

Figure 3 A) Medieval Wisbech showing the position of the castle and the course of the Rivers Ouse (pre-14th century) and Nene. Scale 1:4000 B) Wisbech markets, showing the altered course of the Wellstream. Scale 1:4000

Ouse or possibly both' (Reaney 1943, 292), a possible connection with Wixna or Wissa having been suggested (Darby 1983, 5). *Liber Eliensis* records that Wisbech was given to Ely *c*.1016:

> At the same time as Aelfgar, Bishop of Elmham … was translated into the realms of Heaven, Aelfwine, a monk of the church of Ely from his boyhood … succeeded to the ministry of that same bishopric. Now, along with him, when he was made an oblate in the church, a gift was made by his noble parents … consisting of … Wisbech — which is a quarter of a hundred of the Isle [of Ely] — with its appendages (Fairweather 2005, 172; see also Pestell 2001, 212, fn 51).

Positioned on the former medieval coastline, the town originally functioned as a port, controlling access to the extensive Nene/Ouse river transport system and egress to the North Sea. It still forms a focus within the surrounding silt fenland and is one of a series of settlements spaced at intervals along the landward side of a medieval flood defence known as the Sea Bank (or 'Roman Bank'). Along the coast to the east, the rise of Bishop's (later King's) Lynn, founded in the late 11th century by Herbert de Losinga, was linked to aspirations 'to control and stimulate trade which could then be taxed, in direct competition to the other major trading sites in its immediate area. At this time, that meant principally Wisbech, which received the bulk of maritime shipping' (Pestell 2001, 211). The development of Wisbech as a port was closely linked to the viability of the Nene outfall and fenland waterways: continuous silting up of the Nene was a recurrent problem. Despite its fluctuating fortunes, the town became a corporate borough in 1549 and by the early 18th century was developing into a major port. This period of prosperity, which continued into the 19th century, is reflected in the surviving architecture of the town (Taylor 1973).

At Domesday, Wisbech was held by Ely Abbey, with a value of ten hides (Domesday Book, i, fos. 192a, 5, 57). Although not the wealthiest of the Ely manors, some status is indicated by the fact that the town had its own hundredal moot at 'an unlocated place called *Modich*, probably in or near Wisbech, certainly by the twelfth century when mentioned in the *Liber Eliensis*' (Pestell 2001, 211; Fairweather 2005, 150). The area around Wisbech has longstanding ties with Norfolk. The relationship between the town and various Norfolk communities, particularly those in Marshland, was complex and reflected — *inter alia* — the co-operative efforts required to meet the physical challenges of drainage and flood protection. Landholders in West Walton, Norfolk (about 4.8km from Wisbech), for instance, were apparently obliged by tenure to repair the castle walls and ditch/moat (Watson 1827, 124). This link may have been of considerable antiquity: it has been suggested that Wisbech's ancient administrative system (based on units called 'ferdings' or 'leets') demonstrates strong links with the Norfolk Marshland villages surrounding West Walton on the eastern side of the Great Ouse/Nene estuary, perhaps indicating that they lay within the same ancient estate: during the 13th century, the organisation of the Bishop's estate suggests that Wisbech was associated with the Norfolk Marshland bailiwick rather than with the remainder of the Hundred of Ely (Rippon 2000, 251).

Wisbech lies within a 'hideous fen of a huge bigness', as described by Guthlac in *c*.650AD (Coles and Hall 1998, 3). The economy of the community described in the Domesday Survey (1086) was predominantly agricultural, reflecting the presence of high quality arable land on the fen islands and pastoral activity in the surrounding wetland. Wisbech benefited from lying on silt fen (rich agricultural land) and yet not far from peat fen resources to the south. Throughout the medieval period, the fen landscape provided major natural resources such as fish, wildfowl, salt and high quality seasonal pasture. Access to both upland and fenland resources resulted in substantial wealth for local landowners. Wisbech's annual catch of eels, for example, was over 33,000 in 1086 (Darby 1987, 35). Building materials were plentiful (including reeds, rush, sedge, willow and alder), along with peat for fuel or building. The use of turbaries for peat extraction began in the Roman period and examples lie to the west of the town at Wisbech St Mary (Hall 1996, 173), as well as further south at Elm and Upwell. Such activity may relate to the major transport route across the fenland — the Fen Causeway — which itself probably began as a canal (Silvester 1988, 173, 189). The other major fenland industry was pottery manufacture, with a notable medieval production centre at Ely (Spoerry 2008). Brickmaking had begun at Wisbech by the mid 14th century (Sherlock 1999) and at Ely from perhaps the 15th century, if not before (Lucas 1993).

As is discussed below, very little is yet known in archaeological terms about the origins and development of Wisbech itself. The Fenland Survey details prehistoric to Roman activity in the town and its surroundings (Hall 1996; Silvester 1988, 151–169). There appears to be no direct evidence for prehistoric finds or sites beneath the modern settlement (Hall 1996, 169), although a fragmentary sword and scabbard of Early Iron Age date were acquired by the museum in 1847 and appear to have come from the town (CHER 04008). Roman finds from Wisbech or its immediate vicinity comprise coins (including a hoard) and pottery (CHER 03889, 03891, 03910, 039334 and CB14764). This period saw the initial phase of settlements on the surrounding marine silts (Silvester 1988, fig.112), generally consisting of settlements and salterns with very little evidence in the parish of Wisbech itself (Silvester 1988, fig.112 and fig.94; Coles and Hall 1998, fig.5.1). Romano-British salt manufacturing sites occupied slightly raised ground (such as roddons) in the area, and a series of Middle Saxon sites lay on similarly precarious sites to the north-east of the town. The only known Anglo-Saxon activity from Wisbech itself consists of two bronze brooches of Early Saxon date recovered in 1858 (CHER 04012), a Late Saxon 'Urnes-style' openwork brooch recovered from the castle ditch in 1846 (CHER 01926a) and two burial urns of comparable date retrieved from the site of Wisbech Museum (Hall 1996, 182). The early brooches are significant as they may indicate the presence of relatively dry land at an early date. Although the scale and character of Anglo-Saxon occupation at Wisbech remains unknown, it is possible that the original manor lay on the west bank of the Wysbeck, possibly associated with the position of the 'old' market (Pugh 1967, 240, 243–246; see Fig. 3B).

After the Conquest, the town's topography was dramatically altered by the imposition of the castle — an 'expedient fenland campaign fortress' (Creighton 2002, 37; CHER 01926). Various dates have been given for the castle's construction, which is traditionally believed to have been built by William the Conqueror, following the submission of Hereward in 1071 (Pugh 1967, 251 and fn 27; King 1983, 40). Its lack of mention in Domesday, however, may suggest a date for its completion in 1087, the last year of William's reign (Anniss 1977, 2), although a date of 1089 has also been cited on the basis of Matthew Paris' description (Pestell 2001, 212). A reference in 1577 to an 'olde little rounde towre' may relate to the Norman keep (Anniss 1977, 4). The whole castle precinct enclosed 1.6ha (4 acres) and may have been of motte and bailey type. It is believed to have had a moat/ditch 12m (40 feet) wide, facing towards the Market Place.

It has been suggested that the Norman castle was dismantled during the reign of Henry II (1154–89; Watson 1827, 125), although neither the evidence for this assertion nor the extent of any alteration is clear (Anniss 1977, 7). King John notably stayed at the castle on 12 October 1216 (Rott Lit Pat, I, intro), during his last journey: his baggage train was engulfed by the tide and lost to the sea. It has long been suggested that this occurred near Wisbech (Walker and Craddock 1849, 212–213), possibly on the road between Walsoken and Wisbech, where the road along the sea bank crossed the Wellstream (Pugh 1967, 252 and fn 29). John died a few days later and his 'treasure' has never been recovered.

The castle was 'utterly destroyed' by marine flooding in 1236 and the floods probably dramatically affected the whole area around the market place. Despite this setback, the castle was rebuilt. The constable or keeper — Wm Justice — is mentioned in 1246 (Watson 1827, 125, 130; Annis 1977, 5). Further building works at the site took place in the 15th, 17th and 19th centuries and the castle's topographical influence is still reflected in the distinctive fan-shaped distribution and wedge-shaped building plots bordering the south side of the Market Place (Fig. 1).

To the north of the outer ditches of the castle, the rectilinear 'New' Market Place lies on the tongue of land bound by the two water courses (Fig. 3B). The large parish church of SS Peter and Paul placed to the east of the castle may have been an early foundation, the earliest part of its surviving fabric dating to the third quarter of the 12th century (Pugh 1967, 247; CHER CB14828). Medieval parish churches are frequently preceded by a chapel within the castle bailey: at Wisbech the physical relationship between the church and castle is particularly interesting. The castle, market and church lie on the 5m contour, presumably forming the highest and driest part of the town. The central point of the area of high ground is, however, dominated by the church rather than the castle. This may suggest that a church was already on the site before the construction of the castle 'forcing the castle construction to take place slightly off to one side of the most topographically favourable location that was already taken by the church' (Cambridgeshire County Council 2002, 21). Similar arrangements of castle, market and church are known at many other settlements, such as Kimbolton in Huntingdonshire, Castle Acre and New Buckenham in Norfolk (Pestell 2001, 212) and, on a much larger scale at cities such as Norwich (Shepherd Popescu 2009): this phenomenon has recently been explored in some depth (Creighton 2002, passim). In the case of Wisbech, the placement of these three key elements may be viewed as

part of a conscious act to stimulate and regulate trade (Pestell 2001, 212). The subject site at Market Mews lies within the New Market just to the north of the castle, in a key area for investigation within the town.

Wisbech Market Place
by Lesley Hoyland
(Fig. 3, Plate 4)
There seem to be no illustrations of the Market Place prior to the 19th century, and most of these are contained within the various histories of Wisbech written at this period. Many photographs were taken of the town from the mid-19th century onwards, most notably by Samuel Smith in the early 1850s: these are held in Wisbech Museum.

Markets and Fairs
Markets in Wisbech have a lengthy history (Fig.3B). The absence of charters relating to their inception implies an origin in the pre-Conquest period. Since the medieval period, the town has had several distinct and economically important markets, selling products in their own separate market places. The Old Market place, described below, is still the focus of financial and banking activities in the town, and in the 1930s it remained the focus of local farming trade. Until the 1950s some stalls were still set up on a Saturday.

The Timber Market (not illustrated) was held next to the Wisbech canal near the present day Norfolk Street. It was noted in the early 19th century that the timber came from Northamptonshire and was traded to the Navy in vast quantities (Lysons 1806).

The Horsefair in July was held at the north-east tip of the peninsula, at the confluence of the Wisbech Canal and the Nene, and the Butter Market was held in Bridge Street, but the most important market by the mid-19th century was the Corn Market, held behind the Old Market on the North Brink. By the 1840s over 250,000 quarts of corn were traded, making it the second largest corn market in England after Wakefield (Pugh 1967, 262).

The right to hold the Trinity Fair was granted to Wisbech in 1327 by Bishop Hotham and under the terms it lasted over nineteen days. Bishop Alcock's survey in 1492 to 1493 shows that a market was usually held on a Saturday (as in the present day), and that the Trinity Fair had moved to become associated with the feast of SS Peter and Paul, to whom the church adjacent to the castle was dedicated (Pugh 1967, 262).

By the end of the 18th century five fairs were recorded: the Saturday and Monday over Palm Sunday for hemp and flax, the Monday and Saturday before Whitsun, 25 July was the Horse Fair, and 1–2 August was for the sale of hemp. In 1806, Lysons also mentions a fair on the day before Lady Day and Lammas Day. In the 1930s fairs were held on the Saturday after 14 February, the second Thursday in May, 25 July, the first Thursday in August, and the third Wednesday in September (Pugh 1967, 262).

The New Market: An Historical Survey
The earliest markets are likely to have been held on the present site of the Old Market, situated on the west bank of the Nene, probably under the influence of the Saxon manor on this side of the river (Pugh 1967, 240 and 243–246). There are no specific records of when the market moved to its present 'New Market Place' site, but this is likely to have occurred soon after the Conquest,

Plate 4 Market Mews in the late 19th century (from Gardiner 1898, opp. p. 58)

when the Normans built the castle. The market reflected in its geographical shift the new political power-base and its medieval development outstripped that of the Old Market area.

By 1221 the first references to the New Market appear: tenants in military service are listed and a William de Longchamp is noted as having 'a messuage in the New Market thereto'. The terrible floods of 1236 damaged the Norman castle and the whole area around the Market Place was affected; the assessments of 1251 of tenants holdings were drastically reduced and de Longchamp's messuage was destroyed by the sea along with at least half of the land belonging to him (Pugh 1967, 245).

The area covered by the present Market Place is certainly much smaller than its medieval counterpart, as title deeds dating from 1471 refer to all the land from the bridge to the present Market Place as New Market. No streets are mentioned by name. In 1492, the Terrier of Bishop Alcock shows that there were 115 tenants in the New Market Place as opposed to 32 in the Old Market, indicating how much the New Market Place was becoming the focus of the town.

With the inception of the Corporation of Wisbech in 1549 came the systematic recording of town affairs and it is from these detailed accounts and records that nearly all information about the Market Place and its environs comes, prior to the first map of the town made in 1830. The public-spirited Corporation paid accounts in 1549 'for the payving of the Market Place, and for raggestone, sand and workmanshippe of the same £17.2.2'. Another reference in the same year refers to the presence of a Market Cross 'for lead, tymber and workmanshippe of the crosse in the Markett place £4.3.4' (trans. Walker and Craddock 1849).

This market cross was reputedly built by John de Feckenham, a Catholic recusant held prisoner in Wisbech Castle, who died in 1585. It was located at the west end of the Market Place and was replaced in 1765 by an obelisk (Pugh 1967, 263).

One significant reference to events in the Market Place is contained in a report to the Session of Sewers of 1570 concerning Crab Mersh Bank: 'which bank from Crabmersh gate was decayed in Bishop Goodrich's time, and part thereof carried (by consent of the Bishop) for the pavement of the market place in Wisbeche, and part by Mr Wm Bloomfield, for the making of a windmill there' (Corp. Rec. i). Bishop Goodrich was in charge of the diocese between 1534 and 1554: the above reference mentions that the bank was decayed at this time but it is less clear exactly when the bank was redeposited in the Market Place. Since the Market Place was first paved in 1549, it could be that material was deposited at this time, the bank earth forming a level foundation. The reference to a windmill is also interesting as the present Market Place was frequently referred to as Market Hill (the present day Hill Street was formerly known as Ship Lane), indicative therefore that in former times it may well have formed slightly higher ground relative to its surroundings than it does at the present time.

The next major work undertaken in the Market Place was in 1591 when an order was issued by the Corporation for the erection of the Butchers Shambles on the Market Hill and the placing of stalls there for the butchers. Unfortunately, contemporary records say nothing about the construction, building details or exact location of the Shambles. All available information comes from writers collating information well after the event of the

10

demolition of the Shambles in 1811. It is therefore likely that the nature of the Shambles, and the adjacent Shire Hall which was demolished at the same time, may have been altered and modified through the centuries, and for this reason the Shambles and the Shire Hall will be discussed below with the discussion on the general improvements to the Market Place in 1810–1811. There is a Corporation account for the purchase of 20,000 tiles in 1591 which may have been related to roofing the Shambles, but little else is recorded apart from routine maintenance and repair work. A market house is recorded as being repaired in 1614, and seems to have been rebuilt on a more substantial scale near the river, probably on the site of the Butter Market (Pugh 1967, 263). In 1595, the Shambles cost £107.7.00. and were let at an annual rent of £7.10.00 (Corp. Rec. iii).

There is however, an indirect reference to a building which was generally thought to be much older than the buildings around it. Watson, interviewing a 94 year old citizen in 1827, records that in Butchers Row (the space between the Shambles and the houses opposite on the south-west side of the Market Place) there was a very old building with 'some rude carved work in front, on wood, which seemed to be a man felling an ox, and other devices, with an inscription in Saxon characters, unintelligible' (Watson 1827, 312). This building was also demolished in 1811 but the fact that it is so distinctly different than the rest of the Shambles of the late 18th / early 19th century (and yet with a carving of a man felling an ox — a butcher?) may indicate remnants of an earlier phase of the Shambles.

There are many accounts in the Corporation Records of sundry repairs to the wells and pumps in the Market Place, which must have supplied not only the traders but the townsfolk as well. In 1638 'the towne bailiff was appoynted to pay unto William Harvie his bill of laying out in repaire of the backside and getting uppe the pump on the Markett Hill and other layings out £3.17.0' (Walker and Craddock 1849) and in 1640 the well or pump on the Market Place had to be repaired. A well was ordered to be cleaned and ropes and buckets provided in 1661. Another paving of the Market Place was undertaken in 1665 and the well was disannulled. Later in the same year a pump was ordered for the well in Market Hill and in 1676 a new pump was erected and supplied by a new well.

The records of 14 April 1680 indirectly mention the old Shire Hall, which was demolished at the same time as the Shambles in 1811. Exactly when the building was erected is obscure and there are no records to indicate it was built by the Corporation. The record refers to the letting 'to Robt Squire the shope under the Shire house' for 13 shillings per annum. As with the Shambles the only account of the actual structure is from Watson (1827), and the above account would suggest that the building was of two storeys, the lower used for commercial purposes.

The Market Place received upgrading in 1683 with an order to pave the street near the Shambles and that a well and pump be constructed at the east end, providing the neighbours contributed £7. Other sanitation works are recorded in 1753 when a substantial iron grate was laid down 'where the crying stone lately stood, in the Market Place for carrying of the waters'. This implies that the crying stone, where the town crier made his announcements (and which Watson in 1827 noted as

positioned near the Rose and Crown in the High Street) had at one time been situated in the Market Place.

Another paving of the Market Place 'at the expense of the town estates' occurred in 1764, and in the following year a pump was moved, its new position uncharacteristically detailed: 'upon the Market Place .... from the place where it is now stand and be set down opposite or nearby opposite to Mr Jim Massingale(?) seven or eight feet from the water way opposite the said.' Both the 1753 and the 1764 records show that open sewers ran through the Market Place at this time.

In 1765, the town bailiff was instructed to erect four dials on the obelisk in the Market Hill: it replaced the old Market cross at the west end of the market and it is not entirely clear whether the obelisk had been erected earlier than this date. The obelisk, removed in 1811, was designed by Burgess. From an ink drawing made by Burgess, Gardiner (1898) states that the obelisk appeared to be 32 feet high with no inscription but had an urn placed at its top and its pedestal much blackened 'by bonfires, which, in those days, were kindled near its base, when public rejoicings took place'. There are also references in a private diary held in Wisbech Museum of abusive inscriptions and an effigy which were placed there after a robbery in 1770 (Pugh 1967, 263). Gardiner (1898) cites the location of the obelisk (and by implication the old market cross) as facing Messrs Dawson's door (present day No. 28 Market Place), slightly off-centre to the main axis of the modern Market Place.

In 1772 a repair order for the engine house on Market Hill was sent out: this is peculiar in that there are no other references to an engine house in the New Market Place but there are many which refer to the building and repairs of the engine house in the Old Market. Other repairs were ordered in 1775 when the obelisk and a pump in the Market Place had to be repaired.

One of the most dramatic and significant changes seen in the Market Place must have been the Improvement Act of 1810 which introduced the 'taking down and removing the Shambles therein, for paving, cleansing, lighting the said Town'. Under this Act, the Corporation resolved in 1811 'that the Town Bailliff do cause the obelisk standing in the Market-place to be sold by auction as now standing, and to be taken down, and that he request the magistrates to give an order for the taking up and removal of the cage and stocks adjoining the old shambles' (Walker and Craddock 1849, 437). Prior to this, there had been a footpath next to the shops which was bordered by posts but with no chains between them. The Market Place was also paved at this time and in 1849 Craddock and Walker described it thus: The Market Place 'forms a parallelogram of 380 feet by 94, of which 310 by 37 are appropriated to the stallage, and the rest as thoroughfare. The stallage portion is slabbed on the portion intended for passengers, and cobble-paved where the stalls stand. It was completed in this form in 1811 at a cost of £1170' (Walker and Craddock 1849, 437). A photograph of the Market Place taken in 1857 by Samuel Smith clearly shows the distinctive arrangement of the cobbles and flagstones, as well as contemporary street furniture (WM 049: Wisbech Museum). Much of the distinctive character of the Market Place must have been lost when the new developments took place and the Shambles, Shire Hall and obelisk were removed.

As has been noted above, there are almost no references to the Shambles at any period apart from the notes that Watson made in 1827 when collecting the reminiscences of elderly townsfolk. Butchers Row was the name of the alley formed between the Shambles and the houses opposite on the south-west side of the Market Place. The house with the carved frontage (noted above) was here. Gardiner (1898) refers to the evaluation of the Shambles carried out by several interested parties prior to their demolition, and he quotes a sketch and notes from the diary of the grandfather of a Mr Forster. These show the Shambles as a rectangular building with a smaller rectangular lean-to at its north-east corner, with its long axis running north-south at right angles to the main building. It lay adjacent to, and east of, Shire Hall. The Shambles is described as being a wooden building roofed with grey slate, forming a covered market with posts supporting a large chamber over it. Gardiner (1898) notes that the diary included the dimensions of posts, beams, rafters and boarding but mentions no other architectural details. This upper storey was used for corn storage and was reached by a broad stepped external ladder. The butchers' stalls occupied the covered area below. Until the early 19th century, poultry and eggs were sold from trestles at the side of the Shambles facing Mr Oldham's shop (presently No. 29 Market Place). There are records of a temporary portable structure being erected for the sale of poultry, eggs and butter after the Butter Market was demolished in 1856 (Gardiner 1898, 112). The Shambles and Shire Hall had been in poor repair at the time of demolition — valuations ranged from £217 to £400 — and for some time prior to demolition there were only three shops left in the Shambles.

Gardiner (1898) also describes the Shire Hall as a one-storied building with a semi-octagonal end. The principal door was in the central division of this semi-octagon with semi-circular headed windows at each side with the pillory sitting on the flat roof. The building faced Messrs Dawson's shop (presently No. 28 Market Place) with its side towards the Ship Inn (presently No. 40). This description states that it was one storeyed, but this is at variance with the letting in 1680 of a shop below the Shire Hall, implying at least another storey. There may be several ways to interpret this: the name 'Shire house' may have referred to the upper storey of the Shambles, it may have referred to an earlier building, possibly not at this present location, or that the flat roof of the Shire Hall as it was described in 1811, may indicate that it did at one time have more storeys, which were later pulled down thus leaving the curious flat roof. The fact that the pillory was here also indicates reasonable access which again could indicate that there was formerly another storey.

The stocks, cage and pillory were all centred around the Shambles and when they were removed, punishments were meted out on a wagon drawn up at one of the corners of the Market Place (Gardiner 1898). The Market Place has also been the scene of many civil celebrations: a dinner to celebrate peace was held there in August 1814, and in 1837 over 4000 people sat to dinner to celebrate Queen Victoria's coronation. In 1865 a platform was erected in the middle of the Market Place, and the central lamp-post converted into a fountain to celebrate the first piping of water from Marham springs to the citizens of Wisbech. Queen Victoria's Golden Jubilee was again commem-

orated in grand style in the Market Place with dinner, and a tea-party for around 2,500 children.

In 1900 further developments took place: the cobbles surrounding Market Hill were covered in asphalt and the remaining area was given a new coat of tar and gravel. Further repairs were made in 1910.

In 1964, recommendations were made for the removal of the disused horse-trough situated at the west end of the Market Place and which had been erected to the memory of the Jackson family. General upgrading of the street furniture was also called for as well as the removal and re-siting of the lamp-posts. The horse-trough was duly replaced by low bollards at the High Street and Church Street ends of the Market Place and it was also recommended that the telephone kiosks and post-boxes be situated towards the public toilets at the east end of the Market Place (The Wisbech Society 1964). The location of these public toilets is very unfortunate: since they lay at the east end of the Market Place and were built underground, they may well have destroyed any trace of the old Shambles and Shire Hall if they encroached upon their location.

In 1987 the Horsefair and Church Mews development was undertaken over an 8 acre site to the north of the Market Place. The development comprises a supermarket and twenty-one shop units as well as a new bus station. The scheme was completed in 1988. There was unfortunately no archaeological monitoring of the development.

Historical Survey of the Area Around the Market Place
The Market Place has been discussed in detail above, although in reality the area immediately around the Market Place forms an integral part of its function and position within in the town. The discussion below highlights some of the historical aspects of High Street, Union Street, Hill Street and Market Street, giving the wider context within which the development site lay (Figs 1 and 3).

Market Street
Market Street is the most recent of the streets to be formally planned. It was built by J. Medworth in 1813 when, as owner of Wisbech Castle, he developed the castle estate into the present day Crescent properties. An untitled and undated map, probably from the end of the 18th century, shows the proposed layout of the Crescent with Market Street clearly marked. It is interesting to note that this would have been the first direct access route from the castle to the Market Place: previous access seems to have been via the north-west gate towards Bridge Street, and the south-east gate past the church. Walker and Craddock (1849) note an inscription in Market Street, now gone: 'The entrance to this street from the Market Place is the freehold property of Mr Joseph Medworth of Bermondsey, purchased by him at £400 for the accommodation of the town of Wisbech'. Under the 1810 Improvements Act, the houses and street were regarded as private property and therefore outside the Corporation's concern: Watson in 1827 remarks that Market Street had only recently been paved and gravelled.

Bridge Street
Bridge Street was formerly the site of the Butter Market. In 1688, a wooden shelter was erected near the bridge,

although two years later it is recorded as being in great disrepair due to bad workmanship (Pugh 1967, 263). The 1792 Castle estate map shows the site of the Butter Market as the Customs House. The Butter Market building was erected at the foot of Bridge Street in 1801: it was a rectangular building comprising an upper storey supported by open arches, and with a hipped roof. This building was demolished in 1856, a portable and temporary wooden framework being erected in the Market Hill where eggs and butter were sold. Gardiner reports that the situation was still as such in 1898. The site of Butter Market is where the Clarkson memorial now stands. Gardiner (1898) mentions that the vaults under Mr Exley's premises (No. 4 Bridge Street) are supposed to have originally connected with those from the castle. Interestingly enough, these vaults are not on the listed building records and it may be that this building had been redeveloped prior to their compilation.

High Street and Union Street
The date for the emergence of the modern street pattern around the Market Place is not clear, but the map of castle estates in 1792 shows Bridge Street and High Street, with houses marked between the castle boundaries and the High Street and Market Place. There are many old buildings in both Union and High Street and Gardiner (1898) states that there are vaults under the premises of Mr Broadberry (No.? Market Place), Mr Leach (No. 26 High Street) and Mr Oldham (formerly Mr Dieppe) at No. 29 Market Place (Walker and Craddock 1849, 416 and fig. opp.). The latter premises was recorded as having a three-bayed groined vault, although only one survives to the present day (CHER 10493). It is medieval in date, and it has been speculated that it formed the undercroft of the old Guild Hall, whose exact site remains unknown, but was probably in the Hill Street / High Street / Union Street area (Pugh 1967, 255). It is interesting to note that the premises mark the modern junction of Market Place and Union Street.

There are few Corporation records which relate specifically to High Street and Union Street. The latter was widened under the 1810 Improvement Act. Watson (1827) states that in the 1740s the High Street was partially paved with cobbles next to the houses. In 1756 the centre of the Street was paved with large cobble stones, with a gutter running down its centre. He also quotes reminiscences of Mr J. Stanroyd, a 94 year old senior resident in the town who remembered that prior to 1810, the streets were covered in 'loose silt' (similar to the layers seen in the Market Place test pits; Hoyland 1992) and during the winter planks were laid down, due to the mud. An open sewer ran on the north side of the High Street with three little bridges across it: posts edged the sewer and were used for tethering horses. Next to the Rose and Crown the open sewer was covered with flagstones upon which three steps were raised and fronted by a small wall three feet high: it was here that the Town Crier made announcements, the dais thereafter called the Crying Stone.

One of the oldest buildings in Wisbech is the Rose and Crown Inn (No. 25 Market Place), which is recorded under its older name of the Horn and Pheasant in 1475 (Gardiner 1898).

Hill Street
This street was originally divided into Lower and Upper Hill Street until the 1950s when the modern, all-inclusive name of Hill Street was adopted. Formerly it was known as Ship Lane, and was probably renamed in 1825 when a schedule for Ship Lane/Hill Street is listed in the Corporation Records.

In 1681 a tunnel and grate was laid down in Ship Lane, and in 1714 a well, with pump, was sunk there. It has been suggested that the Guild Hall stood in Hill Street, perhaps where the Town Hall, and later the Grammar School were situated (Pugh 1967, 255).

In 1814 the girls' school was built in Lower Hill Street and was closed in 1928: in 1953 the building was being used as auction rooms. The first recorded post office was established in Upper Hill street in 1793, where it remained until 1851. No. 17 Hill Street was the Food Office until the late 1950s, and there was a fire station in Lower Hill Street until 1932 (Pugh 1967, 261).

The Town Hall stood here until the new one was built on North Brink in 1810–1811. Gardiner (1898) remarks that a windmill stood at the end of Upper Hill Street where a Mrs Hampson lived (location not known) and photographs of the High Street looking towards the Market Place, taken by Samuel Smith in 1854, show the windmill sails appearing above the rooftops in the background.

The Development Site
Little is known of the early history of the development site at Market Mews itself, although it once lay at the eastern edge of the New Market. A number of 17th- and 18th-century buildings are known to have existed and these earlier structures were replaced by a Victorian shop: local residents recall the use of this building as a fishmongers. The late 19th-century character of the Mews is amply demonstrated by a contemporary photograph (Plate 4).

V. Archaeological Background
(Fig. 1)

The Market Place
No formally recorded fieldwork had been conducted in the town before the Market Place assessment in 1991, although interested individuals had briefly recorded their findings during the redevelopment of some Market Place properties. Wisbech Museum's Accessions List of 1983 records that a fragment of slipware pot with brown and yellow trailed slip glaze was found on the site of the Mermaid public house (No. 37 Market Place). The pottery is post-medieval in date, but no other information is given.

Finds recovered during alterations to the Market Place in the early 1990s (CHER 10489) include carved bone, pottery, architectural fragments and broken gravestones (the latter from Market Street). It has been suggested that a crypt or undercroft located beneath a shop within the Market Place may have related to the old Guild Hall, the exact location of which, as noted above, is unknown (CHER 10493).

It is unfortunate that there was no systematic recording of these sites, nor of more recent developments which have been undertaken in and around the Market Place, as more detailed and structured recording may well have yielded significant information on the development of the heart of the town.

Three small test pits (measuring 2m x 2m) were excavated within the Market Place in 1991 and were positioned towards the west, middle and east end of the Market Place (CHER 10312; Hoyland 1992). Test Pit 1 was excavated to an approximate depth of 0.95m below the tarmacadamed surface. Two substantial postholes were found and may represent the remains of old pump foundations. In Test Pit 2, two distinct groups of features consisted of a line of stakeholes associated with a gully and posthole and a sub-circular arrangement of stakeholes associated with two postholes. These features were interpreted as former market stalls prior to the paving of the stallage area in 1811. The layer at the base of the test pit showed further evidence for post- and stakeholes. All of the features recorded were post-medieval in date, with a single fragment of possible late medieval reduced ware. Test Pit 3 provided further evidence for postholes and gullies, again indicative of market activity before 1811. A square posthole may indicate the position of a pump. One layer had a high organic content and may indicate the remains of Crab Mersh bank, which was redeposited into the Market Place in the early 16th century (see p.10).

The Castle Site
A plan of 1795 shows the castle as it existed at the end of the 18th century, prior to the development of the area into its current form of a regency villa, constructed in 1816 by Joseph Medworth who also designed and built the late Georgian houses of The Crescent. This villa once sat adjacent to Thurloe's Mansion (built in 1656, now demolished) and atop the remains of the former Palace of Bishop Morton (built in 1487). All of these buildings and those of The Crescent, Union Place and Ely Place occupy the site of the original Norman castle and bailey.

Although little excavation has taken place at the castle site until very recently, late medieval and post-medieval finds had previously been recovered from the moat along the south side of the Market Place (as well as an Anglo-Saxon brooch; see CHER 01926a above). In the Annual Report of the Wisbech Society for 1956 (Anniss 1977, 2–3 and fig.3), Mr J.E. Bridges reported finds including shoes, late medieval pottery and a 15th-century gilt spur from the site of Mr Knightley's building (Nos 15–17 Market Place). Bridges also reported finding a wall and evidence of the extensive castle moat. The approximate location of the finds is towards the rear of the south-west wall at No. 17. The bulk of the assemblage consisted of coarse domestic ware of the 15th and 16th centuries. Unfortunately, there are no further references to the wall or ditch found here.

Entries in the Accessions Book of Wisbech Museum show that pottery from the demolished premises of Messrs Dawbarn (Nos 19–21 Market Place) was deposited in the Museum in 1928. The pottery is recorded as being found six feet below the surface during demolition and the descriptions indicate an early post-medieval date.

At Wisbech Library, within the bounds of the castle site, evaluation by Oxford Archaeology East in 2008 revealed over 3m of archaeological deposits, including a ditch or terrace which may relate to the castle moat (CHER ECB 2970; Phillips 2008). At the base of the sequence were flood deposits at c.0.5m OD. Radiocarbon dating of deposits thought to be medieval and castle-related unexpectedly produced a Middle Saxon date (AD 660–780 at 95.4% probability, SUERC-19888, GU-17214, 1285±30BP). Subsequent investigations (CHER ECB

3101; Fletcher 2009) revealed a large ditch aligned east to west, with an organic waterlogged primary fill: this again may be part of the castle moat. Pottery from the ditch has been dated to the 11th to 12th century, while radiocarbon dating of seeds from the primary fill returned a date range of AD 1220–1310 (at 80.9% probability; SUERC-23938, GU-18845, 715±40BP). This work also revealed evidence of a cellar which may relate to the Georgian houses known to have existed here. Large blocks of architectural stone recovered from the cellar backfill may indicate demolition rubble from Thurloe's Mansion.

Subsequent work in the central part of the castle site in 2009 (CHER ECB 3252; Fletcher in prep.) took the form of a community excavation, the objective of which was to locate any remains of the Bishop's Palace. Four trenches and forty 1m by 1m test pits were investigated within the lower gardens, the vaults, the upper garden and in the memorial garden. This work indicates that the ground surface at the time of the construction of Thurloe's Mansion lay at around 0.80m OD: given the previous use of the site for gardens, this level is likely to have remained unchanged since the Norman period. The trenches exposed large medieval ditches and pits, flood silts dating to the 12th to 13th century and a significant deposit of post-medieval building rubble. Sequences of 12th- to 13th-century flood silts were also recorded beneath the vaults, continuing to depths below sea level. The test pits here gave an insight into the constructional techniques used in the vaults, as well as evidence of a possible earlier structure. The flood deposits recorded appeared to lie within the moat, with truncated upper levels of 3.25m OD and lower levels of 1.5m OD. The adjacent site at No. 4 Ely Place (ECB 3332) had similar sequences of flooding, with the uppermost flood deposit being recorded at 3.50m OD (again truncated), with its base at 2.71m OD. The evidence at both sites is believed to relate to the flood of 1236.

Other Recent Sites
Other work conducted in the town since the Market Mews excavation by Oxford Archaeology East includes sites at Church Terrace and New Inn Yard. The site at New Inn Yard (CHER ECB 2878; Mortimer forthcoming) lay c. 150m to the west of the Market Mews excavation. The lower part of the sequence revealed medieval flood deposits, of similar character to those found at Market Mews, although most activity on the site dated to the 16th century or later and included numerous pits and the remnants of buildings, with evidence for both 'industrial' and domestic waste, the former including waste from tanning and horn working.

Work at Church Terrace (CHER ECB 2143; Hatton 2004) in 2004, to the south-east of the Market Mews site, took place immediately to the east of the castle and the Church of SS Peter and Paul. The investigation demonstrated that the site was marginal to the main focus of occupation, which lay to the north and north-west. The almost complete absence of occupational evidence here can perhaps be attributed to the ever-present danger of flooding: sandy silt layers representing flooding episodes were evident, and were the result of the River Ouse bursting its banks, and may have also resulted in the river changing its course. Further to the south-west of the river were midden deposits and occupation layers dating to the 13th–15th centuries.

Work at Sandyland Street in 2004, conducted by Archaeological Project Services, c.300m to the north-west of the Market Mews site again revealed evidence for significant flooding (MCB 17440; Williams 2005). The earliest deposits of laminated silts (spanning c.1.50 to 2.00m OD) were laid down under low energy marine conditions at an unknown date. The local conditions gradually changed to a fresh water environment possibly representing shallow open water (with an upper level of c.2.50m OD), again undated, with no evidence of stabilisation of the ground in this area until the 17th century.

VI. Fieldwork Methodology
(Fig. 2)

The total development area recorded at Market Mews in 1996 measured approximately 33m east to west by 16m north to south. The area available for evaluation was limited to 26m east to west by 15m north to south since a building, due to be demolished, still stood at the western end of the site. A 6m strip on the Little Church Street frontage was unavailable for evaluation as this area was to be left undisturbed by foundation trenching. The physical limitations within the development area in terms of space and access requirements largely determined the positioning of the evaluation and excavation areas, and due to these constraints the work took place in three main stages.

Stage 1: Evaluation, Area 1
An area measuring 12m east to west by 4m north to south was positioned 1m from the eastern site boundary and was opened using a JCB (Area 1). Archaeological deposits consisting of clay floors, beamslots and postholes associated with post-medieval timber-framed structures were encountered directly below the compacted rubble of the recent demolition, 0.20m–0.30m below current ground level (c.6.60m OD).

Given the requirement to establish the nature and depth of the surviving archaeological deposits the western end of the trench was increased in width to c.7m north to south over what appeared to be a uniform area of mid brown clay devoid of intrusive features. This deposit and the underlying light brown fine silt were removed to a depth of 1.20m from the current ground surface to allow the investigation of more deeply stratified deposits.

Due to the fact that there was only a break of four days between the end of the evaluation and the commencement of the excavation, no separation of the evaluation and excavation archives was made. The scope of excavation was agreed in consultation between the County Archaeology Office and Garnett Netherwood.

Stage 2: Excavation, Extension of Area 1
The excavation took place largely within the bounds of the evaluation trench, building upon the results of the first stage of work. Prior to excavation a further strip c.2m wide was machined along the southern edge of the site, down onto the top of the latest surviving archaeological phase, in order to clarify the layout and alignment of these structures. Buildings, pits and flood deposits (Phases 8–12) were subsequently excavated along the length of the evaluation trench before time restrictions and health and safety considerations prompted the reduction in size of the excavation and its sub-division into two separate areas.

Stage 3: Deep Excavation, Areas 2 and 3
In order to excavate the deeply stratified deposits safely, two areas were selected for shoring using sheet piling supplied and installed by the clients. Area 2, at the eastern end of the evaluation trench, measured 3m east to west by 2.50m north to south and Area 3, at the western end measured 3m square.

Excavation by hand within Area 2 reached a depth of 4.20m OD, c.2.40m below pre-development ground level. The use of an auger for a further 1.70m (to a depth of 2.50m OD) seemed to indicate the continuation of archaeological deposits to this depth.

Excavation by hand within Area 3 reached a depth of 3.80m OD. The use of an auger for a further 1.20m to a depth of 2.60m OD suggested the continuation of archaeological deposits to this depth. The auger results however, were by no means conclusive given the small diameter of the borehole required to obtain a sample.

Site Recording
All features and other deposits were recorded using CAM ARC's single context recording system. Given the severe time restriction associated with this project however, it was often necessary to allocate context numbers to broad sequences of occupation deposits or floors relating to a particular phase of development. This has resulted in an over-simplification of the surviving sequence within individual buildings. The level of detail obtained from those deposits selected for thin section micromorphological analysis and micro-excavation is indicative of the complexity and state of preservation of the sequence as a whole (see Milek and French, Chapter 5).

Project Archive
All site records are currently held at Oxford Archaeology East's headquarters at Bar Hill and stored under the site code WIS MM 96. Finds are stored at the Cambridgeshire County Council stores at Landbeach, using the same site code.

VII. Phasing

Evidence for 13 distinct phases of activity was identified (Phases 1–13), each individual phase being defined as an episode of activity which was subsequently sealed by semi-sterile riverine silts deposited either as a result of flooding or deliberate dumping. Each phase has been assigned to a site period, the date of these being largely drawn from ceramic assemblages:

Period 1: 13th to mid 14th century	Phases 1–3
Period 2: mid 14th to mid 15th century	Phases 4–6
Period 3: mid 15th century to c.1500	Phases 7–10
Period 4: 16th century	Phases 11–12
Period 5: 17th century to present	Phase 13

Within a single phase more than one episode of activity is often indicated but, due to the limited area of excavation, it has not always proved possible to determine whether this evidence represents the laying of new floors and internal re-modelling within an existing structure, or complete rebuilding. This is particularly problematic within the earliest excavated phases where space and time were most limited.

VIII. Research Objectives

The research objectives for the project as outlined at the assessment stage (Hinman 1997) were:

- to test and develop existing models of the topography of medieval Wisbech;

- to compare the results of the excavations with those from other fenland towns;

- to examine the changing character of land use of the site in relation to the surrounding medieval and post-medieval settlement;

- to contribute to the development of the local pottery type series and its implications for the study of the local and regional economy;

- to examine the faunal assemblage in relation to the diet and economy of medieval Wisbech;

- to examine the evidence for medieval metalworking;

- to examine the macrobotanical, palynological and sedimentary evidence in relation to diet, climatic conditions, changes in land use and building function;

- to contribute towards a developing research framework for the town.

The contribution of the Market Mews project to each of these aspects is discussed in Chapter 6, with more detail in relevant specialist chapters.

Chapter 2. The Archaeological Sequence

I. Period 1: 13th to mid 14th century

All three of the buildings identified within this period (Buildings 1–3; Phases 1–3, Area 3) were characterised by the presence of relatively thick accumulations of finely laminated floor deposits. These floors appeared to have accumulated through the gradual deposition of domestic debris within the confines of individual buildings.

Phase 1: Building 1
(Figs 4–6, Plate 5A)

Ceramic dating
This phase is dated by a single sherd of Unglazed Grimston or Blackborough End ware (6g), post-dating *c*.1200.

Phase 1.1: Occupational deposits within Building 1, Area 3
A sequence of four floors interspersed with thin layers of apparently sterile silts was observed within the sides of a foundation trench (127; Figs 4 and 5). These floors appeared to be far less substantial than the earliest surface recorded in plan which consisted of a floor 0.15m thick, comprising compact, finely laminated dark grey-brown silt (133). This floor was present across the full extent of Area 3 (limited at this stage to an area of 1.50m by 1.40m towards the centre of the southern limit of Area 1) and was not excavated due to lack of time.

Relating to the floor were several features. A foundation trench (127), measuring 0.57m wide by 0.45m deep, was aligned east to west, with a butt end to the west. Its northern and southern sides were lined with a series of six roughly hewn wooden posts, three having been placed on either side of the cut. These were roughly square in section (measuring 80mm across), with rounded corners and flat bases, spaced at intervals of between 0.10m and 0.15m. One of the northern line of posts had been placed on a postpad consisting of a flat fragment of limestone. The posts were presumably held in position by the fill or packing of the foundation trench which consisted of a dark grey-brown sandy clay-silt with moderate inclusions of yellowish brown clay and occasional charcoal (126). This fill contained an iron nail (SF 28).

The posts appeared to have been truncated at the surface level of the contemporary floor indicating either the collapse or deliberate removal of this wall prior to the laying of a subsequent floor. The apparent absence of any trace of demolition debris overlying floor 133 may suggest that internal elements of Building 1 were removed, presumably with the intention of re-using the salvaged materials.

The posts were inclined to the south at an angle of up to 25° from the vertical, suggesting that complete rebuilding of the property was prompted by subsidence. The ground upon which this and later structures were built was clearly unstable and would appear to have been moving downslope to the south-west. Close examination of the extent of floor 133 indicated that it may have been dragged southwards, partially obscuring the top of foundation cut 127 and indicating post-depositional movement of deposits. The cause of this subsidence may have been the presence of a small drainage gully or erosion channel adjacent to the site under the present line of Market Mews, the presence of which is suggested by the nature of deposition of a series of deposits along the southern limit of Area 3 (most clearly illustrated during Phase 7; see below).

To the west, a beamslot or trench for a plank-built partition (132), 0.20m wide and 0.40m deep, extended into the northern limit of excavation and terminated to the south as a posthole (129) on the same line as foundation 127. No evidence of any structural remains was visible within the fill of the beamslot (131) indicating the deliberate removal of this wall prior to re-modelling. Posthole 129, which measured 0.38m by 0.34m and was 0.35m deep, was rectangular in plan with rounded corners, near vertical sides and a concave base. The character of its fill indicates that this post was deliberately removed prior to the laying of a subsequent floor and was almost certainly re-used.

Further to the south was a postpad (130) consisting of a large flat fragment of limestone (measuring 0.15m by 0.14m) which retained the decayed impression of a square wooden post with a diameter of 60mm.

This group of contemporary features clearly demonstrates the presence of a fairly substantial building, utilising a mixture of timber walling and earthfast posts. The excavation area was insufficient to determine whether foundation trench 127 was an example of clay/stud construction or was intended as a footing for some form of raised sill prior to box frame construction.

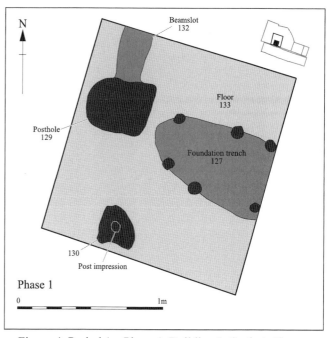

Figure 4 Period 1 – Phase 1, Building 1. Scale 1:50

A

Floor 89
Flood deposit 45

Floors 92 and 46

110

Floor 114

Flood deposit 121=124

125

133

Foundation trench 127

B

42

Flood deposit 86 and 43
Floors 96 and 89
Flood deposit 45
Floors 92 and 46
Floor 48
114 and 110

Flood deposit 121=124

125

Plate 5 a) Detail of west-facing section within Area 3 (Fig. 5, Section 3), showing flood deposits (pale silts)
interleaving with floors and occupation deposits (b) Detail of north-facing section within Area 3 (Fig. 5, Section 1),
showing the thick flood deposit 121=124 (Phase 2.2) towards the bottom of the photograph

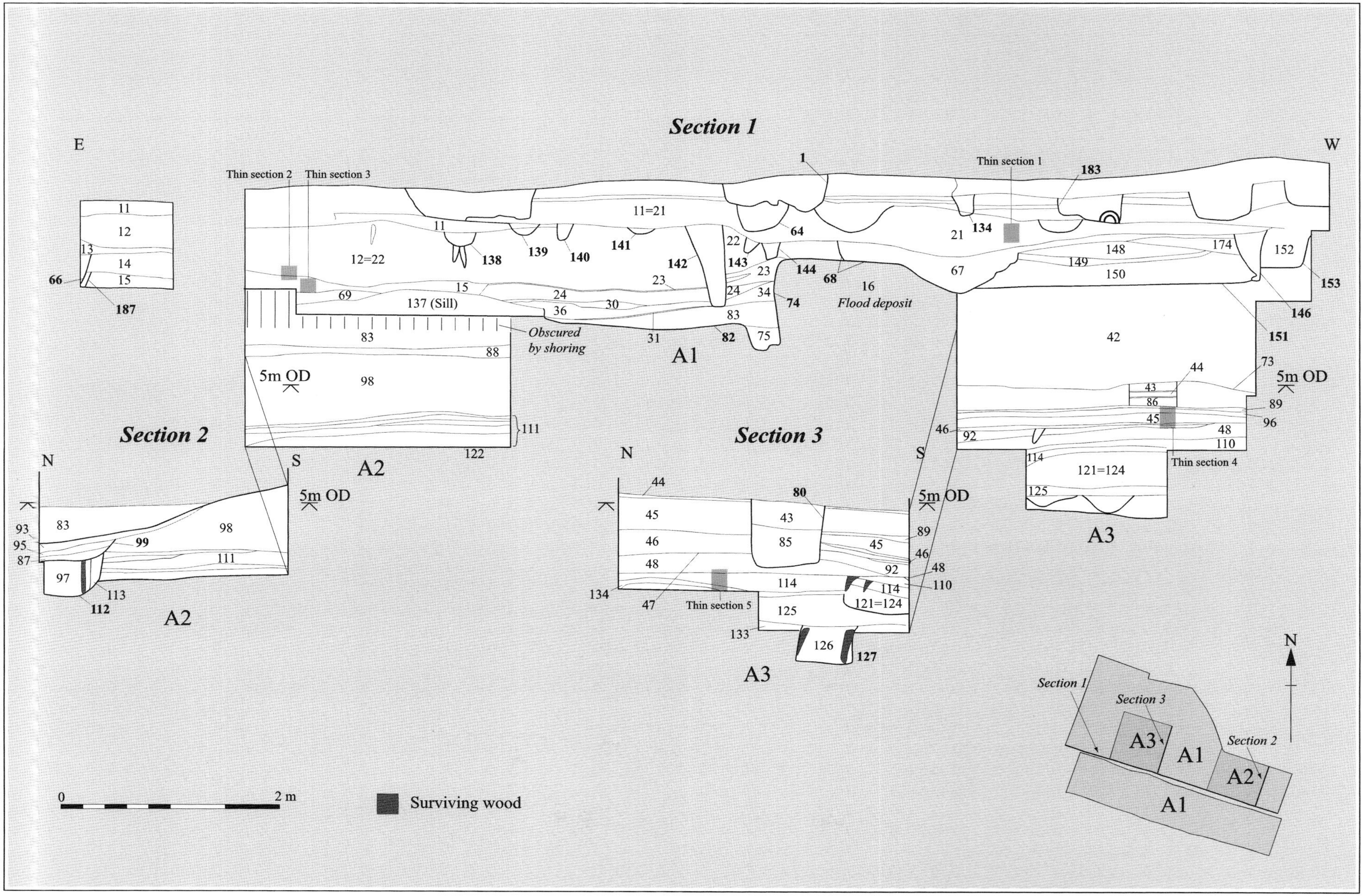

Figure 5 Main sections. Scale 1:50

19

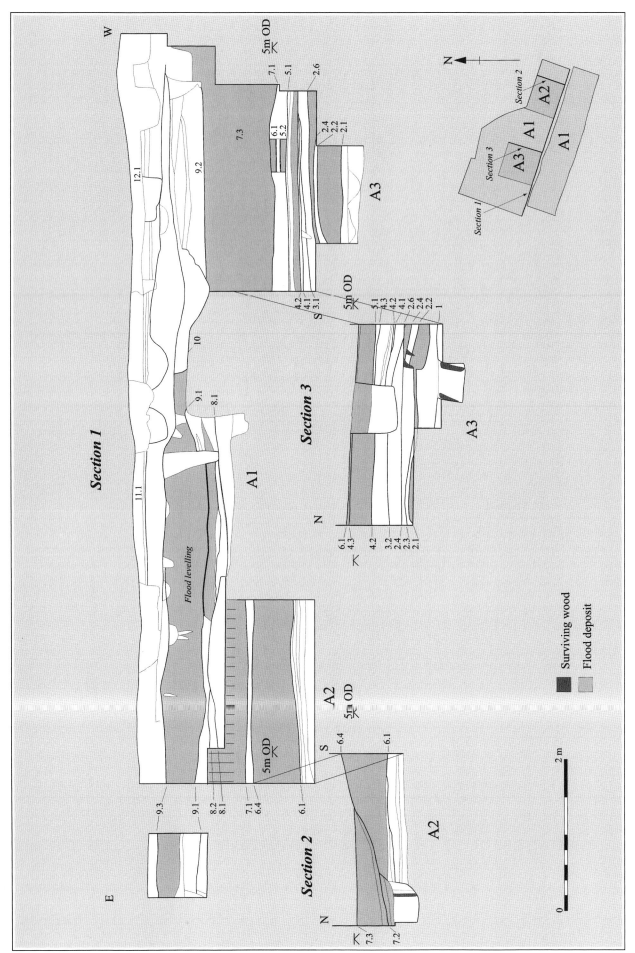

Figure 6 Main sections, showing site phasing and flooding episodes. Scale 1:50

Surviving wood

Flood deposit

20

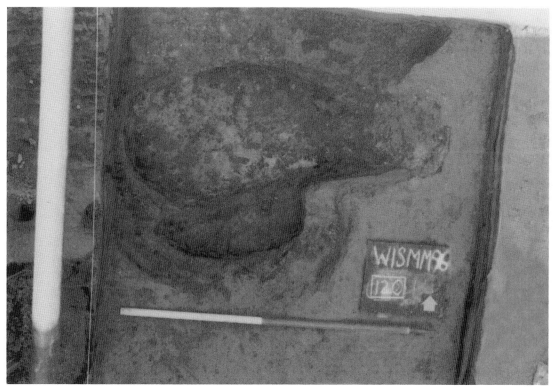

Plate 6 Oven 120 (Phase 2.3, Building 2)

Phase 2: Building 2
(Figs 5–7, Plates 5B and 6)

Ceramic Dating
A small assemblage of 13th-century pottery (33 sherds; 0.175kg) was recovered from deposits assigned to this phase, consisting largely of Grimston, Unglazed Grimston or Blackborough End and Ely wares. The presence of Early Medieval ware may indicate an initiation in the early 13th century (Spoerry, Chapter 3.IV).

Phase 2.1: Occupational deposits within Building 2
Following the deliberate demolition and removal of internal divisions associated with Building 1 a new floor was laid, prior to the construction of what is assumed to be a new building. No evidence for this demolition was apparent between flooring episodes.

The new floor (125) varied in thickness from 0.10m to 0.28m and was laid directly onto the top of floor 133. It comprised a series of finely laminated layers of dark grey silty clay interspersed with lenses of ash. In addition to fragments of pottery, occasional charcoal, mussel shell and animal bone (including a cod vertebra which had been cut width-ways) were noted to have been trampled into the floor surface. A large bone needle (SF 11, Fig. 24) was recovered from this floor: it was probably used for coarse work, such as making or repairing sails or nets (Faine, Chapter 3.VII). Given the limited evidence, however, this object does not provide reliable evidence for any specific activity taking place within Building 2.

Broadly following the course of the earlier foundation (127), another internal wall (116) was aligned east to west (1.80m long, 0.23m wide, 0.50m deep), terminating to the east with a D-shaped post which survived to 0.60m in height. This post may indicate the presence of a doorway.

The sides of the wall 'slot' were near vertical with a sharp break of slope at the top and base of the cut. Its 'fill' (115; possibly actually representing the remnants of the upstanding wall) of mid to light grey clay-silt contained the decayed remains of eleven wooden stakes measuring *c.*0.05m in diameter placed at intervals of 0.10m along the length of the cut. No evidence for a baseplate to hold these stakes in place as part of a structural panel was observed: the reason such a trench should need to be cut into such well compacted but soft ground for what would appear to be a fairly flimsy structure remains unclear. The wall was originally recorded as a foundation trench and thus stratigraphically later than those deposits, including floor surfaces, that it appeared to truncate. Had it acted as a free-standing internal wall, this feature may have been constructed immediately after the laying of floor 125. This internal division appears to have survived the inundation marked by the presence of a flood deposit (see below).

Phase 2.2: Flood deposit within Building 2
Overlying the earliest phase of Building 2 was a flood deposit (121=124, Plate 5B) consisting of a fine pale brown sandy clay-silt layer 0.25m thick, increasing in depth towards the southern limit of excavation. This deposit represents the surviving evidence of what appears to have been a highly destructive episode of flooding.

Phase 2.3: Reflooring and associated oven within Building 2
Sealing the flood deposit was a floor (134), 0.10m deep, consisting of a very dark grey-black compacted silty clay with frequent carbonised organic material. The make up of this floor was similar to the carbonised organic materials present within the base of a contemporary oven (see below). Micromorphological analysis has identified that prior to the use of the oven this floor consisted of

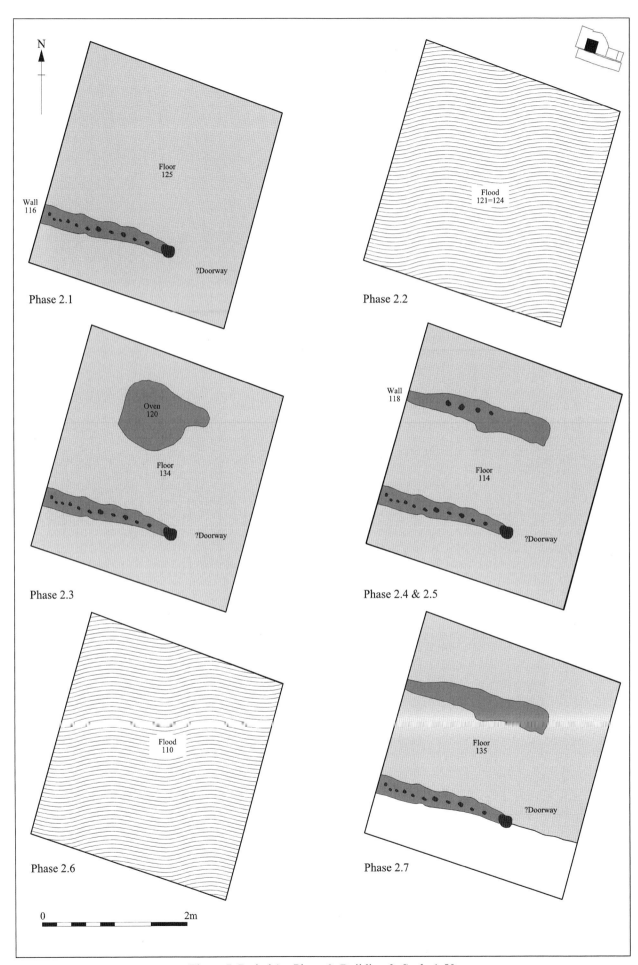

N

Floor
125

Wall
116

?Doorway

Phase 2.1

Flood
121=124

Phase 2.2

Oven
120

Floor
134

?Doorway

Phase 2.3

Wall
118

Floor
114

?Doorway

Phase 2.4 & 2.5

Flood
110

Phase 2.6

Floor
135

?Doorway

Phase 2.7

0   2m

Figure 7 Period 1 – Phase 2, Building 2. Scale 1:50

compacted fine silty sand, horizontally bedded, decomposed organic remains, with a range of phytolith types and food preparation debris such as fragments of bone, egg shell, ash and charcoal (Milek and French, Chapter 5; Thin Section 5).

Oven 120 was keyhole-shaped in plan, with the sub-circular oven area to the west (0.90m in diameter) with a stepped profile forming a shelf along its southern edge and an elongated flue exiting to the east (Plate 6). The sides of the oven were lined with clay, which subsequently partially fired and discoloured a mid orangey red as a result of exposure to heat during its use. Analysis of the environmental samples taken from the primary fill (123) indicates that the oven was fuelled using a mixture of oak, alder and birch (including twigs) as well as a mixture of herbaceous (grasses/rushes/sedges) stems and leaves (Schlee, Chapter 4.IV, Sample 24). After each firing, spent fuel was removed from the oven and scattered upon the surrounding floor, subsequently becoming incorporated into that surface through trampling (Milek and French, Chapter 5, Thin Section 5). This was probably a deliberate action driven by the desire to raise floor surfaces above the level of flooding events. Despite the excellent state of preservation of these deposits there is no clear indication that the oven was being used for anything other than cooking.

The subsequent oven backfill (119; Sample 23) consisted of a loosely compacted mid to light brown clay-silt, representing the deliberate backfilling of the oven and levelling of the immediate area prior to the laying of a new floor (114; see below). This backfilling material was quite distinct from earlier and later flood deposits. It was far less compact and uniform, containing moderate inclusions absent from those silts laid down as a result of flooding. This event has been identified within Thin Section 5 (Milek and French, Chapter 5, Plate 11) as a horizon of redeposited river sand containing randomly orientated, rectangular aggregates of laminated levee material (contexts 119.1–119.3). The size of the aggregates in context 119.1, their random orientation, and the lack of disturbance of a fine organic lens (119.2), all suggest that the deposit was the result of rapid dumping.

Phase 2.4: Reflooring within Building 2
Sealing the infilled oven although still relating to wall 116 to the south, a new floor (114) 0.18m thick comprised a series of alternating layers of decomposing organic matter and compacted sandy silt-loam. It contained iron nails. Micromorphological analysis of the relevant thin section has confirmed that these layers represent the episodic build-up of debris through trampling and the subsequent scattering of plant material, including reeds and grasses, to provide a fresh floor covering. This floor level was significantly different from all of the other floors recorded in Thin Sections 1, 4 and 5, both in the type and quantity of accumulated debris. Floor 114 contained less bone, no ash or egg shell, and more herbaceous material (Milek and French, Chapter 5, Thin Section 5, 114.1–114.6; Plates 11 and 13). This may suggest a change in use of space and/or methods of maintaining the floor, perhaps prompted by a decline in the quality of the climate and consequent rise in the water table.

Further information comes from the environmental samples. Of all the samples taken during excavation, the sample taken from floor 114 (Sample 22) was one of the richest in terms of quality of preservation and range of species represented (Schlee, Chapter 4.IV). The floor make-up contained fish bones, marine mollusc fragments, field beans and hazelnuts in addition to a wide range of non-charred weed seeds. The presence of significant quantities of charred cereals, chaff and straw fragments suggests that, if not derived from the earlier oven, the Sample 22 assemblage is derived from another such feature in the immediate vicinity. This seems to indicate the continuity of an almost identical domestic activity to that evident in Phase 2.3, but now associated with floor 114.

This high quality and range of environmental preservation may point to a change in the status, function or layout of Building 2, perhaps in response to the impact of flooding. The weed assemblage from this floor (together those from the preceding phase) provides evidence that local conditions were consistently or periodically wet, with pondweed and water flea eggs indicating the presence of standing water. These conditions may account for the deposition of both domestic waste and freshly gathered organic materials in order to raise floor levels: this pattern is repeated until Period 3, Phase 9.

Phase 2.5: Internal division within Building 2
While floor 114 was still in use, a remodelling took place within Building 2. A new partition wall was inserted 1.10m to the north of earlier wall 116, terminating at the same eastward point as the pre-existing wall and directly overlying the earlier oven. The new wall consisted of a slot (118) aligned east to west which contained an upstanding clay sill (117), 0.93m long, 0.30m wide and 0.20m high. The clay sill preserved the impressions of four stakeholes, still containing the decayed residues of circular wooden stakes of *c*.0.05m diameter, spaced at 0.20m intervals. The flattened top of the sill may indicate the presence of a beam that, with the stakes, once supported a panel to provide an internal division within the building.

Sill 117 clearly overlay the majority of deposits constituting floor 114, although a further 10mm of occupational debris (not allocated a separate number during excavation) accumulated over the base of the sill prior to the relaying of the entire floor (see Phase 2.7). This deposit (which included lumps of ferruginous concretion) was indistinguishable by the naked eye from floor 114. Both the remodelling of the internal space and the apparent absence of a high degree of carbonised material may indicate a change in use within the building.

Phase 2.6: Flood deposit
A very light grey-brown clay-silt (110), 0.10m thick, survived adjacent to the north-facing section (Figs 5–6) and probably represents evidence of a relatively minor flood, or was possibly floor levelling utilising riverine silts.

Phase 2.7: Internal remodelling and final floor associated with Building 2
A subsequent floor (135) of mid to dark grey silty clay 0.13m thick was differentiated from earlier flooring deposits due to the lack of clearly visible lamination within the context as a whole, suggesting that it had been laid as a single event. This floor was delimited to the south by wall 116, although partition 118 may not have remained in use at this stage.

Phase 3: Building 3
(Figs 5–6)

Ceramic Dating
The small pottery assemblage from this phase again consists of the three key types of the preceding phase (34 sherds; 0.230kg), implying a date of *c.*1250 to *c.*1350.

Phase 3.1: New floor within Building 3
Wall 116 was removed and was sealed by the laying of the next floor. Despite the similarities in make-up between successive floors, Building 2 was probably removed or extensively re-built, when the new floor was laid. This floor (48, Fig. 5), 0.30m deep, was similar to underlying floor 135 and appeared to have been laid as a single episode of dumping, sealing all underlying features. It contained a bone needle. In addition to a small quantity of charred cereal grains, environmental processing of a sample taken from this floor (Schlee, Chapter 4.IV, Sample 20) recovered charred pulses, hazelnut and cherry stone fragments, leather shoe and strap fragments (Fletcher, Chapter 3.VIII, SF 9 and 10) and a few fly pupae.

Phase 3.2: Flood deposit
A pale brown clay-silt layer (47, Fig. 5), varying in depth up to a maximum of 0.30m, was located within the north-eastern quadrant of the area (thinning out to the south and therefore appearing only as a thin deposit in section). This flood event appears to have provoked a new phase of building.

II. Period 2: mid 14th to mid 15th century

All four of the structures assigned to Period 2 (Buildings 4–7; Phases 4–6, Area 3) contained less substantial floor deposits in comparison to preceding phases, suggesting that they did not remain in use as long as their predecessors. The reduced thickness of these floor deposits combined with the increased depth of silts between phases may indicate an increase in both the frequency and severity of flooding during the period.

Phase 4: Building 4
(Figs 5–6 and 8)

Ceramic Dating
A total of 119 sherds of pottery (0.316kg) was recovered from this phase, indicating a date of mid to late 14th to mid 15th century (Spoerry, Chapter 3.IV).

Phase 4.1: Organic floors within Building 4
A series of finely laminated floor surfaces and make-up dumps with a maximum thickness of 0.15m (92) sealed earlier activity and contained what may be a residual iron brooch/buckle with white metal inlay (SF 33, Fig. 17), of possible Anglo-Saxon, Anglo-Scandinavian or Norman date, although a date of origin within the later medieval period is possible (see Crummy, Chapter 3.II). At least six distinct, major divisions were visible within this context during excavation and the layer as a whole was noticeably springy underfoot. One excavator actually noted that this context was as soft as a carpet to stand on whilst recording. The reason for this was apparent from the moment the upper surface of this layer was exposed: the impressions of partially decayed plant stems up to 0.40m in length were clearly visible as thin light brown strands apparently scattered in a random fashion across the darker organic remains of the previous floor covering. The preservation of these plant impressions was so clear that rushes were distinguishable amidst the general scatter of material.

A concentration of burnt and partially burnt clay and ash formed a distinct lens within these finely laminated surfaces and was present towards the north-eastern limit of excavation. This dump of burnt material was thought to derive from an oven or hearth. Whilst this is almost certainly the case, no additional evidence to support this possibility was gained from an examination of the environmental sample taken for this purpose. Occasional bones of pig, sheep and cattle had become incorporated into the general floor make-up.

An assessment of the pollen from a monolith sample taken through this flooring material (Wiltshire, Chapter 4.V) identified the dominant taxa to be those of cereal type grasses and heather. The lower layers appeared to contain more heather and taxa derived from damper soils including sedges, sphagnum moss, bracken and other ferns. The upper layers appeared to contain a higher proportion of cereal type grasses, and herbs characteristic of weedy grassland or meadows. The most abundant woody taxon was hazel, although alder, birch, pine and oak were also recorded. All of the tree and shrub taxa recorded in the deposits are wind pollinated but were probably growing in the catchment area.

Due to the visibly high non-carbonised organic content of this floor a block sample of this deposit was taken for micro-excavation and peroxide flotation along with the more familiar bulk environmental samples. This was intended to establish the level of information being lost through conventional bulk processing: the sample proved to contain cereal straw and rush stems (Schlee, Chapter 4.IV, Sample 17).

A series of shallow 'post' impressions (101, 103, 105, 107 and 109) was present towards the southern limit of excavation. The full extent of these features northwards is unknown due to truncation by a later feature. The deepest of these features (101) was only 0.12m deep, the remainder varying in depth between 20mm and 50mm. Traces of decayed wood were present within the fill of feature 103, with all other 'cuts' being filled with uniform dark greyish brown silts. Given the soft, spongy consistency of the underlying floor it is possible that these were impressions left after the removal of heavy objects, perhaps furniture, from this surface prior to the relaying of the floor (Phase 4.2). The degree of truncation, combined with the limited excavation area meant that it was not possible to identify any pattern within the positioning of these impressions.

Phase 4.2: New floor within Building 4
A subsequent floor consisted of a compact, dark grey/black finely laminated clay-silt layer 0.24m thick, set on an intermittent base of mid-brown clay (46). A number of artefacts were recovered from the surface of this particular floor, including two identical stone spindlewhorls (Crummy, Chapter 3.V, SF 3 and 5, Fig. 23), a copper alloy strap loop of late 12th to 15th century date (used to hold the belt strap end in place; SF 7, Fig. 17), a copper alloy buckle or strap-end plate (SF 6), two iron fragments (possibly chain links; SF 46) and a jet seal matrix or die

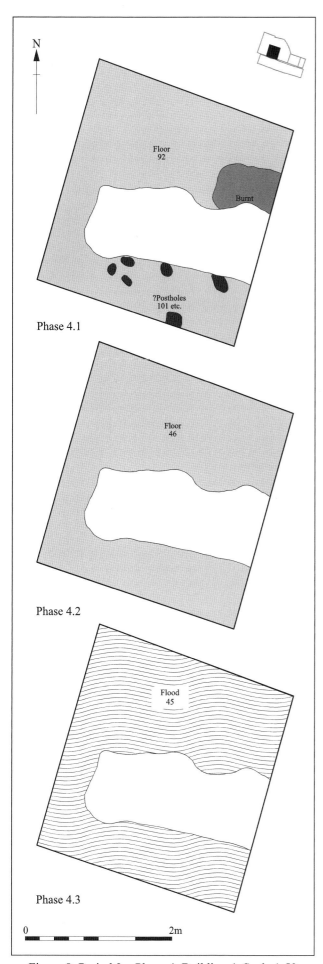

Phase 4.1

Floor
92

Burnt

?Postholes
101 etc.

N

Phase 4.2

Floor
46

Phase 4.3

Flood
45

0   2m

Figure 8 Period 2 – Phase 4, Building 4. Scale 1:50

dating from the mid 13th century to *c*.1300 (Rogerson and Ashley, Chapter 3.VI, SF 4, Fig. 23).

Numerous fish bones (dominated by herring and eel) were recovered from the floor make-up (Curl and Locker, Chapter 4.II), along with low quantities of charred cereals and fly pupae (Schlee, Chapter 4.IV, Sample 14). Weed flora represent generally dry conditions, but with some wetland species indicated.

Micromorphological analysis of Thin Section 4, taken through floor 46, identified a series of fifteen finely laminated deposits of variable composition (Plates 10 and 12). Four floor surfaces were identified (46.7, 46.9, 46.12 and 46.14) on the basis of the compaction of the underlying sediments. The significantly higher concentration of organic and anthropogenic inclusions (Milek and French, Chapter 5) and the horizontal bedding of the organic component, particularly the amorphous organic fine material, is the result of *in-situ* decay of plant material. The floors in Thin Section 4 were generally characterised by fine material, high organic contents and a broad suite of domestic debris such as different types of bones (including fish) egg shell, charcoal and ash. This material would seem to be indicative of domestic 'kitchen' activities. The sediments separating the floor deposits had variable origins, including gradual accumulation, flooding, drying out and post-depositional bio-turbation.

The level of detail provided by thin section analysis provides an indication of the type of living and/or working conditions within the area of Market Mews during the mid 14th to mid 15th century. Within the lifetime of the building indicated by the presence of floor 46, it appears that flooding was still a relatively frequent occurrence, although on current evidence it is not possible to establish at what interval this occurred. Periodic abandonment of the building due to flooding is indicated by contexts 46.10 and 46.11 and the changing level of the water table must have kept these floors damp for prolonged periods. This may suggest that the building or structure was not eminently suitable for domestic habitation but clearly occupation did continue despite such adverse conditions.

Phase 4.3: Flood deposit within Building 4
A subsequent flood layer (45) consisted of pale light-brown sandy clay-silt, 0.30m deep. The flood event evidenced by this deposit would appear to have been of sufficient severity that it required the abandonment of Building 4 and instigated a new phase of building. The quantities of riverine silts deposited as a result of this event must undoubtedly have caused extensive damage. It would appear that following this flood the inhabitants of this area quite literally 'upped sticks', pulling up any surviving building materials and building a new structure on the same plot of land.

Phase 5: Building 5
(Figs 5–6 and 9)

Ceramic Dating
Pottery consisted of two sherds of Unglazed Grimston or Blackborough End ware, post-dating *c*.1200 (8g), although stratigraphic evidence indicates a date of mid 14th to mid 15th century.

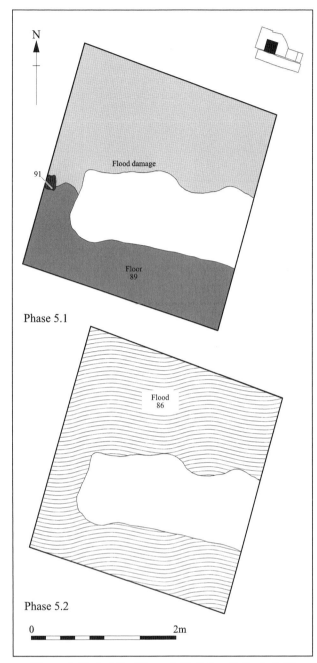

N

Flood damage

91

Floor
89

Phase 5.1

Flood
86

Phase 5.2

0   2m

Figure 9 Period 2 – Phase 5, Building 5. Scale 1:50

Phase 5.1: Floors and other features associated with Building 5

A layer of mid brown clay 30mm thick (96) was only present adjacent to the south-western limit of excavation. The interpretation of this deposit is unclear due to the poor level of preservation, although it is likely to represent the partial survival of a newly laid floor surface or the base of a clay sill.

A subsequent floor (89) consisted of a series of finely laminated very dark grey silty clay deposits 0.10m thick, present along the southern limit of excavation. These deposits were consistent in terms of their make-up, with the continuing accumulation of waste on occupation surfaces evident within earlier phases. During the excavation of this deposit seeds, eggshell and fish bones were all clearly visible and had evidently been trampled

underfoot. Patchy, thinly spread deposits of a white chalky substance thought to be lime were also observed during excavation.

In the western part of the floor was a posthole (91), rectangular in plan with vertical sides and a concave base, retaining the impression of a wooden post. This provides the only direct evidence for a structure associated with this phase. The posthole fill of yellowish brown artefactually sterile silt was extremely loose and showed no sign of compaction. The absence of decayed wood within the posthole strongly suggests that the post had been deliberately removed, presumably soon after another flooding event.

The fact that the only remaining evidence for this entire building and occupation phase survives partially intact along the southern limit of excavation within Area 3 is an indication of the devastating effect that flooding was having within the town. The interior surfaces, and presumably also parts of the building fabric and structure, appear to have been swept away by the power of receding floodwaters.

Phase 5.2: Flood deposit sealing Building 5
Another flood deposit consisted of a light yellowish brown silt containing occasional fragments of coal, brown clay and cess (86). This deposit increased in depth from west to east across the area, to a maximum of 0.12m adjacent to the eastern limit of excavation. The presence of coal fragments may indicate that the metalworking activity witnessed within Area 2 during the subsequent phase was already underway at the time of this flood.

Phase 6: Buildings 6 and 7
(Figs 5–6 and 10, Plate 7)

Ceramic Dating
An assemblage of 416 sherds (7.967kg) of pottery was recovered from deposits assigned to this phase. The group contains two complete vessels: a jug and a storage jar, used in association with metalworking in Building 7. A date of c.1350 to c.1450 is suggested.

Phase 6.1: Buildings 6 and 7

Domestic activity and drainage within Building 6, Area 3
A floor layer (44), 60mm thick, consisted of a series of finely laminated very dark grey-black occupational deposits interspersed with lenses of sterile light brown riverine silts. It is not known whether the silt lenses represent occasional flooding episodes, were deliberately laid floors, or were wind-blown accumulations. Environmental samples (Samples 12 and 13) taken from this context contain a variety of weed seeds in addition to a low presence of charred cereals and chaff fragments along with fish bones, egg shell and fly pupae, suggesting a domestic context (Schlee, Chapter 4.IV). A group of eight stakeholes was observed cutting into the floor within the north-east quadrant of the excavation area. The function of these stakeholes remains unknown. In addition to the ubiquitous scatter of broken pottery and animal bones trampled into this floor, a single silver long cross penny dating to 1280–1301 (SF 2) was recovered, along with iron wire and nail shanks. The coin was probably lost during the 14th century (A. Popescu, Chapter 3.I).

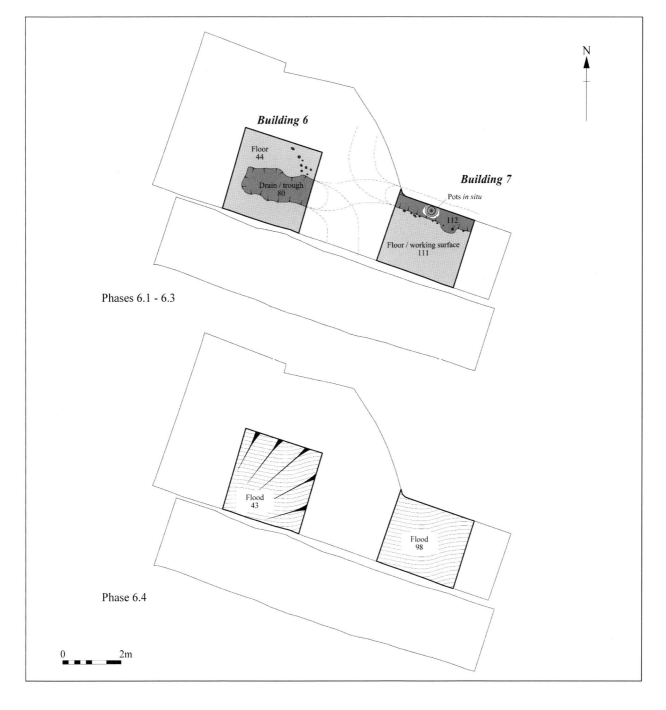

Figure 10 Period 2 – Phase 6, Buildings 6 and 7. Scale 1:125

Cutting into the floor was a possible drain or trough (80), 0.80m wide and 0.60m deep with vertical sides and a flat base. The cut was aligned east to west and extended 2.40m into the excavated area. The western terminal end of the cut was squared. The fact that this cut did not appear to be present within Area 2 further to the east may indicate that it changed course or formed a trough-like feature (see comments on feature 112 below). Flood deposits sealing this feature indicate that the weather was about to take a dramatic turn for the worse and it is also possible that this drain was intended as a temporary feature cut within Building 6 at the onset of flooding in an attempt to direct the rising waters out of this property. The '/drain fill, a brown silt (85), became noticeably darker and wetter towards the base of the cut, with an increasing frequency of mid brown clay fragments thought to represent portions of a disturbed lining.

It is unknown whether these activities were contemporary with the metalworking evident in Building 7. They may have taken place within different rooms of the same building or, given the limited quantity of metalworking debris from Building 6, within entirely separate structures on different plots of land. The largest assemblage of fish bones from the site was recovered from Building 6 (N = 321), dominated by herring (N = 114; Curl and Locker, Chapter 4.II and Table 10).

27

Metalworking activity within Building 7, Area 2

An unexcavated surface (122) of compact dark greyish brown silty clay represents the limit of excavation within Area 2 and was probably laid at the same time as floor 44 in Building 6. Sealing surface 122 were at least three distinct phases of activity associated with the use of Building 7 for a variety of processes necessary for different forms of metalworking. This provides the clearest identifiable evidence from the site for what can be considered commercial/industrial, rather than domestic, activity (Mortimer, Chapter 3.III).

Overlying surface 122 was a heavily compacted floor or working surface 0.13m thick, consisting of a series of discrete episodes of dumping (111). These partially cemented dumps consisted of a mixture of coal, copper alloy waste, ferruginous concretion, ironworking slag and hearth lining. Discrete dumps of coal, slag and lenses of riverine silts were observed during excavation, although the separate sampling of these deposits was not possible due to the time constraints placed on the excavation. A sample from this composite layer (Sample 21) indicates the presence of metalworking waste and low quantities of domestic waste (including uncharred pea and hulled oats; Schlee, Chapter 4.IV). Fragments of copper alloy and ironwork present within this deposit (including an iron strip) suggested that the re-use of scrap metals was taking place within the building, notably including a semi-complete iron barrel padlock (Fig. 16, SF 57).

Phase 6.2: A wood-lined feature within Building 7, Area 2
Cutting through surface 111 was a linear feature which may have served as a drain, water channel or trough. The construction cut (112) was aligned east to west (0.38m deep) and extended into the northern limit of excavation. This feature was initially sealed with clay and then lined with wood. No trace of a lining survived along the base of the cut, although the decayed remains of wooden planking preserving disturbed fragments of the underlying clay (113) were present along its southern side. In addition a line of stakeholes, parallel to the edge of the cut, indicate that stakes were driven into the clay lining at intervals of between 0.15 and 0.20m. These stakes were presumably intended to stabilise the clay and perhaps provided a means for holding the wooden planking in place. Lining 113 contained a copper alloy barrel padlock (Fig. 16, SF 20) and a near-complete bowl-shaped hearth (Mortimer, Chapter 3.III).

The fact that this apparently linear feature did not continue within Area 3, less than 5m to the west, suggests four possible interpretations: 1) that the feature turned south-westwards to equate with ?drain 80 in Building 6; 2) that the feature terminated in a butt end to the west; 3) that the feature turned northwards; 4) that the feature turned southwards (Fig. 10). The butt ended option is favoured, suggesting that this feature was localised and associated with a specific structure or process: the most likely option appears to be that it was a holding tank or trough for water or some other liquid. The two complete ceramic vessels recovered from its backfill may have been buried *in situ* (see Plates 7–9 and Spoerry, Chapter 3.IV), suggesting a secondary use.

The 'trough' was not only cut through a dense concentration of metalworking debris but was also backfilled by material from the same types of process and

Plate 7 Ely ware jar (SF 19) under excavation in fill 97 of wood-lined drain 112 (Phase 6.3, Building 7)

was undoubtedly used during the production of varying types of metalwork.

Phase 6.3: Backfilling of wood-lined feature, Building 7, Area 2
Two complete ceramic vessels, a storage jar and a jug, were recovered from the backfill (97) of wood-lined feature 112 (SF 19 and 56; Fig. 18, Plates 7 and 8), having probably been deliberately placed for use within the 'trough'. The Ely ware storage vessel (SF 19; see also Spoerry 2008, cat. no. 64) was found upright but crushed by the pressure of the surrounding compacted metalworking debris. The Grimston ware jug (SF 56, Fig. 18) was found intact, lying on its side within the larger vessel. The larger vessel appeared to have formed a reservoir for water, with the smaller vessel found inside it used as a portable secondary cistern (Spoerry, Chapter 3.IV). The Grimston jug was heat-damaged. A near-complete copper alloy hand- or cow-bell (SF 12, Fig. 17) was found within the large storage jar, along with other copper alloy objects comprising metalworking debris, a barrel padlock case and further fragments of another barrel padlock (all SF 8). In addition to metalworking debris, the fill of the Ely ware jar was found to contain low quantities of bone, mussel and egg shell fragments and other remains including pea and oats (Schlee, Chapter 4.IV, Sample 19).

Feature 112 itself was backfilled with a wide range of metalworking and associated debris (97). At 7.800kg, the metalworking waste recovered represents more than half the total weight of such debris from the site (Mortimer, Chapter 3.III). Analysis of the materials indicates that the range of processes represented whilst the feature was in use were the same as those represented during backfilling. As well as the items listed above, other metal objects associated with this feature included iron nails (SF 22, Fig. 17).

As has already been noted, despite the proximity of the two excavation areas, coal, slag and other metalworking debris was only recovered in low density from contemporary floor deposits in Building 6: this may indicate the presence of a division or physical boundary between the two areas, which may have formed rooms within the same building or two separate structures.

Phase 6.4: Severe flooding
A flood deposit above Building 6 (43), 0.38m deep, sealed floor 44 and partially filled associated drain 80. The steeply sloping contours of this deposit indicate the presence of a naturally formed drainage channel exiting from the south-west of the excavation area. This channel may have formed as water levels receded and the direction of flow may have been influenced by the presence of existing features within the immediate area. In this instance it appears that the presence of Building 7 was obstructing the flow of flood waters directly to the east. Above Building 7 a similar major flood deposit (98) consisted of pale light brown sandy clay-silt, 0.40m deep. This layer completely sealed the underlying phases of metalworking activity and marked a distinct change of use for the area.

III. Period 3: mid 15th century to *c*.1500

Three separate buildings of this date were identified (Buildings 8–10; Phases 7–10, Areas 2 and 3). Flooding would appear to have reached new levels of destruction during this period, depositing unprecedented depths of waterborne silts across both excavation areas.

Phase 7: Building 8
(Figs 5–6 and 11)

Ceramic Dating
A group of 142 pottery sherds (1.169kg) was recovered from deposits assigned to this phase. The key change in the ceramic assemblage from that of previous phases is the presence of Late Medieval/Transitional pottery, although this date is largely derived from one large bowl sherd (Spoerry, Chapter 3.IV). This type, present towards the end of the phase sequence, may indicate a mid-15th-century date, although the remainder of the assemblage does not necessarily support this suggestion. A clear date for the deposition of many contexts within the phase remains uncertain due in part to the small size of the assemblage, much of which could sit comfortably within the preceding period.

Phase 7.1: Building 8

Remnants of a flood-damaged structure, Area 2
A layer of mid-brown clay (88), 70mm thick, survived adjacent to the southern limit of excavation within Area 2. This layer may represent the last surviving trace of

flooring associated with a distinct phase of construction, Building 8. The western wall of Building 8 consisted of a beamslot supporting a number of upright posts (74). The beamslot was aligned north to south with near vertical sides. The base of the cut was irregular, retaining the impressions of three roughly circular posts up to 0.26m in diameter, one of which may later have been replaced. The fill (75) contained an iron knife blade (SF 32, Fig. 17). Another 'posthole' (76), 0.17m in diameter, was visible higher within the stratigraphic sequence. Its fill (77) probably represents secondary infilling of the robber 'impression' resulting from the removal of posthole 81 which it directly overlay.

Occupational deposits within an erosion gully, Area 3
A fine brown clay-silt layer containing occasional pottery sherds, daub and unfired clay fragments (73) varied in depth between 5mm to 10mm. This deposit mirrored the underlying contours of the earlier flood-lain silt (43) and its composition and form was consistent with occupational build-up over newly laid floors noted in other phases. It was, however, an extremely thin deposit, suggesting a short period of usage. Layer 73 accumulated within the erosion gully implied by the underlying contours, indicating that this was an external surface sloping steeply downwards from north to south. Analysis of a sample taken from the deposit (Schlee, Chapter 4.IV, Sample 8) indicates a low environmental content suggesting a lack of intensive occupation. The duration of activity represented by this deposit is uncertain although the presence of a contemporary floor (88) within Building 8 to the east indicates sufficient respite from flooding for reconstruction.

Phase 7.2: Flood damage relating to the destruction of Building 8, Area 2
An erosion gully (99), *c*.0.60m deep, was aligned east to west and extended into the northern, western and eastern limits of excavation. The southern edge of the cut was irregular, sloping gradually towards a concave, but irregular, base. The deepest visible extent of this cut was positioned directly above earlier drain or trough 112 (Phase 6.2) and its irregular nature suggests that it formed as a result of water cutting through earlier deposits during the process of drainage. The direction of flow for these receding flood waters may have been influenced by the presence of standing structures, and previously buried features.

Erosion gully 99 contained a series of fills (87, 95 and 93, in order of deposition), two of which (87 and 93) were found to contain significant quantities of metalworking debris, including both fuel and ore which had clearly been redeposited, having derived from earlier metalworking. Fill 87 also contained an iron strip fragment (pintle/hinge) and a copper alloy fitting and fragment. Fill 93 contained a fragment of lead nail/stud and possible copper alloy slag. One of the small pieces of fired clay from fill 93 has a surface which may have been prepared to give it a smooth finish, possibly as a mould (Mortimer, Chapter 3.III), although the fragment was too small to suggest the type of object being cast. Fill 95, a mid yellowish brown clay, was again redeposited and may represent the redeposition of portions of clay floor (88) from Phase 7.1.

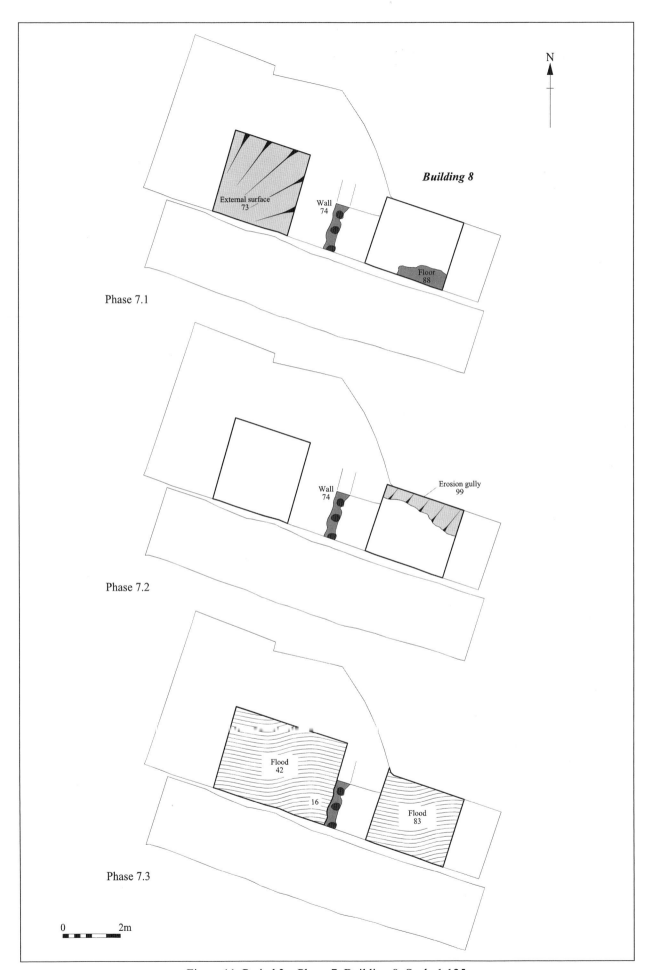

N

Building 8

External surface
73

Wall
74

Floor
88

Phase 7.1

Wall
74

Erosion gully
99

Phase 7.2

Flood
42

16

Flood
83

Phase 7.3

0   2m

Figure 11 Period 3 – Phase 7, Building 8. Scale 1:125

Phase 7.3: A severe flood, Area 1

The single most extensive evidence for flooding at the site is represented by a layer consisting of sterile flood-lain light yellowish brown silt (16 = 42 = 83), which survived to more than 1.00m in depth. Finely laminated streaks were observable within the silt which are presumed to be the decayed remains of reeds and other organic matter torn from the beds of the rising rivers and mixed into the silty suspension. Although largely devoid of artefacts this layer did contain occasional sherds of pottery and the articulated lower limb of a sheep, as well as an iron clench nail.

It appears that the western wall of Building 8 (represented by beamslot 74) remained upstanding during the flood, which swept away the remainder of the structure. The section (Fig. 5) clearly shows the greater depth of the western edge of the beamslot compared to its eastern edge. It is suggested that the wall presented an obstacle to the flow of receding silt-laden flood waters and, in conjunction with other (assumed) structures in the immediate area, formed an effective silt trap. The slight angle of inclination of the impression of this wall from the vertical plane is perhaps explained by the pressure placed on the exterior of the building by the build-up of the flood silts: as a barrier it is probable that the wall served to increase the scouring effects of the floodwaters on other parts of the structure and surrounding deposits. The building itself cannot have survived the severe flooding with any structural integrity and building materials may have been salvaged from it.

Phase 8: Building 9
(Figs 5–6 and 12)

Ceramic Dating

A total of 240 sherds of pottery (1.660kg) was recovered from deposits assigned to this phase and is characterised by the presence of a small quantity of Bourne D type ware, believed to have first been manufactured around 1450 (Spoerry, Chapter 3.IV). The assemblage notably includes a few sherds of Spanish olive oil jar. A mid to late 15th-century date is suggested.

Phase 8.1: Occupational build-up within Building 9

After the subsidence of the floodwaters there followed a period of salvage during which the intact elements of Building 8 were removed, presumably for re-use in the new structure (Building 9). The infilling of the void left by removal of wall 74 (Building 8) was a loose yellowish brown silty clay (75) which may indicate a deliberate attempt to backfill the robbed out foundation trench or, as in previous phases, silt in a semi-liquid state may have simply flowed into the newly created void during salvage. This structural line, however, appears to have continued to function as the rear wall of the building, effectively holding back a 'bank' of flood deposits (42; Figs 5 and 12).

A compacted pale brown silty clay layer (79, not visible in section) less than 10mm thick indicates a trampled surface although rather insubstantial to constitute a floor. Despite its thinness and patchy character a notable quantity of pottery (43 sherds) was recovered from this deposit, along with a piece of copper alloy sheet and a lump of ferruginous concretion. This surface would appear

to represent a relatively short period of use and may have been derived from activity associated with the salvaging of materials from damaged Building 8 or perhaps as part of the construction preparation. Spoerry (Chapter 3.IV) notes that the average sherd size of the ceramic assemblage from this surface is somewhat smaller (9g) than that of the assemblage as a whole (12–13g): this is almost certainly a direct result of trampling.

A clay sill (137) was visible within the north-facing section (Section 1; Fig. 5) although it did not extend into the area of excavation. This sill may have been contemporary with layers 79 and 31, representing an internal division within Building 9.

Floor 31 was a compacted dark greyish brown silty clay layer 0.13m thick, containing occasional lenses of charcoal and daub, along with a copper alloy stud, four iron nails and a sheet fragment. The surface, delimited to the west by the line of earlier wall 74 (the line of which appears to have continued to function as a wall), was noticeably uneven in contrast to all floor deposits from previous phases. Similarities in the content of Sample 1, taken from floor 31, with Sample 7 from later floor 23 (Schlee, Chapter 4.IV) may suggest continuity of use within individual rooms in Buildings 9 and 10 between Phases 8 and 9. It may have lain in a separate room from surface 79 to the east, divided from it by a partition (see below).

Phase 8.2: Further occupational build-up within Building 9

A brown clay-silt deposit (34) 0.10m thick was located adjacent to the near-vertical face of the flood deposit (42). Layer 34 obscured the position of the underlying beamslot trench (74; Building 8) and may represent an attempt to compact the loose backfill of the trench (75), prior to a new phase of building. This layer contained an iron strip and nail.

Further east, a pale brown deposit of riverine silt (36), 0.10m thick, may represent another minor flooding event although equally it could represent a deliberately deposited levelling layer, laid in preparation for the construction of Building 9, or perhaps resulting from a natural accumulation of wind-blown silt particles.

Overlying this deposit was a floor (30) of compacted, dark greyish brown silty clay, 40mm thick, containing lenses of silt, charcoal and clay, as well as an iron nail shank. This thin, patchy, poor quality surface was bounded to the west by the earlier flood deposit (42) and terminated to the east along a straight north to south line, indicating the position of a partition between rooms. Within the subsequent phase (Phase 9) the impression of a heavy linear object, presumed to be a ground beam, was positioned directly over this dividing line.

A dark brown silty clay floor surface (69), 0.10m thick, was bounded to the west by floor 30 and extended into the north, south and east limits of excavation, partially extending above clay sill 137. Although similar in terms of make-up and consistency, these floors may represent the surfaces of different rooms within the same building.

Phase 8.3: Flooding

A pale brown deposit of riverine silt (24), 0.15m thick, sealed earlier floor 30. This silt contained an iron nail.

N

Wall

Building 9

Flood bank?

Floor
31

?Surface
79

Clay sill
137

Phase 8.1

Wall

Building 9

Flood bank?

Floor
30

Floor
69

Clay sill
137

Phase 8.2

Flood bank?

Flood?
24

Phase 8.3

0   2m

Figure 12 Period 3 – Phase 8, Building 9. Scale 1:125

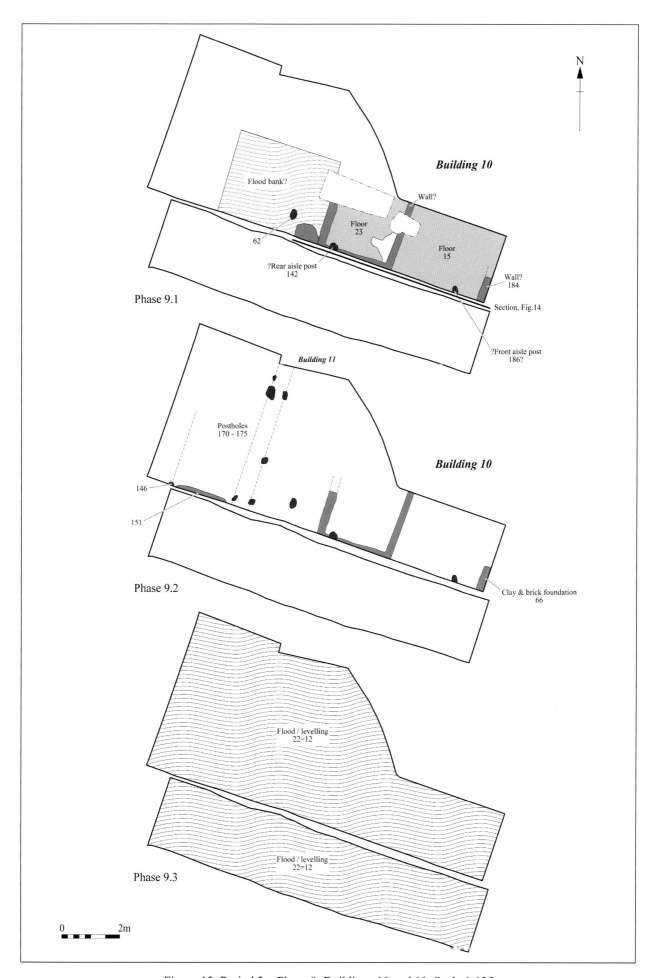

N

Building 10

Flood bank?

Wall?

Floor
23

Floor
15

62

?Rear aisle post
142

Wall?
184

Section, Fig.14

Phase 9.1

?Front aisle post
186?

Building 11

Postholes
170 - 175

Building 10

146

151

Clay & brick foundation
66

Phase 9.2

Flood / levelling
22=12

Flood / levelling
22=12

Phase 9.3

0   2m

Figure 13 Period 3 – Phase 9, Buildings 10 and 11. Scale 1:125

Phase 9: Buildings 10 and 11
(Figs 5–6, 13 and 14)

Ceramic Dating
Some 200 pottery sherds (1.559kg) were recovered from deposits assigned to this phase. The main change from the preceding period is the virtual absence of Ely ware. A date of *c*.1450 to *c*.1500 is suggested.

Phase 9.1: Building 10
Rebuilding on the same ground plan is indicated by the presence of beam impressions delineating the extents of new floors within two rooms. These impressions apparently indicate the former positions of the baseplates for a free-standing timber-framed structure (Building 10), which evidently replicated earlier constructional lines.

Differential deposition within two rooms
Within the westernmost room, the new floor consisted of moderately compacted greyish brown silty clay (23) 80mm thick containing occasional flecks of daub and charcoal, as well as iron nails. As with those surfaces within the preceding phase, the surface of this floor was uneven. It was *c*.2.70m long and appeared to be delineated both to the east and west by slightly raised and level strips 0.20m to 0.30m wide, aligned north to south. The westernmost strip replicated the previous wall line present since Phase 7.1 (74). The constituents of these flattened areas were identical to the remainder of the floor surface, marking the presence of beams (subsequently removed) from a timber-framed structure. That the beams clearly overlay the floors is a clear indication that the surfaces must have been prepared prior to construction of the new building.

In the easternmost room, the new floor (15), measuring *c*.2.80m long, consisted of a compact dark yellowish brown silty clay layer 0.15m thick. It contained a worked bone implement, an iron nail and copper alloy slag. Again, this surface was uneven and was noticeably compacted, with a lower charcoal content than the adjacent floor. The uneven surfaces within these two rooms are attributable partly both to wear through usage and differential compaction, possibly indicating a relatively short period of usage.

The difference in thickness and consistency of the two contemporary floors may suggest that each of the rooms served a different function. Environmental samples were therefore taken in an attempt to identify such possible differences (see Schlee, Chapter 4.IV; Sample 6 (floor 15) and Sample 7 (floor 23)). In the event, both samples produced the same range of charred cereals and pulses in low quantities, although Sample 6 also contained small quantities of bone and egg shell providing limited evidence for a difference in use between the two areas.

Floor 15 was also sampled for micromorphological analysis, with two thin sections taken adjacent to one another in the north-facing section of Area 1 (see Milek and French, Chapter 5; Plates 15–18). These profiles were staggered so that the lowest horizon in Thin Section 2 (contexts 15.3–15.5) overlapped the uppermost horizon in Thin Section 3 (contexts 15.6–15.7), thereby producing a continuous profile over a depth of 0.24m. Context 15 proved to consist of a series of alternating layers of clay and very fine sandy clay loam, originally interpreted as a deliberately laid floor, although micromorphological analysis indicates a composition suggesting mud typical of a swamp, ditch or river pool. The thin sections provide no evidence that these layers were deliberately constructed mud floors, suggesting instead that this deposit could have developed as a result of the presence of a pool next to a tidal creek, which occasionally received an inwash of fine sand, silt fragments and any anthropogenic material incidentally in the vicinity.

Clearly, these two pieces of evidence are initially contradictory: excavation indicated that this deposit was used as a floor, whereas micromorphology suggests that this was not the case. Explanation of this disparity comes from the working conditions and recording methods on the day of sampling. The positioning of the relevant micromorphological samples was opportunistic and determined by gaps in the shoring and it appears likely that what was sampled in the section did not appear in plan, a situation familiar on many sites. A re-examination of the photographic record of the section prior to shoring, during sampling and after sampling, confirms that the thin section is not representative of the deposit sampled in plan. The possibility that a source of water lay adjacent to

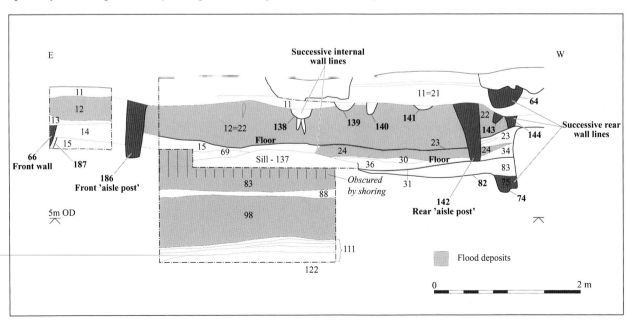

Figure 14 Section showing the interpreted development of Building 10. Scale 1:50

Building 10 is noteworthy: it has already been suggested that post-depositional movement of stratified deposits occurred within Area 3, indicating the presence of a drainage gully or channel below the current line of Market Mews, immediately to the south of the excavation area.

Structural features

Two postholes (70 and 62; former not located in plan) probably formed part of the western wall of Building 10. They were 0.20 and 0.38m in diameter respectively and the former was inclined to the east at an angle of c.40° to the vertical plane, suggesting that considerable pressure had been exerted on the post from the west. An adjacent substantial tapering posthole (142) may represent additional support for the interior of the western wall of the building. It was positioned just to the east of the earlier wall line (wall 74 and its successors) and was set at a raking angle, leaning towards the east, perhaps indicating that it served as a rear 'aisle post' to the building (Fig.14).

At the eastern end of the excavated area, possibly forming the eastern end of the building, was a robbed-out wall foundation (184; 187) and 0.75m to the west by a substantial posthole (186; fill 185). As indicated in Fig.14, these may have formed the front wall and front 'aisle post' of the building. Between these features, two deposits were revealed within a small test pit excavated during the evaluation phase of the project. A silt layer (14) was followed by a deposit of compact mid brown silty clay (13), 80mm thick. The limited east to west extent of these deposits may indicate that, rather than representing floor(s) these deposits may represent an attempt to strengthen the robbed out wall which, when reinforced, would have functioned as a low (c.0.30m high) dwarf wall or buttress within Building 10. The adjacent post (186) may then represent surviving evidence for additional support, forming one of a series of internal studs.

Both of the major front and rear posts (142 and 186) appear to have remained upstanding during subsequent flooding.

Phase 9.2: Alterations to Buildings 10 and 11

At the eastern end of Building 10, the earlier wall (184) was replaced by a clay and brick foundation (66; 65). The bricks were unfrogged, red, and handmade, measuring L: c.10 x W: c.5 x T: 2½ inches (260mm x 130mm x 65mm). This is the first example from the site of a structure with such a foundation and the strengthening of this building may have been intended to facilitate the addition of a second storey.

To the west was ephemeral evidence for the presence of a possible structure (Building 11), delimited to the west by a posthole (146), with construction occurring after a levelling cut (151; Fig. 5). A sequence of layers within this cut (147 to 150) may have formed alternate make-up dumps and floor surfaces. The eastern end of the structure was not visible in section, having been truncated by later pitting although a number of postholes running north to south (170 to 175) may represent a wall line.

Phase 9.3: Flood or levelling

A layer of pale brown silt (22), 0.60m thick, may have resulted from flooding or levelling. This same deposit (12) was identified during the excavation of a small test pit towards the eastern limit of Area 1. Micromorphological analysis of layer 22 (Thin Section 2) proved inconclusive.

The nearly perfect sorting of this layer and the lack of a fine mineral component, offers two potential avenues of interpretation (Milek and French, Chapter 5). The material could have been wind-sorted, having originally derived from coastal sand dunes, or it could have accumulated on the bed of a fairly slow moving 'river'. Deposition on the site could therefore have been due to deliberate dumping, in order to elevate the ground surface (although it notably lacks the range of inclusions noted in other levelling layers). Alternatively this deposit may have been entirely natural in origin, representing a river channel infilled with a fine sandy bedload. It appears highly likely that the deposit, as recorded during excavation, represents more than one event.

Phase 10: Pitting
(Figs 5–6)

Ceramic Dating

Pottery from this phase consists of 35 sherds from a single Orange Sandy ware jug (0.672kg), dating broadly to the period 1350–1500, although on stratigraphic grounds the phase may date to the second half of the 15th century (Spoerry, Chapter 3.IV).

Phase 10.1: Pitting

Prior to the raising of the ground level, fragmentary evidence in the form of two small pits suggests a change in use at the western end of the site. One pit (41, not illustrated), 0.35m wide and 0.33m deep, was revealed and partially truncated during the installation of shoring at the western end of the site. Its single fill (40), a light brown clay-silt with frequent light brownish green mottling, contained the remains of the Orange Sandy ware jug decorated with a yellowy green glaze noted above. The mottling within the fill was assumed to indicate the presence of cess deposits although this feature was too small to have functioned as a cess pit. The jug may have been used for the transportation of night soil, although no cess-like concretions were found adhering to it.

The second pit (68, Fig. 5) was revealed during the preparation of the western end of the site to receive shoring. Only a portion of the north-western quadrant of this feature and its fill, which was 0.35m deep, was excavated and comprised a series of finely banded clays and silts (67) containing occasional animal bone.

IV. Period 4: 16th century

Two buildings of 16th-century date were identified (Buildings 12 and 13; Phases 11–12, Area 1). A change in land use from previous phases is indicated by the presence of a series of intercutting rubbish pits towards the western end of the site. These pits contained a variety of domestic refuse.

Phase 11: Building 12
(Figs 5–6 and 15)

Ceramic Dating

A group of 135 pottery sherds (1.875kg) was recovered from deposits assigned to this phase. The sudden appearance of Cistercian ware (1470, but usually a little later), alongside Bourne D ware (post-1450) and Orange

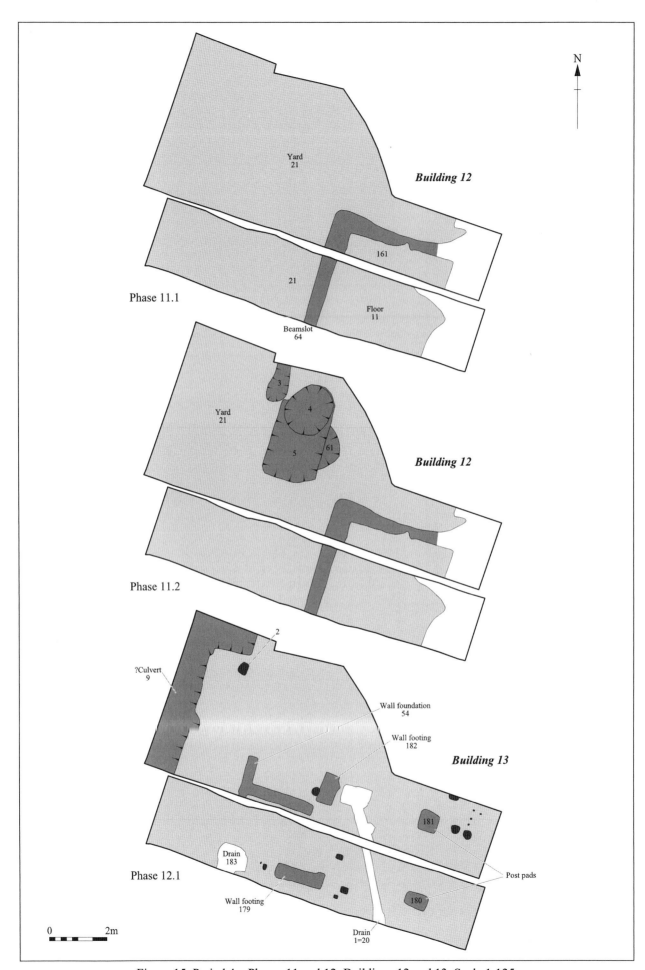

N

Yard
21

Building 12

161

21

Phase 11.1

Floor
11

Beamslot
64

3

Yard
21

4

5   61

Building 12

Phase 11.2

2

?Culvert
9

Wall foundation
54

Wall footing
182

Building 13

181

Post pads

Drain
183

Phase 12.1

Wall footing
179

180

Drain
1=20

0   2m

Figure 15 Period 4 – Phases 11 and 12, Buildings 12 and 13. Scale 1:125

Sandy ware points not only to a later date but also to a change in ceramic supply and possibly the character of activities at the site (Spoerry, Chapter 3.IV). A date shortly before 1500 is the earliest possible date for this phase, continuing with types dating to the 16th century but no later.

Phase 11.1: Construction and use of Building 12
The western limit of Building 12 was marked by the presence of a beamslot (64) aligned north to south, which returned eastwards at its northern end (161). The impression left after the removal of this beam was filled with fine light yellowy brown silt. No indication that the beam had decayed *in situ* remained and it appears likely that this particular structural element was salvaged for re-use. The western wall replicated the line of the back walls of Buildings 8–10, indicating continued definition of the same plot of land.

The rather shallow depth of features within the preceding phase may indicate a degree of truncation, probably caused by levelling prior to this phase of rebuilding. A layer of light yellowish brown silty clay up to 0.35m thick extended across the whole of Area 1 (11=21; Fig. 15) and served to raise the ground level and provide a stable surface for renewed building activity, the presence of horizontally-bedded pottery and animal bone fragments to the east indicating that this also formed a trampled floor surface. The deposit contained small fragments of red brick, possibly derived from the demolition/destruction of the preceding wall due to flood damage. Layer 11 also contained an iron ring.

Analysis of micromorphological samples from the eastern part of layer 21 (Thin Section 1; Plates 19–22) revealed a wealth of information not visible to the naked eye. Three main horizons were evident within this context (Milek and French, Chapter 5). The earliest horizon (21.4–7) contained randomly deposited fragments of anthropogenic materials (such as bone, egg shell and also, lime plaster and clay) which may indicate building activity. Included here were two fine, horizontal layers (21.4 and 21.6) of articulated phytoliths (the silica 'skeletons' of decayed plants) in an extraordinary state of preservation due to their rapid burial. These plant remains are evidence for the laying down of whole herbaceous plants and grasses during the initial stages of construction. The second horizon (21.2–21.3) was composed of a virtually sterile clay loam just over 10mm thick, and was laid over the second layer of plants and grasses. Laid above this, the final horizon (21.1) was compacted in a manner characteristic of trampling and may be interpreted as the newly laid floor: it consisted of a mixed accumulation of domestic debris including pottery, bone, and coarse lime plaster, presumably from the internal walls of the building.

Phase 11.2: Pitting
A series of pits was excavated towards the western end of the site within what is assumed to have been the back yard of Building 12. These were restricted to a relatively small area of the site and were used for the disposal of a variety of domestic waste.

The earliest feature, a rubbish pit (61), was probably roughly circular in plan although it was subsequently truncated to the west by later pit cuts. Its fill, a very dark grey clay-silt with orange-red flecks (60), contained

frequent ash and charcoal and occasional red brick and tile. The flood-derived silts into which the base of this pit had been cut were discoloured, the light pinkish brown colouring indicating that hot ashes had been dumped here.

Cutting into the earlier pit was a sub-rectangular rubbish pit (5), 1.70m long by 1.50m wide and 1.20m deep with vertical sides and a concave base. Its fill (50) consisted of a moderately compact dark grey clay-silt which contained a mixture of domestic debris including two goose radii which had been part sharpened, perhaps for use as styli. Other finds included an iron ?slag and nails.

A subsequent rubbish pit (4) was roughly circular in plan, 1.60m in diameter, with near vertical sides and a concave base. Its fill (17) was a dark brown silty clay containing occasional red brick fragments, tile, animal bone, pottery, oyster and mussel shells. In addition a dagger cross-guard of late 15th- to mid 16th-century date (Crummy, Chapter 3.II, SF 30, Fig. 17) was recovered from this pit, along with a number of iron nails, a fragment of window glass, a copper alloy fragment and an iron plate (SF 53, Fig. 17).

To the north-west was a small, elongated pit (3), which was planned and numbered during the evaluation but left unexcavated.

Apart from cattle, sheep and pig the faunal assemblages from pits 4 and 5 are of interest due to the presence of a range of bird bones (Faine, Chapter 4.I). These include goose, chicken, mallard and kittiwake, the wild species suggesting the exploitation of the surrounding fenland.

Phase 12: Building 13
(Figs 5–6 and 15)

Ceramic Dating
A group of 105 sherds of pottery (1.098kg) was recovered from deposits assigned to this phase, dating to *c.*1450–*c.*1550.

Phase 12.1: Structural features associated with Building 13
As with the preceding phase of development, a degree of truncation and levelling of underlying deposits occurred prior to construction. As a result no evidence for the destruction, through demolition or otherwise, of Building 12 survived within the archaeological record. In turn, the final phase of construction within the excavation area removed all traces of floors and upstanding walls associated with Building 13. The only features to survive had been cut into the surface of the underlying layer (11=21). Although the footings to this building were fairly shallow, the use of foundations marks a change in both construction technique and building materials.

Two drains were recorded, one of which (1=20) was constructed using red brick and glazed ceramic piping and was aligned north-west to south-east. Its construction was similar to that of the second drain (183) further west, only the northern end of which was recorded within the excavated area. Both features had clearly become redundant due to blockages. The fills of both drains contained considerable quantities of lime, presumably used in attempts to clear obstructions.

To the north-west, a wall foundation (54; 55), contained a single north-south line of red unfrogged bricks (L: 11½ x W: *c.*4 inches (290 x 100mm) x T unknown). It is assumed that, given the rather unusual dimensions of these bricks, they were probably locally made.

A number of wall footings (179 and 182) and post pads (180 and 181) are thought to have been contemporary, possibly forming part of the same building. Numerous post and stakeholes (155–169 and 176–178) may also have been internal features within Building 13. An isolated posthole (2; fill 6) indicated building activity above earlier rubbish pitting in the area. It contained an iron nail.

The function of a substantial cut (9) to the west of Building 13 is uncertain. Partially excavated during the evaluation stage of the project, this trench was seen to extend across the whole of the western end of Area 1. Its fills (7 and 8) demonstrated steep alternating tip lines of sandy clay silt and clay silt indicating that this feature was cut to a substantial depth, although excavation by hand ceased after 0.50m. Fill 7 contained a copper alloy strap end of probable 14th-century date (Crummy, Chapter 3.II, SF 51, Fig. 17), while fill 8 contained four iron nails (one with wood attached) and a copper alloy buckle plate (Fig. 17, SF 50). It is possible that this was the eastern side of the construction cut for one of the many brick-built culverts known to run beneath the modern town.

V. Period 5: 17th century to Present

No archaeological traces remained of any buildings of 17th- and 18th-century date. The final phase of construction recorded within the archaeological sequence was represented by a Victorian building (Building 14) which had been demolished prior to redevelopment of the site. The foundations of this building consisted of a series of reinforced concrete blocks supporting a raft present within the south-eastern corner of the development. A tiled floor, of probable Victorian origin, survived on this raft.

Immediately following the successful conclusion of the fieldwork element of this project, work began on the construction of a new phase of buildings, now complete, initially occupied by John Menzies and subsequently, in 2000, by the Iceland supermarket chain.

Chapter 3. The Finds

I. Coin
by Adrian Popescu

A long cross penny of the type introduced in 1279 by Edward I was found on the floor of Building 7. The condition of the coin, which appears to have been burnt, is such that it is impossible to obtain a precise date for its production but it definitely belongs to one of the issues struck between 1280–1301. Assessing the wear is not straightforward but the parts of the surface of the coin which are not affected by oxides suggest that it did not circulate too long before being lost: the period of deposition is probably 14th century.

Edward I (1272–1307)
Obv. +ᵃDWR...hYB
Rev. CIVI-TAS-LON-[DON]
AR VI 0.92g
Penny, London mint, class 3–9, 1280–1301 (lost before 1351?)
SF 2, Floor 44, Building 7, Phase 6.1, Period 2 (1350–1450)

II. Metalwork
by Nina Crummy
(Figs 16–17)

The assemblage of 69 items of metalwork (quantified by material in Table 1) derives for the most part from only a few contexts in, or associated with, Buildings 4, 7, 8, 12 and 13, with smaller groups of material from Buildings 9 and 10, only small scraps of metalwork from Buildings 1, 2, and 6, and nothing from the other structures. Many of the objects derive from floors, but none can be closely dated and only in Building 7 do they provide information about the activities conducted there.

In contrast to the group of small personalia and domestic craft items in Building 4 (see spindlewhorls below), the objects from Phases 6.1–6.3 in Building 7 relate to an industrial process during the mid 14th to mid 15th centuries. Features and floor surfaces in the building produced a considerable quantity of metalworking debris, including both copper alloy waste and iron-working slag (Mortimer, below), The recovery of three padlocks from the building (two copper alloy, one probably brazed iron: SF 8, 20 and 57) suggests that they are products of the metalworking activity, and a cow- or hand-bell (SF 12) found with them may be another. However, one padlock (SF 20) has part of a spring from the iron bolt stuck in an aperture of the bolt-plate, which suggests that it was used before being discarded; all these items may therefore have been collected and brought to Building 7 for recycling. Most were found inside the Ely ware storage vessel in 'trough' 112.

Nevertheless, the idea that the padlocks are the products of the smith working in Building 7 is supported by the recovery from the metalworking debris of iron wire or rod fragments similar to those used to decorate SF 20 (Mortimer, below), and stylistically by the use of a heart-shaped key aperture on SF 8 and SF 20. The use of live applied strips on SF 57 is idiosyncratic, but the surface of the cylindrical cases was often ornamented by rods and strips applied in various ways, with many patterns apparently being individual in one way or another. The full-length tab between the case and bolt-collar on SF 57 and SF 20 is a common feature on medieval padlocks, occurring at, for example, Winchester, London, King's Lynn, Beverley and York (I.H. Goodall 1990a, 1001; Egan 1998, fig. 72, 257; Goodall and Carter 1977, fig. 132-1-3; I.H. Goodall 1992, fig. 82, 418; Ottaway and Rogers 2002, fig. 1442, 12563, 15085). Copper alloy padlocks are not as common as iron ones, but some again have full-length tabs (A.R. Goodall 1992, fig. 176, 154).

The interpretation of the bell as either a rejected casting or scrap brought in for recycling is also uncertain. It lacks its clapper, which may either have been lost, or never fitted, and no bell-mould fragments appear to have been recovered from the building (Mortimer, below).

In Building 8, all the objects were associated with the destruction phases of the building; the erosion gully (99) and flood layers (42 and 24) contained small copper alloy fragments, a lead nail or stud shank, several iron nail fragments, and an iron strip that is probably part of a pintle, a hinge pivot for a door, window or similar structural feature; a small knife (SF 32) came from the wall trench (74). Most can be defined as general debris, which may have originally derived from Building 8 or been brought in during the inundations. The knife is more unusual; it small size suggests it is a personal item rather than a craft tool.

The floors in Buildings 9 and 10 produced only small scrap items, mainly iron nails, all of which may have been residual in the make-up material, and the floor (11) in Building 12 contained only a small iron ring, again

Object type	Copper alloy	Iron	Lead	Quantity
Brooch/buckle	0	1	0	1
Buckle/ strap-end plate	2	0	0	2
Cross-guard (dagger)	0	1	0	1
Fitting	2	0	0	2
Fragment	3	4	0	7
Hand-/cow-bell	1	0	0	1
Knife	0	1	0	1
Nail/shank	0	35	1	36
Padlock/?padlock	4	1	0	5
Plate	0	1	0	1
Ring	0	1	0	1
Sheet	1	0	0	1
Slag/?slag	1	1	0	2
Strap-end	1	0	0	1
Strap-loop	1	0	0	1
Strip	1	2	0	3
Stud	1	0	0	1
Wire	2	0	0	2
Total	**20**	**48**	**1**	**69**

Table 1 Metalwork by object type and material

presumably residual. Two refuse pits associated with Building 12 contained a limited range of items, mainly iron nails and small metal scraps, part of a broad iron strip, and the iron quillon-type cross-guard from a dagger (SF 30) came from pit 4. Unusually, there are no small copper alloy pins, lace-ends and other small dress accessories that often occur in rubbish pits of this period. The dagger fragment, being plain, should probably be classed as a weapon, but daggers were also often perceived as an essential item of dress for some levels of society, and this example might equally well have been considered as a personal accessory.

The possible culvert (9) may have been contemporary with Building 13 and may have eventually been used for rubbish disposal or redeposition of material from the locality or elsewhere. Again it contained mainly nails and no pins or lace-ends, but it did produce a large strap-end (SF 51) and a folded buckle-plate (SF 50), though the former at least is most likely to be a residual 14th-century item.

Apart from the objects from Buildings 4 and 7, this assemblage therefore contains little that can provide evidence of the types of activities that took place in this part of Wisbech over the medieval and early post-medieval periods. The paucity of metalwork, and in particular of small personalia, might be taken as evidence that the area was used for industrial rather than domestic occupation, but there is an equal lack of craft tools. The absence of such artefacts suggests either that there may have been sufficient advance warning of the floods to allow the contents of the buildings to be removed, or that the force of the waters may have effectively flushed the buildings clean — the latter suggestion does not, however, accord with the presence of fragile environmental evidence (*e.g.* eggshell). Other than the small groups of finds recovered from Buildings 4 and 7, there is certainly little *in-situ* evidence for the abandonment of household goods or industrial equipment in the face of sudden and overwhelming natural disaster.

The following catalogue of illustrated items is arranged by building number, and within building by period, phase, context, and material.

Building 4

SF 33 Fig.17. Fragment of an annular **brooch** or circular or D-shaped iron **buckle**, decorated with white-metal inlaid wire. The wire is set in a shallow groove that spirals about the hoop; most of the iron of the hoop has decayed, leaving voids in a patch of iron-stained clay. Analysis of Anglo-Scandinavian white-metal inlays at York showed that they are usually tin, or a tin-lead alloy (Ottaway 1992, 721–5). Diameter 50mm; section circular, diameter 6mm.

The use of white-metal inlay suggests a Saxon, Anglo-Scandinavian or early Norman date for this fragment, and it may therefore be residual here. However, two annular copper alloy brooches from London have panels of grooved cabling (with no inlay surviving) and both were associated with late 13th- to mid 14th-century pottery (Egan and Pritchard 1991, fig. 160, 1312, fig. 162, 1315). It is unusual to find the inlay passing right round the diameter of the ring on the Wisbech fragment. The cabling on the two London brooches is only on the upper face, as is that on a D-shaped inlaid iron buckle from an 11th- to mid 12th-century context at Winchester (I.H. Goodall 1990b, fig. 136, 1266), but another 13th- to 14th-century copper alloy annular brooch from London has inlaid lead strips and is decorated on both sides; it could be worn with either face uppermost (Egan and Pritchard 1991, fig. 161, 1314). There is, therefore, some possibility that the Wisbech inlaid iron fragment is another example of a double-sided medieval brooch and is contemporary with its context.
Floor 92, Building 4, Period 2, Phase 4.1

SF 7 Fig.17. Thin trapezoidal copper alloy **strap-loop** with internal projections and a knop in the centre of the longest side. Length 21mm, maximum width 28mm. Similar examples date broadly from the late 12th to 15th centuries, but some from later contexts need not necessarily be residual (Geddes and Carter 1977, 289, fig. 130, 13; A.R. Goodall 1984, 339, 347, fig. 190, 68; Crummy 1988, fig. 18, 1740, 1743; Hinton 1990, fig. 143, 1353–4, 1356; Egan and Pritchard 1991, 233; Garrard 1995, fig. 446, 521; Ottaway and Rogers 2002, 2903).
Floor 46, Building 4, Period 2, Phase 4.2

SF 6 Fig.17. Fragment of a copper alloy **buckle- or strap-end-plate** with one side bent down at right angle to enclose the leather strap. There is a rivet hole in each surviving corner and one in the centre. The plate is embedded in clay layered with organic material. Maximum dimensions 23 by 24mm.
Floor 46, Building 4, Period 2, Phase 4.2

Building 7

SF 57 Fig.16. Brazed iron barrel **padlock**, at least partly encased in a ferruginous concretion, and with one corner broken off but present (unseen; described from X-radiographs). The tab between the narrow bolt collar and the case is full length, and there are five evenly-spaced applied strips passing around case, tab and bolt collar, with the end strips sealing the junctions of the end-plates and the case, which is empty. Length approximately 75mm, diameter approximately 38mm.
Floor 111, Building 7, Period 2, Phase 6.1

SF 12 Fig.17. Copper alloy **open hand- or cow-bell** (Brown 1972, 112–13), with a moulding at the rim, encrusted with organic material and small fragments of metalworking debris. The clapper is missing. Height 94mm, maximum diameter 89mm.
Fill 97, from within Ely ware storage vessel in 'trough' 112 associated with metalworking, Building 7, Period 2, Phase 6.3

SF 8 Fig.16. a) Large lump of clay mixed with metalworking debris, with a copper alloy **padlock case** embedded within it. The bolt-plate of the case is solid, the end-plate has a heart-shaped aperture for the key, probably the same form as that on SF 20 below, and has an external binding strip. Length approximately 65mm, diameter 37mm. b) Three fragments of bent **copper alloy sheet** also with metalworking debris attached (not illustrated). One may be the bolt collar and part of the tab from a padlock case. Another is curved and may also be part of a padlock case. Maximum dimensions 51 by 26mm, 52 by 38mm, 45 by 17mm.
Fill 97, from within Ely ware storage vessel in 'trough' 112 associated with metalworking, Building 7, Period 2, Phase 6.3

SF 22 Fig.17. Iron **nail** with what may be part of the shank of a second nail attached. The head is only slightly larger than the rectangular shank. Length 68mm.
Fill 97, from within Ely ware storage vessel in 'trough' 112 associated with metalworking, Building 7, Period 2, Phase 6.3

SF 20 Fig.16. Copper alloy **barrel padlock**, the outer face of the case decorated with applied thin iron rods. There is a full-length tab between the narrow cylindrical bolt collar and the cylindrical case. On the end-plate the area around the key aperture is damaged, but it was set at the base of the plate and appears to have been heart-shaped, as that in SF 8 above. The bolt-plate is damaged, but had three apertures for the bolt-spring, one containing part of its iron strip. Length 52mm, diameter 26mm, height with flange 58mm.
Clay lining 113, from within Ely ware storage vessel in 'trough' 112 associated with metalworking, Building 7, Period 2, Phase 6.3

Building 8

SF 32 Fig.17. The tang and part of the blade of a small iron **knife**. Both back and edge are more or less straight before curving together towards the tip. Length 74mm, maximum width 16mm.
Fill 75, within wall trench 74, Building 8, Period 3, Phase 7.1

Building 12

SF 30 Fig.17. Iron **cross-guard** from a dagger, with curved and knobbed side bars (quillons). Length 160mm, width at blade slot 20mm, thickness at slot 20mm. The date is probably late 15th century to mid 16th century (Bradbury 1990, 1080).
Fill 17 of pit 4, associated with Building 12, Period 4, Phase 11.2

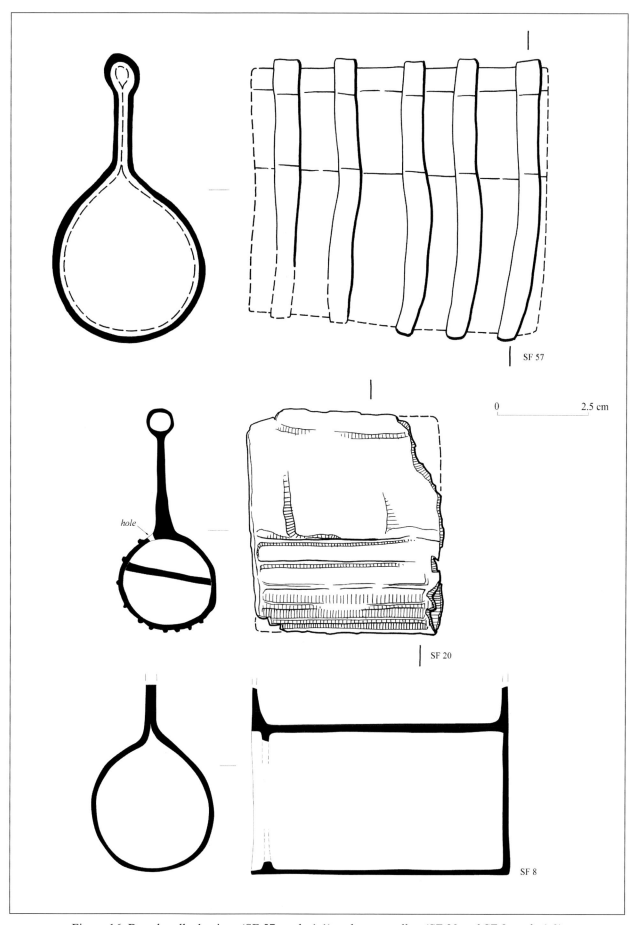

hole

SF 57

SF 20

SF 8

0   2.5 cm

Figure 16 Barrel padlocks: iron (SF 57, scale 1:1) and copper alloy (SF 20 and SF 8, scale 1:2)

41

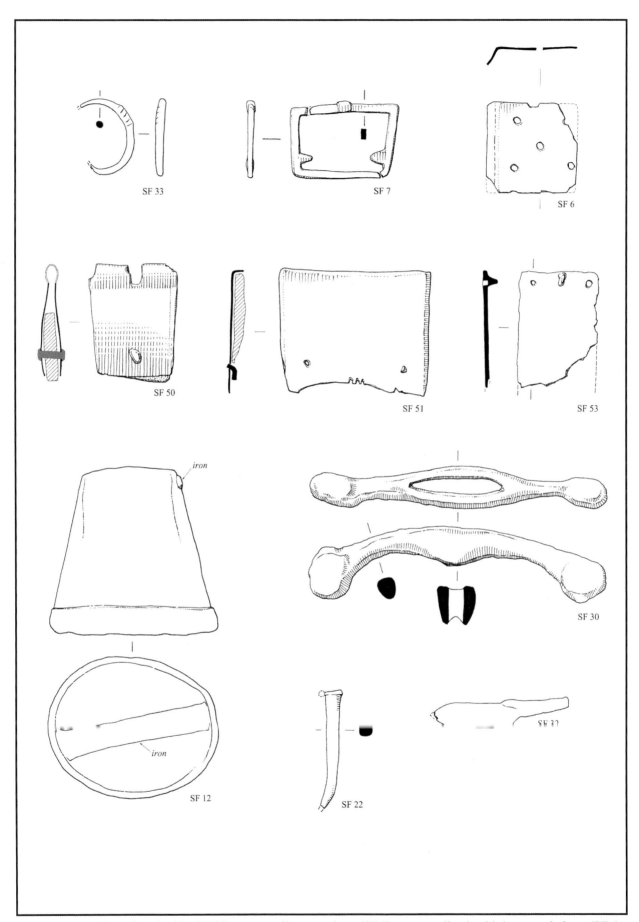

Figure 17 Iron brooch or buckle (SF 33); copper alloy strap loop (SF 7); copper alloy buckle/strap-end plates (SF 6, SF 50 and SF 51); iron plate (SF 53); copper alloy cow/hand bell (SF 12), iron nail (SF 22); iron knife (SF 32); iron dagger cross guard (SF 30). Ironwork at scale 1:2, copper alloy at scale 1:1 (except SF 12 at 1:2)

SF 53 Fig.17. Fragment of a square or rectangular iron **plate** of thin rectangular section, with a rivet hole in the two surviving corners. Length 76mm, width 48mm.
Fill 17 of pit 4, associated with Building 12, Period 4, Phase 11.2

Building 13?

SF 51 Fig.17. Front plate of a large two-piece trapezoidal copper alloy **strap-end** with fragments of the strap preserved on the underside. Three of the sides are plain and bent over to enclose the sides of the strap, the fourth is open and concave, with three notches set off-centre. There is a rivet hole in each corner at this end. The surface is plain. Length 32mm, width 41mm. Wide strap-ends from London of this type are varied in form, and are often from 14th-century deposits (Egan and Pritchard 1991, 135–6).
Fill 7 of feature 9, possibly associated with Building 13, Period 4, Phase 12

SF 50 Fig.17. Copper alloy folded **buckle-plate**, slightly tapering, with the end of the leather strap preserved between the front and back plates and secured by a single dome-headed rivet in the centre of the inner edge. The front-plate is decorated with pairs of marginal grooves. Length 30.5mm, maximum width 24.5mm.
Fill 8 of feature 9, possibly associated with Building 13, Period 4, Phase 12

III. Metalworking Waste
by Catherine Mortimer
(Tables 2 and 3)

Introduction
A total assemblage of 12.638kg of metalworking waste was recovered from the site, of which more than half came from the wood-lined drain/trough dating to the mid 14th to mid 15th century (Phase 6, Period 2). Visual analysis, using a binocular microscope, allowed the identification of the material types (Tables 2 and 3). The material was weighed, using scales which are accurate to 2g (up to 126g) or 5g (up to 2.5kg). A magnet was used to confirm the identification of iron objects and of hammerscale. Further analysis was carried out where necessary to identify the type of copper alloy using non-destructive surface X-ray fluorescence (XRF), which identifies the main metallic components present (Table 3).

The Material
A large amount of the material recovered was furnace/ hearth lining or vitrified furnace/hearth lining. From the evidence of the hearth found in context 113 (see below), it may be that the structures at this site are more likely to have been hearths (pit-like) rather than furnaces (with superstructures, generally related to smelting). During many high-temperature processes, especially amongst metalworking activities, clay may be fired so strongly as to cause the lining to react with the fuel, and then partially or completely melt. The clay used for linings may have been less refractory (able to withstand high temperatures) and less carefully prepared than that used for the manufacture of crucibles and thus more vulnerable. The lining may keep some of its form, preserving some areas as fired clay (either reduced or oxidised), despite heavily slagging on the other side. Where the hearth lining was heavily vitrified, it may have run off or been raked out as separate dribbles of dark, glassy 'slag'.

Many of the pieces of hearth lining have traces of corroded copper alloy on them, which suggests that they were used in connection with melting copper alloys. In most cases, the form of the lining fragments mean that they may well have come from structures similar to the small near-complete bowl-shaped hearth found redeposited in context 113 (Building 7, Phase 6.2, Period 2), which is heavily slagged and has copious amounts of copper alloy deposits. This is an unusual find. Amongst the interesting features are the rough, irregular clay walls (13–20mm thick), suggesting that a small pit (diameter about 110mm, 80–90mm deep) was dug into the ground and then clay was used to line the pit. The irregularity of the walls strongly argues against this being a crucible as such, since most metalworkers would strive to minimize stresses and strains within the crucible walls by making them of an even thickness. On the outside (the side in contact with the soil), the clay is reduced-fired in most areas although there is a hole through the side around which the clay is oxidised. There is no evidence for intense vitrification of the clay in the area of this hole, which would be expected if this was the tuyère (bellows nozzle) position. Instead, the hearth was clearly subject to very high temperatures directed in from above, as the entire preserved length of the rim is very strongly vitrified; most medieval crucibles are heated from the outside and are thus vitrified both outside and inside. Possibly the copper alloy to be melted was held in a crucible placed within the hearth, although there is no evidence of any crucible fragments at the site; presumably, if a crucible was used, the melt must have been partially or totally unsuccessful, given the substantial amounts of copper alloy on the hearth itself. Alternatively, it is possible that the copper alloy was melted directly in the hearth, under a layer of charcoal (some of which can still be seen within the vitrification and copper alloy deposits) and then tapped off into a mould or moulds lying downslope from the hearth. It is extremely unlikely that the hearth was used for primary copper alloy smelting, as the nearest copper sources are far away, and ores were rarely transported long distances in an untreated form.

As some of the hearth lining and vitrified hearth lining has no copper alloy deposits, some of this may relate to ironworking rather than copper alloy working. Small amounts of copper alloy waste were found, some of which clearly show that they were molten when they hit the ground. One piece of sheet copper alloy was found concreted with other materials in a lump of ferruginous concretion (see below) in context 79 (Building 9, Phase 8.1, Period 3).

Another common material at the site is ferruginous concretion. This is iron-rich material, which contains a variety of inclusions — pieces of fuel, stone, pottery, fired clay, hammerscale, slag, pieces of copper alloy and iron objects — bound together by iron corrosion products. This material would be formed in a damp and iron-rich environment. It can therefore be seen as the man-made equivalent of iron panning, and ironworking deposits laid down in an area which was prone to flooding would presumably be more likely to form ferruginous concretions than they would in dry areas.

The amounts of true ironworking slag (rather than iron-rich vitrified hearth lining) are relatively minor compared to many other sites, but they do indicate that iron was worked at or near the site. The precise nature of the ironworking involved is not immediately clear, as much of the material is non-diagnostic. Certainly none of it is tap slag (which would have indicated making iron from ore) and much of it can be classified as smithing slag, albeit with small areas of 'runnier' material. One fragment from context 111 (Phase 6.1, Period 2) may be part of a smithing hearth bottom, a small plano-convex block of ironworking slag, formed in ironsmithing. The spherical hammerscale recovered from some of the environmental samples and from context 97 (Phase 6.3, Period 2) suggests that at least some of this ironsmithing involved primary working (*e.g.* removing slag particles from iron billets) rather than secondary working (*e.g.* making iron artefacts by forging), which would normally produce flake hammerscale. Many of the iron objects found in or with the ferruginous concretion have corroded into small flakes, which may mask the presence of some flake hammerscale. The iron objects include some short lengths of wire or rod. The relatively large quantities of ferruginous concretion (nearly 4kg) are also evidence for ironworking being carried out in the area. Fuel is also relatively frequently found: there are several large deposits of coal, but charcoal and possibly coke were also present.

Minor material types included within the 'industrial debris' samples are fuel ash slag (formed by the reaction of clay with plant materials at high temperatures), fired clay, pottery and organic material (probably cess). One of the small pieces of fired clay from the fill (93) of an erosion gully (99; Building 8, Phase 7.2, Period 3) has a surface which may have been prepared to give it a smooth finish, possibly as a mould. Two unidentified samples may be pieces of fuel and ore.

Distribution

The largest amount of material came from context 97 (7.8kg, more than half the total weight at the site; Building 7, Phase 6.3, Period 2), and it included evidence for high temperature processes involving both copper alloy and iron. This is the backfill of the wood-lined drain or trough 112, and the feature cut into surface 111 which comprised 'compacted slag' (actually a mixture of copper alloy waste, ferruginous concretion, ironworking slag and hearth lining). The lining of the drain (113) contained the hearth and other vitrified hearth lining. The other contexts with notable weights of metalworking material are 93 (Building 8, Phase 7.2, Period 3; which has a mixture of metalworking debris of a rather similar character to that in contexts 97 and 111, and was therefore perhaps redeposited) and 117 (Building 2, Phase 2.5, Period 1) which is mainly ferruginous concretion.

XRF Analysis

Analysis was carried out on a small selection of corroded copper alloy materials (casting waste or deposits on ceramic materials). Surface analysis of corroded copper alloys is problematic, in that corrosion may have preferentially removed or enhanced particular elements. Furthermore, where copper alloys are at a high temperature, metals such as zinc tend to be driven off as vapour, thus reducing the amount detected in metal deposits on ceramics (although at the lips of crucibles zinc levels may be high). However XRF analysis does indicate that the copper alloys at the site included tin-containing alloys (bronzes), zinc-containing alloys (brasses) and some alloys which contained zinc, tin and lead (quaternary alloys). All three types of copper alloy are known to have been used to cast a wide variety of artefact types during the medieval period and — on the basis of the metalworking waste alone — it is therefore not possible to suggest the types of artefacts which were being made at the site (although some suggestions have been made by Crummy, above).

Conclusions

Over 12kg of material from high-temperature processes was examined; a smaller amount of other material which has no obvious links with high-temperature working was also identified and catalogued. Evidence for melting copper alloys was discovered, although the lack of any identifiable mould fragments or part-formed artefacts means that it is difficult to say exactly what happened to the metal after it was melted; the alloys indicated by XRF analysis are not characteristic of any particular artefact

Building/feature	Ctxt	ca waste	fas	fc	fe conc	fe obj	fuel	h/fl	slag	vhl/fl	other	Totals
Building 2, Phase 2	114								0.002	0.0026		**0.028**
	117				0.270	0.046					0.002	**0.318**
Building 3, Phase 3	48						0.008		0.002			**0.010**
Building 4, Phase 4	92			0.255								**0.255**
Building 6, Phase 6	44	0.002	0.010							0.002		**0.014**
Building 7, Phase 6	97	0.110		0.034	2.313	0.008	1.378	0.034	2.893	0.890	0.100	**7.832**
	111	0.014			0.911		0.190	0.485	0.540	0.393		**2.533**
	113									0.367		**0.367**
Building 8, Phase 7	73									0.004		**0.004**
	75			0.006								**0.006**
Flood, Phase 7	83								0.006			**0.006**
	87				0.014			0.030	0.046			**0.090**
	93	0.016		0.010	0.175	0.018	0.046	0.066	0.220	0.270	0.022	**0.843**
Building 9, Phase 8	23						0.002					**0.002**
	34								0.240			**0.240**
	79				0.022		0.002	0.014				**0.038**
Building 10, Phase 9	15			0.002			0.010					**0.012**
Pit 4, Phase 11	17									0.022		**0.022**
Pit 5, Phase 11	50			0.018								**0.018**
	Total	**0.142**	**0.010**	**0.325**	**3.905**	**0.072**	**1.628**	**0.637**	**3.747**	**1.982**	**0.190**	**12.638**

Table 2 Metalworking debris: finds types by context and phase (kg)

Context	SF	Material type	XRF
93	-	CA waste #1 (on vhl)	**Cu** (Pb) (Sn) tr Zn
	-	CA waste #2 (on vhl/fc)	**Cu** tr Pb
97	-	CA waste in ferruginous concretion	**Cu** (Zn) (Pb)
	8	CA waste	**Cu** Pb (Sn)
	8	CA object #1	**Cu** (Pb) (Sn)
	12	CA object #2	**Cu** tr Pb tr Sn
		CA object	**Cu** (Sn) tr Zn tr Pb
111	-	CA waste	**Cu** Pb Sn (Zn)
	2	CA strip	**Cu Sn** (Pb) tr Zn
113	-	CA waste on hearth #1	**Cu Zn Pb Sn**
	-	CA waste on hearth #2	**Cu Zn Pb** (Sn)
	-	CA waste on hearth #3	**Cu Zn Pb**
	20	CA object	**Cu Pb Sn**

Elements in bold were detected in large amounts, those in ordinary type were detected in small amounts, those in brackets were only detected at minor levels and 'tr' = trace. Cu = copper, Zn = zinc, Sn = tin, Pb = lead. Iron was detected in all samples.

Codes for Tables 2 and 3
ca waste = copper alloy waste   CA = copper alloy
fas = fuel ash slag   fc = fired clay
fe conc = ferruginous concretion   fe obj = iron object
h/fl = hearth or furnace lining   shb = smithing
sph hs = spherical hammerscale   unid = unidentified material
vhl/fl = vitrified hearth lining or furnace lining

Table 3 Metalworking debris: qualitative XRF analysis (all from Phase 7)

types. Although it is clearly connected with copper alloy working, the hearth from context 113 remains rather a mystery. No crucible material was identified. Besides melting copper alloys, ironworking, probably smithing, was also carried out at or near the site.

IV. The Pottery
by Paul Spoerry
(Figs 18–22; Plates 8 and 9; Tables 4–8)

Introduction
The excavations resulted in an assemblage of 1,485 pottery sherds, totalling 17.097kg. These were recovered from contexts throughout a sequence of occupation and flood deposition that spans several centuries. The sequence was investigated in three areas within close proximity to each other and direct associations between the episodes in each area have been made.

Pottery type identification is based on accepted common names for the identifiable products of known producers, and known/common vessel types. Data regarding quantities of ware and vessel types within key stratigraphic units was analysed and in addition specific formal and decorational traits were described.

Dating the Sequence
For the purposes of this report the ceramics have been grouped according to site phase. It is immediately apparent that the phase assemblages vary in size quite considerably. In general it is not considered worthwhile studying the statistics for groups of pottery derived from less than 50 sherds (50 individual pieces of data) and on that criterion Phases 1, 2, 3, 5 and 10 are liable to provide data with too much inherent bias. To counteract this problem of division into small sub-units, study of pottery types and styles has been used to differentiate between groups of phases that have different assemblages. The pottery from these groups of phases has been analysed as representative of individual, and roughly datable, periods within the sequence.

The amount of pottery by fabric type is presented for each major phase in Table 4, statistics being calculated based on weight of pottery in grammes (all subsequent percentages in this report are based on calculations of grammes of pottery, unless stated otherwise). It is evident from this table that three fabric types are present

Fabric	Phase 2	Phase 3	Phase 4	Phase 6	Phase 7	Phase 8	Phase 9	Phase 11	Phase 12
BOND	0	0	0	0	0	3	0	37.1	27
CSTN	0	0	0	0	0	0	0	14.2	0
DUTR	0	0	0	0	0	0	0	2.2	0
EMW	14.3	0	0	0	0	0	0	0	0
ESMIC	0	0	0	0	8.9	0	0	0	0
GRIM	37.1	47	7.3	20.6	14.3	26.9	40.5	33	11
HEDI	0	0	0	0	0	0.7	0	0	1.2
LANG	0	0	0	0	0	0	0	0.9	0
LINCS	0	0	3.8	0	0	0	0	0	0
LMR	0	0	0	0	0	0	0	0.5	0
LMT	0	4.3	2.8	0.1	14.6	0	4	6.2	26
UGBB	34.9	21.7	68.7	9.8	31	44.8	52.7	1.3	32.3
MEL	13.7	24.3	15.5	69.2	31.2	19.9	2.8	2.3	2.2
OLIVE	0	0	0	0	0	2.1	0	0	0
OSW	0	0	1.9	0.1	0	0	0	0.1	0
SCAR	0	2.6	0	0	0	0	0	0.2	0
SSHW	0	0	0	0	0	0	0	0	0.3
TUDB	0	0	0	0	0	0	0	1.1	0
TUDG	0	0	0	0	0	0	0	0.1	0
UNK	0	0	0	0.3	0	2.7	0	0.8	0

Table 4 Quantity of pottery fabrics in major phases (by weight)

Period	Phase	Pottery Assemblage Date-Range	Main Identifiers	Key dating horizons
1	1		One sherd only	After 1200
	2	1250–1350	UGBB cooking pots	After 1250
			Highly decorated Grimston glazed ware jugs	
			Some calcareous Ely ware	
	3	1250–1350	As 2 but with both decorated and undecorated Grimston jug sherds	
2	4	1350–1450	UGBB cooking pots dominate	After 1350
			Less Grimston and Ely, and jugs not highly decorated	
			OSW jug sherds appear	
	5		Two sherds only	
	6	1350–1450	Grimston jugs more common (one complete) and fewer UGBB cooking vessels. More Ely ware including a whole storage vessel.	
3	7	around 1450?	Ely ware bowls of both medieval and late medieval style	After 1450
			Bowls in other fabrics (ESMIC, LMT)	
	8	around 1450?	Less Ely ware	
			More Grimston glazed jugs and UGBB cooking vessels	
			Bourne D	
	9	1450–1500	Grimston ware drinking jug	
			LMT bowl	
			Ely ware almost absent	
			UGBB	
	10	1350–1500	One Orange Sandy ware vessel	
4	11	1470–1600	Bourne D ware	After 1470
			Cistercian ware	
			Imports	
	12	1450–1550	More parochial version of the Phase 11 group	

Table 5 Phase dates and key dating horizons

throughout all major phases and that these represent the majority of the assemblage in all those phases with the exception of Phases 11 and 12 (Buildings 12 and 13). These three pottery types are Grimston Glazed ware (GRIM, and hitherto Grimston ware in this report), Unglazed Grimston/Blackborough End wares (UGBB) and Ely Ware (MEL). The definition for Grimston ware used here is that adopted by Little (1994) for both Glazed Grimston A and B wares, but with the majority of the pottery from Wisbech being of the finer A type. Unglazed Grimston/Blackborough End wares include that material called Local Unglazed ware at Grimston by Little (1994). This industry appears to have initially manufactured pottery in the Early Medieval ware tradition (Wade 1980, 443) at Blackborough End (Rogerson and Ashley 1985), with a range of wheel-made bowls and jars being produced for a primarily local market. The author had the opportunity to inspect a collection of Blackborough End wasters at Lynn Museum and was able to establish that the fabric is very like the sherds from Wisbech, but is also hard to differentiate in the hand specimen from the fabric of some glazed Grimston products. The likelihood is that these unglazed utilitarian products were manufactured at

both Blackborough End and Grimston, and perhaps elsewhere in the hinterland of Lynn, to a generic pattern.

The phases have relatively little dating independent of pottery identification. Consideration of all the pottery present within each phase has resulted in the provision of general phase/building dates, as shown in Table 5, which also identifies change points within the pottery assemblage on the site. It is apparent that the whole sequence can be compressed into little more than 250 years up until Phase 11, with the latter adding another century and containing no material definitely later than 1600. It is interesting to note that there are several phases dated within the 15th century, perhaps implying a great need or desire for construction during this time. This may be a result of frequent flood events during this period.

Phase/Building Assemblages

The phase assemblages have been considered independently of each other but, as discussed above, many are too small on their own to provide valuable statistics. To allow for more valuable analysis the phases have also been grouped into site periods which derive from the approximate date-ranges as defined in Table 5; these are

Vessel	Phase 2	Phase 3	Phase 4	Phase 6	Phase 7	Phase 8	Phase 9	Phase 11	Phase 12
A Bowls, dishes etc.		22.6	9.5	2.6	52.9	18	4.5	3	14.7
B Cooking vessels	56.2	14.6	76.1	9.8	23.5	48.1	55	3.2	34.4
C Jugs, pitchers etc.	43.8	62.8	14.4	20.9	23.6	29.8	32.7	40.7	18.6
D Storage jars & cisterns				66.6		4.1			
C or D jug/cistern								37.1	32.3
Cups & mugs							7.8	16	

Table 6 Percentages (by weight) of vessel types in phases

46

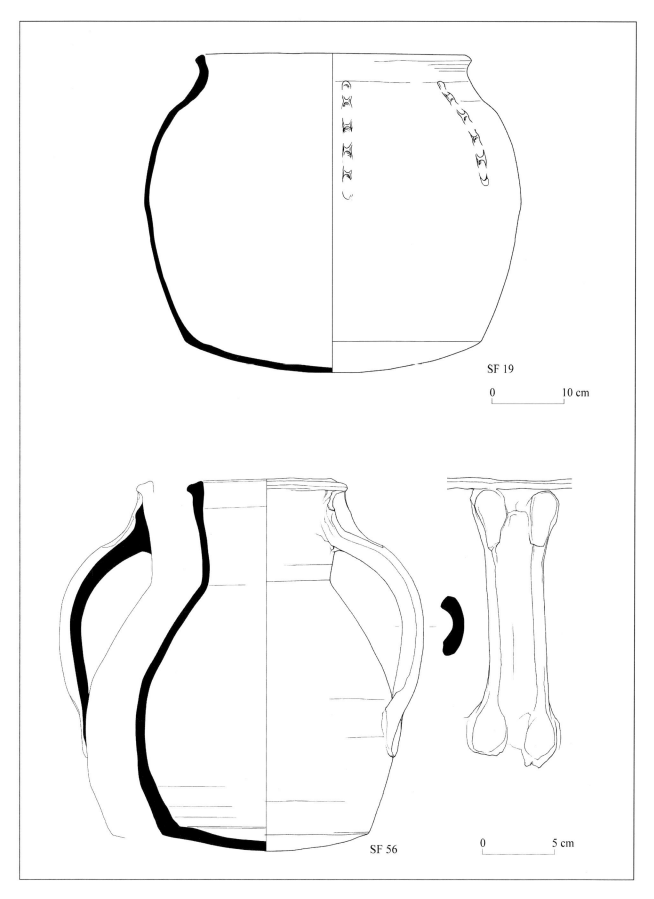

SF 19

0   10 cm

SF 56

0   5 cm

Figure 18 Pottery. SF 19 at scale 1:4, SF 56 at scale 1:2

47

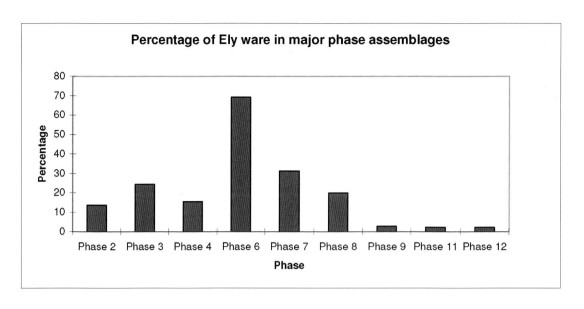

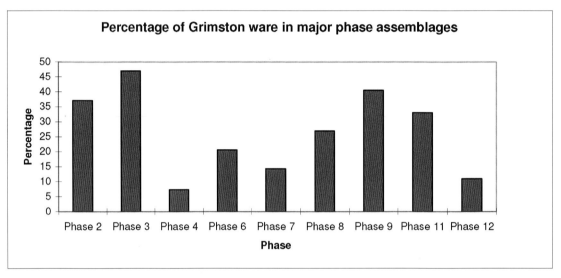

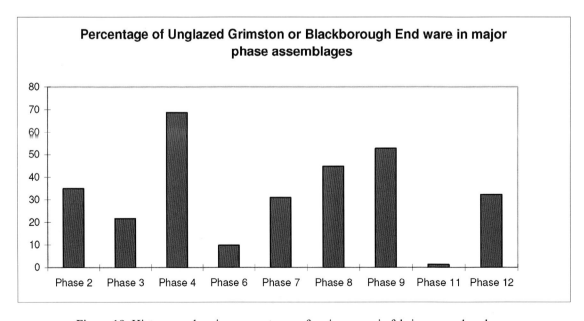

Figure 19 Histogram showing percentages of major ceramic fabric groups by phase

discussed in the next section. All phases and periods have been analysed with regard to the presence of both fabric and vessel types. In addition, individual pieces of more than general significance are discussed within each phase. Vessel types and fabrics by phase are indicated in Table 6.

Phase 1: Building 1
This phase yielded a single sherd of Unglazed Grimston or Blackborough End ware.

Phase 2: Building 2
This group is too small to provide data of statistical value other than in the broadest sense. The tripartite division between Grimston ware, Unglazed Grimston or Blackborough End ware and Medieval Ely ware is a characteristic of the whole sequence (Table 4 and Fig. 19 for this and all other phases), but here Grimston ware includes only glazed jugs, some with highly decorated designs using applied strips, pellets and scales and with an iron-rich painted wash under some areas providing a brown contrast with the usually olive green lead glaze. The presence of Early Medieval ware, a probable precursor to Unglazed Grimston or Blackborough End ware but ceasing to be produced by 1200 or a little before (Milligan 1982, 224), indicates that an early 13th-century date may be appropriate for the initiation of the sequence.

Phase 3: Building 3
Similar to Phase 2, this group is also mainly composed of the three key fabric types and again Grimston ware is most common, although mostly in plainer glazed jug fragments but with highly decorated sherds also present. Unglazed Grimston or Blackborough End ware is exclusively present as cooking pots whilst Medieval Ely ware appears as glazed jugs and one internally glazed calcareous bowl fragment. One piece of buff pottery with a thick green glaze and partially covered in a tarry deposit has been tentatively identified as Scarborough ware. The presence of one sherd of Late Medieval/Transitional ware is undoubtedly the result of error or localised intrusion.

Phase 4: Building 4
This medium sized group is dominated by sherds from several Unglazed Grimston or Blackborough End ware cooking pots, with Grimston ware jugs and Medieval Ely ware jug and bowl sherds also present. A few sherds from glazed Orange Sandy ware jugs may suggest a date after the mid-14th century, a point that may be reinforced by the lack of highly decorated Grimston ware jug sherds, although the small numbers involved demand extreme caution. A highly decorated sandy jug sherd may be from a Lincolnshire source.

Phase 5: Building 5
Only two sherds of Unglazed Grimston or Blackborough End ware were recovered from this phase.

Phase 6: Buildings 6 and 7
This group contains two complete vessels, a jug and storage jar (SF 19 and 56; Fig. 18 and Plate 8) superficially of similar fabric but in fact the former has been attributed to Grimston ware whilst the latter is probably Medieval Ely ware. The presence of these two vessels has skewed the quantification figures for this phase, but it is worth noting that the three most common fabric types have not

Plate 8 The Ely ware storage jar (SF 19), containing the Grimston vessel (SF 56)

changed. There are rather more highly decorated Grimston ware jug sherds than in the previous two phases. This does not preclude a late medieval date, but may indicate more residuality. Other pottery types are only present as single, or occasional, sherds. Vessel type data is even more skewed by the presence of the two whole vessels and cannot be used satisfactorily (Table 6, Fig. 20).

The Medieval Ely ware storage vessel (SF 19, Plate 9) was found upright, but crushed, with the Grimston ware jug lying on its side within it and complete. In addition several metallic objects were found also within the larger pot, these being a copper alloy bell (SF 12), part of a copper alloy barrel padlock (SF 8) and a nail (SF 22) (see Crummy, above). These had all been dumped, or placed, within a wood-lined drain/trough which had also received

Plate 9 The Ely ware storage jar (SF 19)

large amounts of the waste products from various metalworking process including iron smelting, smithing and, most commonly and most interestingly, secondary copper alloy smelting and casting (Mortimer, above). These waste products also characterised the floors through which the drain was cut. These is no reason to suspect that either vessel was primarily an industrial type: both are common in other contexts elsewhere. In addition the Medieval Ely ware storage vessel shows no evidence of use, or exposure to, chemical processes or heating. The Grimston ware jug (SF 56), however, is completely oxidised, when such vessels are more commonly reduced, and has its surface glaze heavily altered through, most probably, the effects of heat. There is a complete absence of internal deposits but externally the glazed parts of the surface are rough and scaled with burnt lumps of overfired glaze. Under this only a very thin, partial, light green glassy layer survives. The vessel is a standard late medieval Grimston ware type with externally-thickened rim, wide strap handle with joining thumbprint decoration at top and bottom, straight, tapering neck and pear-shaped body with sagging base (Fig. 18). The Medieval Ely ware vessel has been broadly categorised as a storage vessel but, in this case there is reason to suspect it may have performed the function of cistern. It is oxidised externally, although that is the more usual finish for such products, and has a fabric that contains much larger quartz temper than that seen in the typical Grimston ware fabric of the jug. A simple, rounded, out-turned rim sits above a very short neck that gives way to the rounded shoulders of a globular body above a sagging base. It has an internal covering of olive green glaze restricted to the very bottom of the walls and the base itself and externally there are four thin, thumbed vertical strips. The only use-related information is a thin, partial covering of limescale in the base and ferruginous concretions where a deposit of iron slag was located during burial. The rather irregularly-shaped rim of the pot provides an aperture of around 24cm

and this, from experimentation, appears wide enough for the Grimston ware jug to be easily placed within. It is therefore suggested that the Grimston ware jug may have been used in conjunction with the Medieval Ely ware vessel, the former acting as a ladle removing water from the latter. The burnt surfaces of the Grimston ware vessel also suggest that it was used during the metalworking processes that characterise this area of the site, repeatedly coming into contact with external heat sources and providing immediate access to small quantities of water, the Medieval Ely ware storage vessel being the secondary supply 'reservoir'.

Phase 7: Building 8
The key change in this assemblage from that which went before is the presence of Late Medieval/Transitional ware, although this is largely derived from one large bowl sherd with an internal glaze under thick limescale. This type may indicate a mid-15th-century date, although the remainder of the assemblage does not necessarily support that. Bowls are more prevalent than in any other phase, with sherds from perhaps nine in Medieval Ely ware, including types that, from the small amount of work executed on the kiln site assemblage, appear to be both 13–14th-century and 14th–15th-century in date. Cooking vessels, all in Unglazed Grimston or Blackborough End ware, and Grimston ware jugs are also present. Fragments of a jug and bowl in smooth Essex micaceous redware Fabric 40 (Cunningham 1985) may point to a date after 1450 for the last deposition in this phase which otherwise appears rather mixed.

Phase 8: Building 9
The presence of a small amount of Bourne D type ware, believed to be first manufactured around 1450 (Healey 1975) characterises this phase. The five sherds from, perhaps, three vessels are all from one context and the security of this deposit must be considered carefully as the

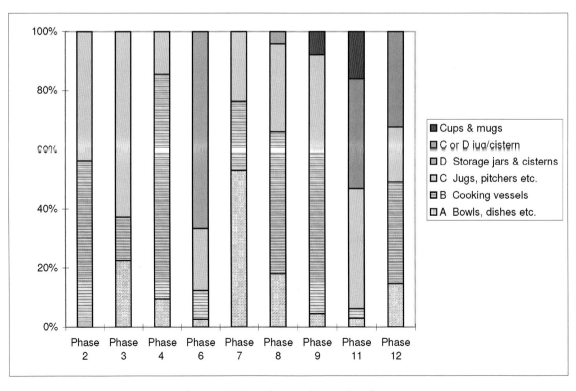

Figure 20 Ceramic vessel types by phase

50

dating of this and the subsequent phases currently rests on the presence of these few pieces. A few sherds of a Spanish Olive jar are the first imports seen in the site assemblage. Vessels are again mostly Unglazed Grimston or Blackborough End ware cooking pots and Grimston ware jugs, with Medieval Ely ware and Unglazed Grimston or Blackborough End ware bowls also present. This assemblage is likely to date from the mid to late 15th century.

Phase 9: Buildings 10 and 11

A virtual absence of Medieval Ely ware in this phase assemblage is the main change from that which preceded it, although this may continue a trend already started in Phase 8. Almost all of the pottery is from Unglazed Grimston or Blackborough End ware cooking pots and Grimston ware glazed jugs, but with a little Late Medieval/Transitional ware also present. This group does not appear very different in date to that of Phase 7. The complete base of a small drinking jug in a Grimston ware fabric is a type not seen elsewhere on the site.

Phase 10: Pits

This phase assemblage constitutes thirty-five sherds from one Orange Sandy ware jug, dating broadly to the period 1350–1500, but perhaps, on stratigraphic grounds, to the second half of the 15th century. This fabric type is of uncertain source (see Spoerry 1998, 72–3) but may well derive from kilns in the Rockingham Forest industry, and/ or from further afield, perhaps from Essex. The jug has a rilled body under clear glaze with thumb impressions at the handle join; all of which are traits seen in the period in a number of producers in eastern England (in Humber wares and at Grimston, for example).

Phase 11: Building 12

The sudden appearance of Cistercian ware (1470+, but usually a little later) alongside much Bourne D ware (post-1450) and Orange Sandy ware (a 'transitional' type at several locations in the eastern counties) points not only to a later date but a change in ceramic supply, and possibly also use or in the activities taking place on the site. The storage and consumption of liquids, mostly ale, seem to be well represented in this phase and not before, although this is symptomatic of general changes in habits in society and may not be site-function specific. A date shortly before 1500 is the earliest possible with this phase including types dating to the 16th century but no later. The appearance of cisterns is the main change in vessel type, these being almost all of Bourne D type ware, whilst cups and other drinking vessels are mainly in Cistercian ware but with a small amount of Langerwehe from the Rhineland also present. A comparative absence of cooking pots is not just a function of the demise of the comparatively local Unglazed Grimston or Blackborough End ware industry, but echoes the general trend in late medieval to post-medieval assemblages. Here it is rather later than in some other regions, although the results correlate well with those from Peterborough (Spoerry 1998) which is upstream of Wisbech.

Phase 12: Building 13

Phase 12 has a more parochial pottery assemblage than that of Phase 11, and would perhaps be dated slightly earlier on this data only there being none of the

characteristically 16th-century pieces seen in the preceding phase. Unglazed Grimston or Blackborough End ware and Late Medieval/Transitional ware, including cooking vessels in both fabrics, are common with fragments of Bourne D cisterns making up the other main component.

Period Assemblages

Period 1: c.1200–1350 (Buildings 1–3, Phases 1–3)

When viewed together these three phases provide an assemblage of 68 sherds (0.411kg). This is dominated by the three key fabrics types, Unglazed Grimston or Blackborough End ware, Grimston ware and Medieval Ely ware, with Grimston ware most common (Table 7, Fig. 21 for this and subsequent periods). As the latter is most commonly present as glazed jug sherds, both here and elsewhere, it is no surprise that over 50% of the pottery from Period 1 derives from jugs (Table 8, Fig. 22). This assemblage is generally in keeping with what one would expect of domestic material, although often in assemblages of this period cooking vessels are more common than jugs. A little Early Medieval ware is also present which, with a demise before the start of the 13th century (Milligan 1982, 224), represents the only fabric type from the site possibly dating to the period prior to the changes in the Fen river system (Darby 1983, 31–4) that may have had such a profound affect on both the economy and topography of the town. The Period 1 assemblage, as a whole, is characteristically mid-13th- to mid-14th-century in date on the basis of the presence of highly decorated Grimston products although an early 13th-century date is possible for the earliest phases.

Period 2: 1350–1450 (Buildings 4–7, Phases 4–6)

The period assemblage constitutes 537 sherds (8.291kg). The period statistics (Tables 7 and 8, Figs 21 and 22) demonstrate that the skewing affect of the presence of two large vessels is less than for Phase 4 only, but it is still evident in the enhanced presence of both Medieval Ely ware and storage vessels. It is likely that the trend in Period 2 would otherwise demonstrate no change in the importance of Medieval Ely ware in the assemblage, and possibly of Unglazed Grimston or Blackborough End ware as well. If the large Medieval Ely ware storage vessel were removed from the figures shown in Table 7 and used to produce Fig. 22 then the proportions of other vessel types would be very comparable to those in Period 1. This may suggest that there is no great difference in the functional assemblage as well as the production origin of these two phase assemblages which implies continuity of ceramic supply and the activities conducted on the site over some considerable time. The possibility that these vessels may relate to the substantial evidence for metalworking that can be dated to this period on the site has been considered and in conclusion it seems probable that they were used in such processes (see further discussion in Chapter 6).

Period 3: 1450–1500 (Buildings 8–11, Phases 7–10)

The Period 3 assemblage constitutes 617 sherds (5.060kg) and Unglazed Grimston or Blackborough End ware is the most common fabric type, replacing Medieval Ely ware in respect of Period 2 and Grimston ware in Period 1. As before, Unglazed Grimston or Blackborough End ware is

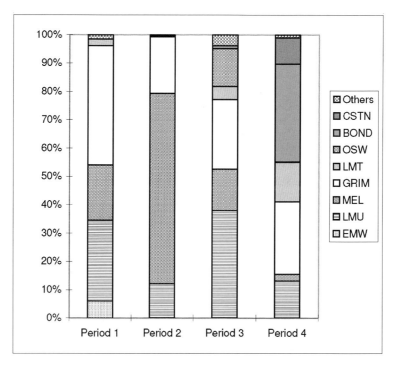

Figure 21 Ceramic vessel fabrics by period

mostly present as cooking vessels, however, sooted bowl sherds are also evident indicating that these were also used on the fire, perhaps also in food preparation. The tripartite medieval assemblage is supplemented here by pottery types characteristic of the end of medieval, and transitional, periods. Late Medieval/Transitional ware, a Norfolk product from perhaps 1450 onwards (Jennings 1981, 61) is the most common arrival, but there is a little Bourne D type ware as well. In addition there are several sherds of a Spanish Olive jar, not a particularly datable type but the earliest foreign import recorded at the site (Hurst *et al* 1986, 66). The high incidence of Unglazed Grimston or Blackborough End ware and hence, but to a

lesser extent, cooking vessels in this period assemblage is rather surprising, as the diversification of pottery types and decline of the ceramic cooking vessel are well known phenomena at the end of the medieval period (McCarthy and Brooks, 1988, 90). The persistence of these types at Wisbech is in keeping with the picture seen at Peterborough (Spoerry 1998). The amount of Medieval Ely ware in the Period 3 assemblage is similar to that seen in Period 1, and may not be very different to that in Period 2 after removal of bias derived from the presence of one large vessel. Whilst extrapolating data from one site only is dangerous, it may well be that Medieval Ely ware was consistently the third most important bulk ceramic

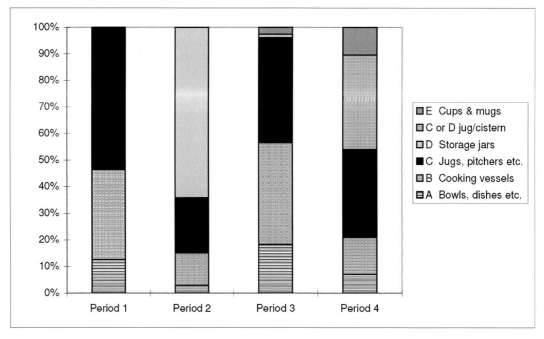

Figure 22 Ceramic vessel types by period

product found in Wisbech during the whole of the period in question. This point needs consideration when a medieval assemblage from the town is next analysed.

Period 4: 1500–1600 (Buildings 12–13, Phases 11 and 12)
A total of 240 sherds of pottery weighing 2.973kg was recovered from deposits assigned to this period. The marked difference between this group and all preceding assemblages is obvious, stemming from both pottery fabric types and vessel categories. Unlike the preceding phase, this does mirror expected changes in the general ceramic assemblage by the end of the medieval period. The persistence of medieval types such as Unglazed Grimston or Blackborough End ware and Grimston ware is, however, surprising, but this cannot be entirely blamed on residuality as Medieval Ely ware does not show the same trend. If there were a major medieval residual component then all three common medieval types would be expected to be represented. Late Medieval/ Transitional, Bourne D ware, particularly cisterns, and Cistercian ware cups are the key new types in this period, affecting both fabric and vessel statistics. The first two of these were present in Period 3, which befits their mid-15th-century start dates. It seems, however, that neither was a major component in this assemblage until after Cistercian ware was also present; the key change defining the start of Period 4. Cistercian ware was probably produced from as early as 1470, but may have been uncommon in this region until some decades later.

Variations Over Time
Variations in the contribution of individual pottery fabric types and vessel categories have been discussed in the sections above concerning individual phases and periods. Some trends that are exhibited over time are, however, worth more direct comment. Figure 19 shows trends in the contribution of the three most common fabric types to the phase assemblages. Percentages have been adjusted to account for the large bias that is introduced into the data as a result of the presence of two complete vessels in Phase 6. Figure 19 therefore represents a truer picture in terms of the trends exhibited, but not in the actual numbers themselves. Unglazed Grimston or Blackborough End ware, Grimston ware and Medieval Ely ware constitute at least 80%, and usually more than 90%, of all of phase assemblages 1 to 9, although by the last of these phases Medieval Ely ware had declined substantially while the other types had not. In Phase 11 their combined

contribution was much less (see Table 4). During the two and a half centuries or more represented by these phases, however, trends and changes are evident, most notably in the presence of Medieval Ely ware and Grimston ware. The former increased in quantity to a peak around Phases 6 and 7, but then steadily declined in importance in all assemblages from then on. Grimston ware was the most abundant type at the start of the sequence, highly decorated jugs being particularly noticeable at that time, but it dropped in importance in the site assemblage after 1350, becoming more common again in the Period 3 phases (peaking in Phase 9). Unglazed Grimston or Blackborough End ware was generally the most common ware and is a continuing presence in the late medieval sequence, but later on (Phase 11) it was perhaps replaced by newer types such as Bourne D and LMT, suggesting that this unquestionably 'medieval style' unglazed coarseware fabric was less favoured once more modern alternatives were available. Medieval Ely ware, although a provider of both glazed bowls and jugs during the middle part of the sequence, ceased to be even a secondary supplier to this assemblage by Phase 9. Grimston glazed pottery slumped throughout the period when Medieval Ely ware was most common, and this coincides with the end of highly decorated pottery production in the 14th century of which Grimston was initially a specialist supplier. It appears to have become more common during the latter part of the 15th century, however, and this may suggest that it was more resilient in the face of a changing market than the more coarse, and 'medieval', Ely product.

Conclusions
Although not large, the specific nature of this assemblage, being a snapshot of episodic inundation and occupation, allows valuable temporal analysis. It is evident that the assemblage is mostly domestic in character, but that in Phase 6 the suggestion that metalworking is occurring may well provide a reasonable explanation of the function of the pair of complete vessels. Although metalworking is the sort of anti-social activity that could be banished to the edges of medieval settlement, this was not always the case. Current knowledge of medieval craft production does not preclude domestic and industrial activities taking place together, rather it specifically suggests that to be the case within individual properties. Thus the assemblage from this site could easily represent the general ceramic assemblage from urban edge 'industrial settlement'.

The ceramic sequence provided here may only be representative of one part, or even one property, of medieval Wisbech, but it still represents an enormously valuable temporal progression against which other work in the town can be compared. The identification of the contribution to the ceramic assemblage of producers from, in particular rural Norfolk and Ely, is significant as it fills a geographic

Fabric Type	Period 1	Period 2	Period 3	Period 4
EMW	6.1			
SCAR	1.5			0.1
UGBB	28.5	12.2	38	12.7
MEL	19.5	67.1	14.6	2.3
GRIM	42.1	20	24.6	24.9
LMT	2.4	0.2	4.6	13.5
OSW		0.1	13.3	0.1
BOND			1	33.4
ESMIC			0.2	0.4
IMPORTS			0.7	2
CSTN				9

Table 7 Percentages (by weight) of fabric types in period assemblages

Vessel	Period 1	Period 2	Period 3	Period 4
A Bowls, dishes *etc.*	12.6	2.9	18.3	7
B Cooking vessels	33.8	12.2	38.3	14
C Jugs, pitchers *etc.*	53.6	20.7	39.6	33
D Storage jars		64.3	1.3	
C or D jug/cistern				35.5
E Cups & mugs			2.6	10.4

Table 8 Percentages (by weight) of main vessel types in period assemblages

gap between urban ceramic data from sites in the medieval Fenland ports of Ely (Spoerry 2008; Hall 2001), Peterborough (Spoerry 1998) and Cambridge (Edwards and Hall 1997 and pers. comm.), and large ceramic groups from the other outfall of this river system at King's Lynn. The decline in importance of Medieval Ely ware in the Wisbech assemblage after 1450 is significant, as is the late date of change away from ceramic cooking vessels and towards the provision of ceramic cisterns and drinking vessels. The c.1450–1500 date for this development mirrors that seen at Peterborough (Spoerry 1998) and points to a conservatism in ceramic manufacture and use which may seem surprising on the eastern seaboard within easy reach of changes occurring across the North Sea. It may well be that the everyday ceramic market was driven more by internal factors than through contact via the Fenland hithes with new ideas from abroad. Grimston ware and Unglazed Grimston or Blackborough End ware were produced in rural sites in North Norfolk and presumably were carted overland to King's Lynn and then upstream to Wisbech on barges, this being one of the major routes for Fenland traffic. Medieval Ely ware was made close to the waterfront on the edge of the city (Spoerry 2008) and it would have been very simple to transport such products downstream along the Ouse and Wellstream to Wisbech, especially to a riverside location such as this. Lincolnshire and Yorkshire glazed wares appear as occasional types throughout the medieval assemblage but it is only with the growth of Bourne D production after 1450 (Healey 1975) that any product from areas to the north becomes common in this assemblage. This was transported to Wisbech either overland to Peterborough and then down the river Nene, or via the River Glen and the Wash. The only medieval import is pieces of perhaps two Spanish olive jars, with Rhenish stonewares and Dutch redwares conspicuous by their absence until Phase 11, when they are still rare. A little late medieval Essex redware suggests more coastal contact but, in general, the assemblage is local or even parochial and conservative in character.

Catalogue of Illustrated Pottery

SF 19   No. 64 in Spoerry 2008

Large Medieval Ely ware storage vessel with simple, rounded out-turned rim above a short neck, globular body and sagging base. This vessel is in a medium coarse sandy fabric with very occasional calcareous inclusions, with buff-brown surfaces, orange-brown margins and a mid-grey core. It has a partial green glaze internally under a layer of limescale. It is believed to have been used as a cistern in a 15th-century metalworking workshop.

Fill 97, 'trough' 112, Building 7, Period 2, Phase 6.3

SF 56   Late medieval Grimston ware pear-shaped jug with externally thickened rim, tapering neck and sagging base, with wide strap handle. The vessel is completely oxidised and has a heat-altered partial glaze. The fabric was probably originally reduced grey and the glaze glossy green, in common with most Grimston products of this type, but the colouration of both have been altered through heating during its use in a metalworking workshop.

Fill 97, 'trough' 112, Building 7, Period 2, Phase 6.3

V. Stone Objects
by Nina Crummy
(Fig. 23)

A group of items from the floor surface in Building 4 (Phase 4.2) consists of two small stone spindlewhorls and several metal objects (see above). The recovery of the whorls is evidence that spinning remained a female domestic craft in the medieval period, carried out between other household activities, though weaving had become a male-dominated trade. This distinction between fibre-production and cloth-production can be seen as early as the late 9th and 10th centuries at the manor of Goltho, Lincolnshire, where spindlewhorls were mostly found in the hall and bower and were probably used by women of all social levels, while weaving and finishing equipment came from the weaving shed and the adjacent part of the courtyard. At this period most of the weavers were probably unmarried girls engaged full-time in the craft, allowing the creation of a surplus of cloth, over the needs of the manor itself, that could be sold on in urban markets like Lincoln (Beresford 1987, 55–7, 68; Crummy 2002,

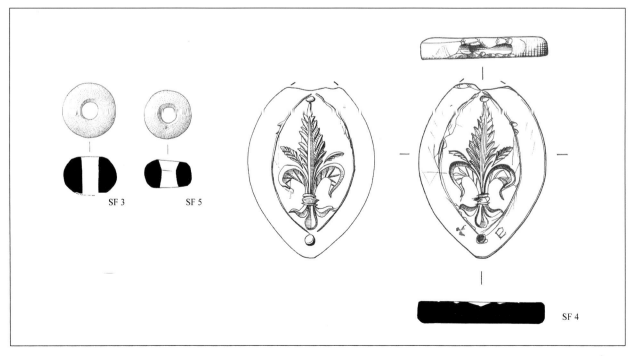

Figure 23 Stone spindle whorls (SF 3 and SF 5), scale 1:2; jet seal matrix (SF 4). Scale 1:1

SF 3   SF 5

SF 4

38). Though no fair specifically for the sale of cloth is recorded for medieval Wisbech, at the end of the 18th century there was a hemp and flax fair (see Chapter 1.IV). The location of Wisbech at the confluence of the Wellstream and Wysbeck would have provided an excellent location for the retting pits used in flax-processing, and the fibre was in considerable demand in the medieval period, when England tried, but failed, to avoid importing it (Walton 1991, 322).

The Market Mews spindlewhorls are made from a fine-grained hard grey limestone (or calcite mudstone), other examples of which come from King's Lynn and Northampton (Geddes and Dunning 1977, 315–17; Oakley and Hall 1979, 286–9). They weigh only 11 and 16g, which places them within the lighter of the two weight ranges defined by both the Northampton and King's Lynn whorls. No distinct clustering was noticed for stone whorls from Winchester and York, and, though it might be expected that small whorls such as those from Wisbech were used for producing fine yarn from either wool or flax, Walton Rogers has pointed out that more complex factors were involved, such as the method of manufacture for the whorls and the spinning technique used (Woodland 1990, 218, fig. 45, g; Walton Rogers 1997, 1743–5).

SF 3   Bun-shaped **spindlewhorl** of hard grey limestone, spalled around the spindle hole on one side; diameter 29mm, thickness 18.5mm. The spindle hole is slightly figure-of-eight-shaped, the profile typically formed by drilling the hole through the whorl from each side; diameter 8.5 to 10mm. Weight 16g.
Floor 46; Building 4, Period 2, Phase 4.2

SF 5   Bun-shaped **spindlewhorl** of hard grey limestone as SF 3 above, slightly narrower on one side; diameter 26mm, thickness varies from 13 to 15mm. Weight 11g. The spindle hole is figure-of-eight-shaped; diameter 7.5 to 9.5mm.
Floor 46, Building 4, Period 2, Phase 4.2

VI. Jet Seal Matrix
by Andrew Rogerson and Steven Ashley
(Fig. 23)

Pointed oval personal seal matrices came into use in mid-13th-century England and remained popular until *c.*1300, especially amongst women (Harvey and McGuinness 1996, 79–80). The occasional occurrence of matrices engraved with central designs but lacking legends shows that two engravers may have been involved, the purchaser first choosing his die with its off-the-peg design and then ordering the required lettering (Harvey and McGuinness 1996, 16). The very feeble 'S' on the example from the floor of Building 4 at Wisbech is presumably the first letter of *sigillum*, the Latin for seal and the normal first element in a seal with a personal name.

By the end of the 12th century almost all seal matrices were made of metal (Heslop 1987). There has been a huge increase in the number of recorded metal matrices in recent years, as a result of metal detecting. Non-metal examples have survived in small numbers and those made of jet are rare: only two out of one hundred-and-twenty-six 12th- to 16th-century personal matrices in the British Museum listed by Tonnochy (1952) were of that material, while twenty-seven out of twenty-eight matrices in Salisbury Museum are metal, with one of bone (Cherry 1991). Of over eight hundred matrices listed in the Norfolk Historic Environment Record none is of jet. Thus this unfinished example can be seen as a welcome addition

to a class of archaeological find that was always small in number and that is unlikely to see significant augmentation in the future.

SF 4   Jet, pointed oval **seal matrix or die** with incomplete inscription. One end is missing, broken across two obliquely rilled, round-sectioned channels which must have formed part of an arrangement for suspension. The central motif, an elegantly engraved fleur-de-lis, is set within a poorly executed pointed oval border. There is no legend apart from a solitary reversed 'S' very tentatively engraved next to a 1mm deep dot at the base of the fleur-de-lis. A shallower dot at the top is the result of damage. Surviving length 47mm, width 34mm, thickness 5.5mm.
Floor 46, Building 4, Period 2, Phase 4.2

VII. Worked Bone
by Chris Faine
(Fig. 24)

A worked cattle bone (SF 11) was recovered from context 125, a floor of Building 1 (Period 1). Probably a portion of radius or tibia, it has been worked to produce a large needle, with a single hole drilled through the distal end. An implement of this size would only have been of use for coarse work such as maintaining nets or sails. A further unidentified long bone from a floor of Building 3 (Period 2) had been worked into a needle shape, while an indeterminate worked bone implement came from the floor of Building 10 (Period 3, Phase 9.1). Two worked goose bones, both radii, came from pit 5 (Phase 11.2, Period 4). One had been sharpened at the distal end, the other had been partly whittled at the same end, having had its ligamental prominence sliced off. It is possible that these bones had been cut for use as styli.

SF 11   A **net needle** made from the anterior surface of a thick cattle bone such as the tibia. This complete, roughly worked needle is 207mm in length, sharpened to a point at one end. The head is 22mm wide, pierced by a regular hole 4mm in diameter. It is closely paralleled by an unphased find from Norwich (Margeson 1993, no. 1449, p.187). Such large needles must have been used for coarse work, such as making or repairing sails or nets as the head would have interfered with fine work. Undated.
Floor 125, Building 1, Period 1, Phase 2.1

VIII. Leatherwork
by Carole Fletcher

Seven fragments of leather (not illustrated) from three contexts assigned to Periods 1 and 2 were examined using the terminology proposed by Thorton (1973). Although small, all of the fragments are reasonably well preserved, with cut edges, stitching holes and remnants of the leather's grain surviving. A large fragment of a leather shoe was recovered from floor 48 within Building 3 (SF 9). The small fragments appear mainly to have been scraps cut from shoes, indicating possible reuse of the leather for patching other shoes.

SF 60   Three fragments of leather were recovered. Two pieces were joined to form a roughly triangular piece and the third was a thin narrow strip. The two pieces that form a roughly triangular fragment 56mm long by 36mm high have knife cut edges on two sides: the third is broken with only a small portion of the cut edge surviving. The fragment is 4–5mm thick, although the degree of cracking and abrasion make it difficult to identify the grain or flesh side of the leather and no stitching holes are evident. The fragment appears to be an off-cut from a hide or other leather used to make shoes. 'This triangular shape is often considered to be the hallmark of the shoemakers trade' (Allin 1981, 20).

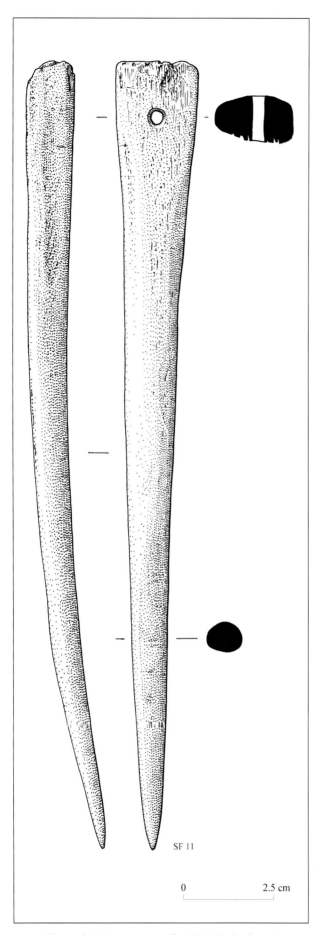

Figure 24 Bone net needle (SF 11). Scale 1:1

SF 11

0 ————————— 2.5 cm

The third fragment of leather is a thin tapering strip 15mm at its widest narrowing to 11mm and approximately 2mm thick. The grain side is discernible, the two sides and the wide end are knife cut, there are no visible stitching holes and this fragment also appears to be an offcut.
Fill 126, foundation trench 127, Building 1, Period 1, Phase 1

SF 9 Two fragments of leather were recovered from floor 48. The first is a roughly triangular fragment with knife cut edges on all sides, with the exception of one very small broken point to the elongated triangle (approximately 70mm long by 20mm high). At the lower part of the fragment, approximately 1mm from the knife cut edge, is a row of stitching holes. These are approximately 7mm from centre of stitch hole to the centre of stitch hole; the leather curves under at this lower edge and it appears that this fragment has been cut from a shoe. The fragment itself formed part of a closed seam although the type of shoe from which this has been cut is not clear. The second strip of leather is 79mm long and 15mm wide and 3mm thick. It is knife cut on three sides, straight on the long edges and diagonally at one end, while the other end has broken along a line of stitches. The upper surface of the leather is cracked along the edges, and the area around the broken end is in poor condition. It is difficult to locate stitching holes on the surface because of this cracking and silt still adhering to the leather. There also appears to be a small iron fragment adhering to the surface.

Small areas of grain survive on the upper surface of the leather. The flesh side of the strip reveals more information and a series of very fine stitch holes or perhaps punched or slashed holes can be discerned. These form a straight line along one edge and looped or curved patterns on the surface. The 'stitches' are approximately 2mm apart and may be decorative rather than functional. It is possible that this strip of leather may be a band from a patten upper.
Floor 48, Building 3, Period 1, Phase 3.1

SF 10 The leather is in poor condition, having broken into small pieces, although two fragments are of sufficient size to permit comment. The largest fragment is 158mm long and 60mm at its widest point. The grain and flesh sides of the fragment can be identified, but there is no discernible grain on the leather's surface. The fragment is from the sole of a shoe, but is irregular in shape with only a short length (48mm) of cut edge surviving. This section shows evidence of edge to flesh stitching in the form of stitch holes between 1.5 and 2mm wide by 4mm apart. It appears that this surviving portion of the sole represents the seat, waist and part of the tread, the latter showing the greatest disintegration and wear. The second fragment, also in poor condition, is approximately 70mm long by 9mm wide and appears to be a narrow strip of the edge of a turnshoe. The fragment is curved, as if from close to the toe or heel of a shoe with what appear to be grain to flesh stitch holes approximately 2mm wide and between 4 and 5mm apart. The fragment may form part of the upper shoe rather than the sole. No discernible grain could be identified on the leather's surface.
Floor 48, Building 3, Period 1, Phase 3.1

SF 61 Two fragments of leather were recovered from the possible drain/trough. The first is a narrow piece of leather 60mm long and 9mm wide, tapering to 5.5mm at its narrowest end. It is approximately 1.5mm thick and is knife cut along its sides and possibly at both ends. The leather is slightly curved and a row of stitch holes is visible along its length, approximately 7mm from centre of stitch hole to the centre of stitch hole. Small areas of grain survive on the upper surface of the leather. The flesh side shows an area of iron corrosion product attached to the surface and there also appears to be a small iron fragment adhering to the edge of the piece of leather. This fragment of leather is likely to have been trimmed from a shoe.

The second fragment is a narrow, roughly triangular piece of leather, 43mm long, 6mm wide at one end narrowing to 4mm, and 5mm thick. Both ends are broken, though the edges are cut; stitch holes are visible and are edge to flesh. This type of stitching and the shape indicate that it is part of a pierced rand from a shoe.
Fill 97, drain/trough 112, Building 7, Period 2, Phase 6.3

Chapter 4. Zooarchaeological and Botanical Remains

I. Animal and Bird Bone
by Chris Faine
(Figs 25–31; Table 9)

Summary
A total of 477 fragments of animal and bird bone was recovered, with 197 being identifiable to species (41.2%). Although animal remains were recovered from all phases, most came from a series of rubbish pits and floor layers assigned to Phase 11 (16th century). Sheep/goat dominate the assemblage (53.6% of the identifiable sample), with lesser proportions of cattle, pig and horse. The majority of the bones from domestic mammals come from adult animals, with 51.7% showing signs of butchery. The domestic assemblage represents waste discarded during butchery, with elements showing evidence of use of a heavy knife or cleaver. A number of small mammal bones were found in the later rubbish pits, while a variety of wild and domestic bird remains indicate exploitation of the surrounding area.

Methodology
All elements identifiable to species and over 25% complete were recorded. Loose teeth, caudal vertebra and ribs without proximal epiphyses were noted but not included in any quantification. Elements not identifiable to species were classed as 'large/medium/small mammal' but again not included in any quantification. All elements were assessed in terms of siding (where appropriate), completeness, tooth wear stages (also where applicable) and epiphyseal fusion. Completeness was recorded in terms of percentage and zones present (after Dobney and Reilly 1988). The identifiable assemblage was quantified in terms of number of individual fragments (NISP) and minimum numbers of individuals MNI (see Table 9). The ageing of the sheep/goat population was largely achieved by examining the wear stages of mandibular cheek teeth (after Grant 1982; Payne 1973; Hambelton 2000).

Species	NISP	NISP%	MNI	MNI%
Domestic mammals				
Sheep/Goat (*Ovis/Capra*)	103	56.5	43	50
Cattle (*Bos*)	42	23	23	26.4
Pig (*Sus scrofa*)	12	6.6	10	10.4
Horse (*Equus caballus*)	1	0.5	1	1.2
Small mammals				
Cat (*Felis domesticatus*)	4	2.2	1	1.2
House Mouse (*Mus musculus*)	3	1.6	1	1.2
Rabbit (*Oryctolagus cuniculus*)	3	1.6	1	1.2
Pygmy shrew (*Sorex minitus*)	1	0.5	1	1.2
Birds				
Goose (*Anser sp.*)	6	3.3	1	1.2
Domestic Chicken (*Gallus Gallus*)	3	1.6	1	1.2
Kittiwake (*Riss Tridactyla*)	2	1.1	1	1.2
Mallard (*Anas platyrynchos*)	1	0.5	1	1.2
Teal (*Anas crecca*)	1	0.5	1	1.2
Grey Heron (*Aredea cinerea*)	1	0.5	1	1.2
Total	**183**	**100%**	**87**	**100%**

Table 9 Quantification of animal and bird bone

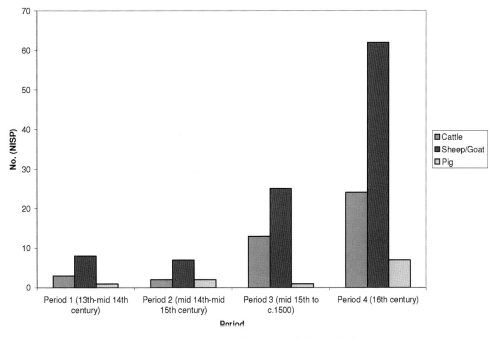

Figure 25 Domestic mammals by period

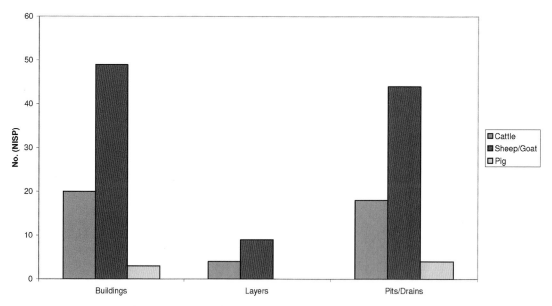

Figure 26 Domestic mammal distribution by feature type

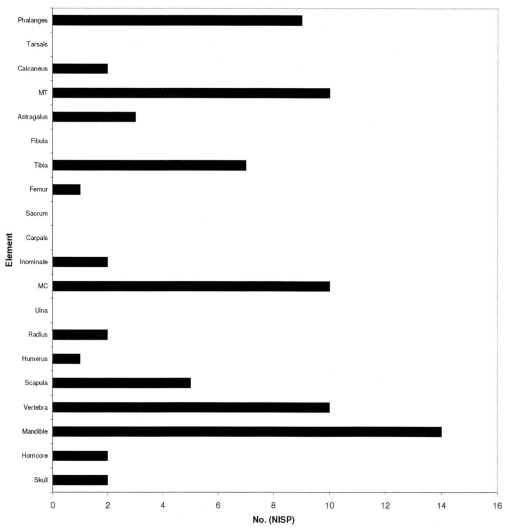

Figure 27 Sheep body part distribution

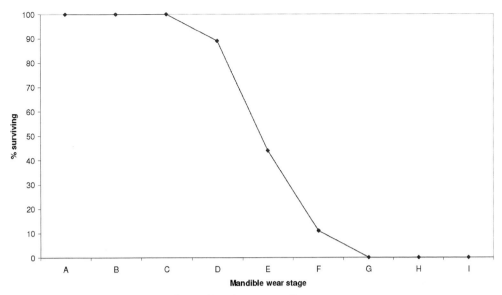

Figure 28 Sheep mortality curve

The states of epiphyscal fusion for all relevant bones were recorded to provide a broad age range for the major domesticates (after Getty 1975). A variety of metrical analyses was carried out according to the conventions of von den Driesch (1976). Measurements were either achieved using a 150mm sliding calliper or an osteometric board in the case of larger bones.

Distribution

The distribution of remains from the major domestic mammals is represented by period in Fig. 25. No bones were recovered from Period 5. In terms of the distribution of the major domesticates, 59% of cattle, 60% of sheep/goat and 63% of pig remains came from a series of rubbish pits (2, 4, 5 and 61) associated with Buildings 12 and 13 (Period 4, 16th century). This distribution reflects the nature of the relevant archaeological deposits (Fig. 26): large quantities of cattle and/or sheep remains are not generally anticipated on the floors of domestic dwellings such as those found at Market Mews. The species

distribution for the remaining phases is generally quite regular, with small amounts of butchered sheep/goat, cattle and pig remains being recovered from floors in all phases. Unsurprisingly, few large mammal fragments were found in the intermittent flooding layers.

Species Represented

Sheep/Goat

Sheep/Goat are by far the most prevalent species in the assemblage, making up 56.5% of the identifiable fragments (MNI: 43). A wide range of elements was recovered, particularly mandibles, front limbs and metapodials (see Fig. 27). Unfortunately much of the assemblage is extremely fragmented, and differentiation between sheep and goat was therefore not possible by either morphological traits or metrical analysis: it is assumed for the purposes of this report that the elements in question represent sheep. Ageing data by mandibular wear stages and epiphyseal fusion is presented in Figs 28

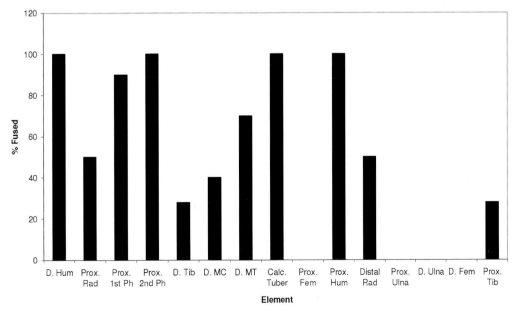

Figure 29 Sheep epiphyseal data

and 29 respectively. From Fig. 28 it is clear that almost all the individuals survived to at least young adulthood, with all being killed off by 36 months. Although epiphyseal fusion data determine the age of an animal once it has reached adulthood, Fig. 29 indicates that, with a single exception, all the animals in the assemblage had reached maturity. Some 56% of sheep/goat remains show evidence of butchery. The majority of long bones had been split midshaft or at the epiphyses. Almost all marks are severe and indicate chopping with a cleaver or large knife. Twelve thoracic vertebrae are chopped longitudinally through the vertebral body.

Only one instance of pathology was found in the sheep assemblage, with a 1st phalange from the fill of pit 5 (Period 4) showing severe lesions both proximally and distally; probably the result of a severe infection. Such a condition would almost certainly have made the animal lame.

Cattle

Cattle are the next most prevalent species in the assemblage, with 42 fragments (23% of the total sample/ MNI: 23). A more limited range of elements was recovered (Fig. 30). Like the sheep/goat remains, vertebrae and front limbs dominate, although with a lesser proportion of metapodia. Unfortunately a large amount of the assemblage is heavily butchered (66% of the identifiable assemblage), leading to problems when analysing the fragments themselves. No intact mandibles could be recovered for tooth wear analysis, although all loose teeth retrieved were from adult individuals. Although limited by sample size and the range of elements present, the population largely consisted of individuals around two years old. It is clear from Fig. 31, however, that the lack of later fusing elements recovered puts limitations on any further analysis. Likewise any metrical analysis to ascertain size, shape and sex was not possible due to the range and fragmented nature of many of the elements.

Several instances of pathology were found in the cattle assemblage. Two 1st phalanges from the fill of pit 4 (Period 4) and flood deposit 22 (Period 3) show evidence of bone growth on their plantar surfaces. This is relatively common and can be a result of general 'wear and tear', rather than the result of a specific condition or trauma. More interestingly, a proximal metatarsal from the fill of pit 4 (Period 4) shows possible evidence of osteitis, *i.e.* inflammation of the periosteum due to repeated trauma. Such trauma could for instance be the result of repeated banging of the leg against a fence or stall.

Pig

A small number of pig remains (19/6.6% of identifiable fragments) were recovered from all phases of the site. The assemblage consists of a range of cranial and post cranial elements, the majority of which (75%) are heavily butchered. Due to this fragmentation and the small size of the assemblage, few conclusions can be drawn about the pig population in terms of ageing and sexing stature. Only one long bone (a distal humerus from the fill of pit 5, Period 4) is sufficiently intact to show epiphyseal fusion, coming from an individual at least 1 year old. No instances of pathology were seen in the assemblage. The butchery marks are for the most part severe, and were probably made by a heavy knife or cleaver. Their positions are largely indicative of butchery for meat, with long bones split midshaft, mandibles split along the ascending ramus to disarticulate the jaw, and scapula chopped above the glenoid.

Other mammals

The fill of pit 5 (Period 4) contained the butchered tuber coxae from an adult horse calcaneus, along with three fragments identified as house mouse. Two fragments of cat bone (a rib and proximal radius) were also recovered. The fill of pit 4 (Period 4) yielded a cat ulna and a distal humerus of pygmy shrew. One cat phalange was recovered

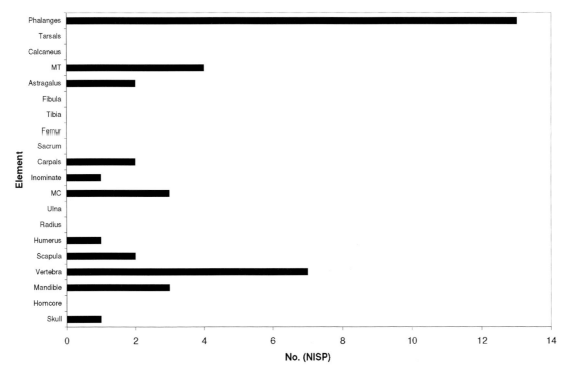

Figure 30 Cattle body part distribution

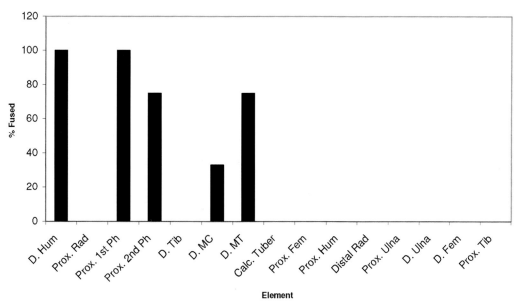

Figure 31 Cattle epiphyseal fusion data

from floor 23, within Building 10. No signs of butchery are evident on the cat remains. It is likely that the other small mammal remains represent accidental deposition or pit falls.

Birds
A range of domestic and wild bird species was recovered, with the majority of the wild species coming from pit 4 (Period 4). Domestic species include six fragments of goose bone (*Anser sp.*) along with three of domestic chicken (*Gallus sp.*). Some 55% of the domestic bird remains show evidence of butchery and two goose bones had been worked into artefacts (see Chapter 3.VII). Wild species include two fragments of duck (one mallard and one teal), along with two fragments of kittiwake (*Russ tridactyla*) and one of grey heron (*Aredea cinerea*). Although not subject to butchery as with many of the domestic species, their presence in a domestic rubbish context may indicate the exploitation of wild birds from the coast and surrounding fens.

Discussion and Conclusion
Most of the assemblage was recovered from deposits dating to the 16th century. The evidence suggests a meat-based economy. Despite the fragmentary nature of much of the assemblage, ageing data demonstrates that cattle and sheep were raised to at least young adulthood before slaughter (sheep being slightly older than cattle generally). Mutton appears to have been the favoured meat during all periods, with cattle of secondary importance. Pig remains, although few, are found in all phases of the site and again the majority are of adult animals. Although there was no evidence for on site breeding, this remains a possibility for pigs which could easily be kept in towns.

Body part distributions for the major domesticates are relatively similar, with large numbers of cranial elements, front limbs and vertebrae, along with lesser proportions of metapodials. Whilst some meat bearing elements are conspicuous by their absence, so are many of the elements indicative of other industries, such as tanning (*e.g.* horn

cores, caudal vertebrae). In this respect, the Market Mews assemblage varies significantly from recent excavations at New Inn Yard, Wisbech, where pits containing waste from hornworking were found (Mortimer forthcoming). It is likely that the Market Mews assemblage represents waste products from meat consumption, with some of the larger meat bearing elements being deposited elsewhere. Evidence of butchery on many of the elements is also similar for all species, indicating heavy butchery with large knives or cleavers.

As would be expected in a meat-based economy, the overall health of the domestic animal population is good, with few instances of pathology noted. Those seen largely consist of lesions on the plantar surface of cattle metapodials, in themselves not indicative of any specific condition.

Few horse remains were found. Horses were regularly exploited for both meat and skins throughout the periods in question, and it is unusual to find so few horse remains, even in smaller domestic contexts such as these. No traces of skinning were found on the few fragments of cat bone, suggesting a commensal population rather than any exploitation for fur, as has been recorded at various other medieval sites such as St Ben'ets, Cambridge (Luff and Moreno-García 1995) and Norwich Castle (Albarella *et al* 2009). Given the repeated flooding at the Market Mews site, the general absence of smaller mammal remains is unsurprising.

The bird remains indicate exploitation of both domestic and wild species. Most of the assemblage consists of chicken and geese of indeterminate species (*Anser sp.*), along with two fragments of duck. Eighty per cent of goose remains showed signs of butchery, along with 33% of chicken (the smaller domestic fowl needing fewer cuts to be disarticulated/butchered). Geese in particular were popular birds, yielding meat, eggs and feathers. The small amount of wild species indicates exploitation of the surrounding coast and fens. No butchery marks were seen on any of these elements, although given the size of the species involved this is not entirely unexpected.

II. Fish Bone

by Julie Curl and Alison Locker
(Fig. 32; Table 10)

Introduction

Amongst the group of 993 fish bones examined (0.108kg), 601 were identified to species (by J. Curl). Of these identifiable bones the vast majority are vertebrae: this is common in fish bone assemblages since vertebrae are the most numerous and robust elements in the fish skeleton. A few other elements were recovered, including scapulae, dentaries, teeth, ribs and dermal denticles.

In general the condition of the fish remains is good. Many vertebrae are complete, as are a few dentaries and dermal denticles. There is little evidence of butchery, a notable exception being a cod vertebral centrum chopped medio-laterally. Butchery marks are most likely to be observable on the bones of the larger fish species such as cod, which may be headed, filleted and divided, but are poorly represented here. Numerous fish remains show evidence of burning, particularly from hearth/oven 120 (Building 2, Phase 2.3). All of the burnt bones are from herring, which may indicate they were prepared for consumption in a different manner to the other species. One butchered fragment, unidentified to species had been gnawed, possibly by a cat.

The Identified Fish

The species are described below and in Table 10 in family order after Wheeler (1978).

Thornback ray, or roker (*Raja clavata*), was identified from three spines and a dermal denticle from occupation layer 48 (Building 3, Phase 3.1). Rays have a cartilaginous skeleton which rarely survives and are usually identified from loose teeth and dermal denticles; these lie under the skin and some show species-specific characteristics. The roker (an East Anglian name of Danish origin) is the most common species and found inshore all round the British coastline. The larger females reach a length of 85cm and weights of 18kg. They were often caught in traps and on lines inshore.

Skate (*Raja batis*) was also identified from dermal denticles recovered from pit 4 (Building 12, Phase 11.2) and floor 114 (Building 2, Phase 2.4). This is the largest of the rays; females can achieve 285cm in length, and adults are found in deeper waters than the roker. A mid water predator, skate were more likely to be caught on lines. Two indeterminate ray denticles came from Building 12 (Period 4).

Eel (*Anguilla anguilla*) is the second most commonly identified species accounting for 19% of all fish bones by number of identified specimens (NISP; see Table 10). A catadromous species, young eels return to freshwater to feed and grow before returning to the sea to spawn. Eels were very common in the medieval ponds, marshes and waterways of East Anglia and were caught by a variety of means including fixed structures across streams, traps and on multi-pronged spears. Eels were so numerous they were also used as a currency to pay rents. Their rich and oily flesh is highly nutritious and can also be salted and smoked for storage. Most of the identified bones were

Date	Period 1 (13th to 14th century)			Period 2 (mid 14th to mid 15th century)			Period 3 (mid 15th century to c.1500)				Period 4 (16th century)				
Building	1	2	3	4	5	6	7	8	9	10	11	12	13		
Species														Subtotal	% of identified species
Thornback ray/roker (*Raja clavata*)		4												4	0.60%
Skate (*Raja batis*)		1				4								4	0.60%
Skate sp												2		3	0.40%
Eel (*Anguilla anguilla*)		1	9	39		30		2	6	20				112	18.60%
Herring (*Clupea harengus*)	77	10		48		114	1	5	11	41		7		328	54.50%
Salmonidae (cf salmon *Salmo salar*)	1			1		2								4	0.60%
Trout (*Salmo trutta*)		5		15										20	3.30%
Pike (*Esox lucius*)	1	3		6		23								33	5.40%
Pike?										1				1	0.10%
Carp	2													2	0.30%
Minnow (*Phoxinus phoxinus*)				2		9								11	1.80%
Cod (*Gadus morhua*)	1	2		3										6	0.90%
Rockling										10				10	1.60%
Stickleback (*Gasterosteus aculeatus*)				5										5	0.80%
Perch (*Perca fluviatilis*)				9					4	11				24	3.90%
Gobidae.		2				3								5	0.80%
Dab (*Limanda limanda*)													1	1	0.10%
Sole (*Solea solea*)				27						1				28	4.60%
Unidentified	45	40		82	3	136		6	24	32		5	2	392	
Total	**129**	**75**		**237**	**3**	**321**	**1**	**13**	**45**	**116**		**14**	**3**	**993**	

Table 10 Fish bones species by building

vertebrae, with a single dentary from Building 10. This fish has nearly double the number of vertebrae per fish of most other species resulting in some over-representation. Of the 21 contexts containing fish bones at Market Mews, nine contained eel, with only herring being better represented by both bone count and spatial occurrence.

Herring (*Clupea harengus*) is the most commonly identified species by NISP, representing 54% of the identified bone, and by occurrence, was found in 12 of 21 contexts (Table 10). The herring fisheries of East Anglia, centred on netting seasonally migrating vast shoals of these small fish, are well documented. They were operating from at least the 7th century to become the first fishing 'industry' of the region centred on Great Yarmouth, though this later failed as other fishing grounds were explored and the processing of fish on the East Anglian coastline lost prestige. These oily fish were eaten fresh, salted and smoked, and were a traditional food in Lent and other fast periods when meat could not be eaten.

Salmonidae (*cf* salmon *Salmo salar*) are represented by four bones, from three contexts. These are all from small fish which may have been caught locally, before the adult fish migrate to the sea. The 20 bones attributed to trout (*Salmo trutta*) are also likely to be a catch from local waters.

The pike (*Esox lucius*), found in lakes and slow running rivers, is a predatory freshwater fish and was held in high esteem in the medieval period. It was identified in six contexts at Market Mews. Pike prey on other fish once they are a year old and 8–10cm long; they can be over 100cm in length, particularly the females which live longer than the males (Maitland and Campbell 1992). Pike are frequently identified in fish bone assemblages from this region and were evidently commonly caught and eaten.

The Cyprinidae, a family which includes carp, roach, chub and a number of other species, are represented by two vertebrae from a single context. Vertebrae are difficult to assign to species in this family. A small member of this group, the minnow (*Phoxinus phoxinus*) was identified and though not in itself specifically fished for food may have been netted with other fish, or as the stomach contents of a predator such as pike.

Cod (*Gadus morhua*) is only represented by six vertebrae, in three contexts. Adult cod could have been caught inshore on the local coastline in the winter months, the fish moving offshore in the summer. A prime food fish, cod were landed at nearby King's Lynn. Prized fresh, there was also an important trade in salted and dried cod. Stored fish, particularly gadids and herring, were a vital commodity prior to the development of icing and refrigeration.

The ten vertebrae attributed to rockling cannot be specifically identified. These are all Gadidae, with several species, found in varying habitats from inshore to deeper waters. They can be eaten but are less prestigious than cod. The bones came from a single deposit and may be one fish.

Stickleback (*Gasterosteus aculeatus*) are small fish, of little value as human food, other than as part of a 'messe' of fish with other small species and, like minnow, may also be the stomach contents of pike. They were only identified from a single context from Building 4 (Period 2). A ubiquitous species, sticklebacks can be found in freshwater through to fully marine conditions.

Perch (*Perca fluviatilis*) is a freshwater species, common in lowland lakes and rivers in a slow current. Line caught, it was a popular food fish together with other freshwater species, such as cyprinids and pike. It is no longer eaten in Britain today, being considered 'bony'. Perch has also been identified from a number of other sites in the region.

Five bones attributed to the Gobidae family were found in two contexts. Common in inshore marine conditions these small fish would have been of little food value for humans and occupy the same niche as minnow and stickleback.

The only flatfishes identified are dab (*Limanda limanda*) from a single context and sole (*Solea solea*) which can both be trapped along the shoreline. The latter is represented by 28 bones, 27 of which came from floor 46 in Building 4 (Phase 4.2, Period 2).

Discussion

It is evident from Table 10 and Fig. 32 that most of the fish came from Phases 4–6 (Period 2, mid 14th to mid 15th century) and in particular Building 6. Many of the contexts are floor levels (which have also been subject to flooding) and may, in part, explain why most of the fish bones are from small species, larger debris having been cleared away. The samples of identified bones are rather too small

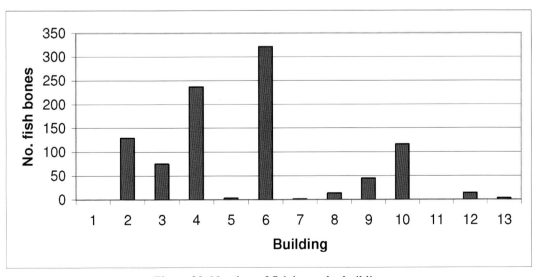

Figure 32 Number of fish bones by building

to be credible as data reflecting any changes or continuity in fish consumption through time and space. However by both NISP and occurrence (which crudely measures how often a species occurs against all contexts) herring is the most common species being found in 12 of 21 contexts. Eel is next in nine of 21 contexts. This reflects the exploitation of most abundant locally available marine and freshwater species. By occurrence pike, perch (both in four of 21 contexts) and small salmonids (three of 21 contexts) emphasise freshwater resources, the latter being equal in occurrence with cod and minnow. However, of these three cod is the more significant food fish by virtue of size. Rays were found in few contexts and are likely to be under-represented for reasons described above. Flatfishes are poorly represented, only by dab and sole, rather than the two most commonly identified species at other sites in the region; plaice (*Pleuronectes platessa*) and flounder (*Platichthys flesus*).

Wisbech, now only 16km from the estuary of the Wash, is well placed to take advantage of the local fisheries in abundant freshwater systems, the estuary and the North Sea. At Domesday, Wisbech was amongst Cambridgeshire's most important fisheries, with access to both freshwater and marine resources (Darby 1940, 23). King's Lynn was another major port only 16km away where many fish were landed. Large cod and ling were identified in a hand collected sample from medieval deposits at King's Lynn from Baker Lane (Wheeler 1977) and also from Austin Street (Locker 2000) where both hand collected and sieved bones were identified. Among the sieved material from three trenches herring was the most numerous species in all samples; although present in smaller numbers, eel bones were found in most contexts. The gadids were important, represented by cod, haddock *(Melanogrammus aeglefinus)*, whiting *(Merlangius merlangus)*, ling *(Molva molva)* and indeterminate gadids, with some cod and ling over 100cm in length. Plaice/flounder were the second most numerous group and found in every context. This assemblage shows a greater variety of marine fish, especially the major food fishes.

Two medieval tenements at South Street, Boston (Locker 1998), some 38km north-west and close to the coast were subject to the same problems of flooding that affected Market Mews. Here, apart from a large number of stickleback remains and eel, the assemblage was dominated by herring. There were a variety of gadids (cod, haddock, whiting and ling) and flatfishes which together with a variety of other marine species also suggest more varied consumption of marine species than at Wisbech. Another very small assemblage from Boston of only 22 identified bones (Locker 2003) included pike, cod, whiting, large gadid and flatfishes, but no eel or herring.

Stickleback also featured strongly in medieval deposits from two sites in Spalding, 26km west of Wisbech. At Holbeach Road (Locker 2004a) the small sample (129 identified bones) included 71 stickleback bones. Eel, herring and plaice/flounder were also identified and pike, by a single bone. Similarly at Springfield, Spalding (Locker 2004b), of 118 identified bones 42 were stickleback, the remainder largely eel herring and flatfish. Only pike and perch were true freshwater species. Neither of the Spalding sites show evidence for fish from a deep water or distant fishery, such as cod or ling.

In conclusion this small assemblage, spanning successive buildings over four centuries, suggests consistent consumption of herring and eel, the latter abundant in the local myriad freshwater systems, together with pike, perch, salmonids and some cyprinids. Marine exploitation was limited to shoreline and inshore waters as represented by rays, flatfishes and winter cod. There is no definitive evidence for consumption of fish from deep water fisheries. In many respects this assemblage is similar to that of other contemporary samples, particularly from Spalding, and smaller rural sites in that it relies mainly on very localised resources. The assemblage lacks evidence of fish being brought in from a substantive deep water fishery as found at Boston, larger towns such as King's Lynn and more distantly at Norwich, where a number of fish assemblages, including a large assemblage at Norwich Castle (Locker 2009 a and b) have been analysed.

III. Mollusca

Small quantities of oyster, mussel and cockle shells were recovered, which, because of their often fragmentary nature, were not enumerated. All of these species would have been available close to Wisbech.

IV. Plant Remains
by Duncan E. Schlee

Introduction
Twenty-one flotation samples of ten or twenty litres were processed. The samples were taken from a variety of surfaces and associated cut features from the major occupation phases encountered during the excavation. These deposits ranged in date from the 13th century at the base of the excavation to the 16th century at the top. The aim of this sampling was to attempt to characterise the nature of the occupation in each phase, and to identify any changes in economic and domestic activities, both in relation to changes in the associated structural features, and in relation to the repeated flooding events of varying severity which occurred throughout the occupation sequence.

Processing
Most samples were processed using a standard flotation machine collecting flots in a 0.5mm mesh and heavy residues in a 1mm mesh. Subsamples from two layers (46 and 92 from Building 4, Phase 4) were processed using peroxide flotation to ascertain whether significantly different results were obtained by this method. Heavy residues were sorted for the recovery of all archaeologically significant inclusions. All charred items were sorted from the flot fractions, while sufficient waterlogged specimens were recovered from each sample to identify the range of plant species represented. Identifications were carried out using reference material and with the assistance of Alan Clapham at the McDonald Institute, Cambridge.

Preservation and Characteristics of Deposition
The stratigraphic preservation on the site was excellent, with a continuous sequence of apparent occupation surfaces and associated structural features, interleaved

with fine clay silts deposited during flooding events. The flood deposits varied in depth from 1mm to up to 1m. Depending on their depth, thickness (intensity and longevity of occupation), and composition, the occupation surfaces were compacted to different degrees, varying in thickness from a few millimetres to more than 5cm. This compaction, combined with periodic flooding, has generally resulted in good organic preservation. Ground water conditions have not, however, remained sufficiently or consistently waterlogged to prevent degradation of the organic remains. As a result, some evidence such as straw, seeds and reeds, which were observed within compacted floor surfaces during the excavation, were only preserved as impressions and pseudomorphs in the fine silts. These did not survive either excavation or processing.

Plant material was preserved both by charring, and through the relatively anaerobic ('waterlogged') conditions created by the fineness of the flood deposits, compaction, and ground water conditions. While the charred material is generally confined to cultivated food crops and weeds associated with agriculture, the waterlogged seeds tend (though not exclusively) to consist of plants representing the prevailing local environment. It is likely however, that at least some of the uncharred material has been introduced onto the site from further afield during the flooding episodes. Not all the deposits were found to possess the same degree of preservation.

Some samples contained large numbers of a wide range of different plant species, while others contained fewer specimens or a much smaller range of species. Broadly speaking, the density and quality of both charred and waterlogged material increased with depth. This partly reflects an improvement in preservation conditions with depth, but may also reflect a change in the intensity and character of occupation in the light of apparently increasingly frequent and severe flooding events further up the stratigraphic sequence. Other evidence of domestic or economic activity and dietary resources was recovered in the form of animal bones (especially fish), marine molluscs (mussels and cockles), bird egg shell, coal and slag. These often formed distinct laminations within compacted floor deposits. These more robust items help indicate the intensity of occupation, where plant material is less well preserved.

Micromorphological analysis of some of the deposits has indicated that there were often several interfaces within floors, and more surprisingly within the flood deposits, that were not always visible during excavation (Milek and French, Chapter 5). These interfaces may represent different phases of deposition within a flooding event, where the silts have stabilised (and small quantities of organic matter and other rubbish have been deposited) before further silts were laid down. These deposits would thus represent periods of abandonment. Alternatively, they may represent continuous occupation but with repeated flooding preventing sufficiently long-lived or intensive activity to allow more substantial floor deposits to develop.

The tight time restrictions within which the excavation occurred, combined with the complexity and fine stratigraphic resolution of the deposits, often made it impossible to separate individual layers within a phase for the purposes of excavation and sampling. The clay silts deposited during flooding episodes did, however, enable the separation of major occupation phases.

Interpretation was also hampered by the limited area that it was possible to excavate. Since only small parts of buildings could be excavated, it is difficult to ascertain whether differences in the characteristics of the floor deposits were due to changes in the activities undertaken within the buildings, or whether the same activities were undertaken, but that individual rooms underwent changes in use and deposition patterns.

The Composition of the Assemblage

Cereals
Charred cereal grains are present in most of the samples, but generally in small quantities, with the exception of Samples 22 (114, Building 2, Phase 2.4), 23 (119, Building 2, Phase 2.3), and 24 (123, Building 2, Phase 2.3). Bread wheat is the most prevalent, generally occurring alongside oats. Barley is only occasionally represented by one or two grains in an assemblage. Rye is present only in Samples 22 and 24.

As would often be expected in an urban situation, there is little evidence for crop processing. The low presence of rachis fragments but absence of other chaff fragments in two samples from Building 12, Phase 11.2 (Samples 4 (17) and 5 (50)) and occasionally, other samples, suggests that these are more likely to be impurities picked out of cleaned grain, or that straw or chaff was used as fuel. Traces of cereal straw were found within compacted floor deposits, presumably used as floor or roofing material, and would thus have been readily available for use in hearths.

Although Samples 22, 23 and 24 contain larger quantities of chaff and straw fragments, these too are most likely to be through the use of whole straw for fuel. Apart from their association with a domestic hearth (oven 120, Phase 2.3, Period 1), the fragments are sufficiently large and few in number to represent single ears, indeed, the rye chaff is represented by an intact ear (from which the rye grains may well have been derived). Many of the oat grains in these samples are also still contained within their awns, suggesting they were from a complete plant, or were for use as animal fodder rather than for human consumption.

Pulses
Peas and beans were recovered from several deposits, although only in small quantities. As with wheat and oats, they are present in all the main occupation deposits throughout the excavated sequence.

Fruit and nuts
Hazel nut shell fragments were recovered from the earlier floor deposits, both in charred and uncharred states. A single apple pip, and two cherry stones were also recovered. Uncharred seeds of bramble fruit and elderberries were also occasionally present. While these may have had dietary significance, they are most likely to derive from plants growing in the vicinity.

Weed seeds
Weed seeds were recovered in varying quantities from the samples. The overall assemblage suggests three main environments from which plant material was coming onto

the site: wet land, waste land and cultivated land. While charred seeds are generally more likely to have had economic, industrial, or agricultural significance, it is less easy to ascertain whether waterlogged seeds have been introduced by human or natural agencies (and therefore what their significance might be).

The likely proximity of the site to a wetland environment, coupled with the evidence for repeated flooding strongly suggests that much of the weed flora is present through natural means. Such environments are, however, the source of many useful plant resources, which may have been intentionally brought onto the site with animal fodder, roofing, or flooring material. The weeds of arable cultivation which are not charred may still have come in with cultivated crops, but could also have been washed in during floods. Material from other environments, represented by non-charred weed seeds, may also have been washed in from further afield, but these species are often sufficiently broad in their habitat requirements to have been growing in or around the immediate vicinity.

Miscellaneous
Many of the samples contain varying proportions of decomposed and degraded organic debris. This was presumably deposited on and trampled into floors during occupation phases. It is also possible that some of it originates from organic matter washed in during flood events. The bulk of this material is too degraded for identification and its origins can only be inferred from the weed seed assemblage and impressions of straw and reeds in floor laminations. A charred fragment of possible bread or dung was recovered from Sample 4 (pit fill 17, Phase 11.2, Period 4). A few fragments of what may have been apple peel were also recovered from this sample.

Fish bones were frequent in many samples, often forming distinct laminations within floor deposits. During excavation, some fish skeletons were found to be articulated. Bird egg shell was also common often forming laminations within compressed floors.

Fly pupae were recovered from several samples. In Sample 4 this would support the interpretation of the pit fill as being cessy. Fly pupae were, however, also recovered from floor deposits, reflecting the presence of fish bones and other organic debris on the floors.

Species Represented (by Environment)

Wet Places
Species present: *Polygonum hydropiper* (Waterpepper), *Schoenus negricans* (Bog Rush), *Menyanthes trifoliata* (Bog Bean), *Alisma ranunculoides* (Lesser Water Plantain), *Ranunculus flamula* (Lesser Spearwort), *Ranunculus scleratus* (Celery Leaved Crowfoot), *Ranunculus aquatilis* (Water Crowfoot), *Scirpus maritimus* (Sea Clubrush), *Cladium mariscus* (Common Sedge), *Juncus* sp. (Rushes), *Potamogeton* sp. (Pondweed), *Cladoceran* eggs (Waterflea eggs).

Plants associated with a variety of wet environments are well represented. Bearing in mind the archaeological evidence for flooding and the presumed close proximity of the River Ouse, it is likely that many of these plants would have been growing nearby. It is also likely that the sedges and rushes would have been utilised for fuel and roofing material. The presence of pondweed and waterflea eggs suggests standing water. Although it may be an accident of differential preservation, both were only present in samples of well compacted floors, suggesting that conditions were far from dry even during periods of more intensive occupation. Bog-bean seeds, occasionally present, and indicating a fen environment, may reflect the use of the plant in brewing, but are most likely to be present coincidentally.

Cultivated/ Wasteland
Species present: *Lapsana communis* (Nipplewort), *Carduus* sp. (Thistle), *Fumaria officinalis* (Fumitory), *Galeopsis tetrahit* (Hemp Nettle), *Stellaria media* (Chickweed), *Hyo-scyamus niger* (Henbane), *Chenopodium album* (Fat Hen), *Polygonum persicaria* (Red Shank), *Polygonum aviculare* (Knotgrass), *Polygonum convolvulus* (Black Bindweed). These are all common in disturbed, cultivated or wasteland, and are likely to have been growing in open areas nearby. Henbane is associated with stony ground, often near the sea, and around human habitation. Chickweed and Red Shank could be associated with stream or bank side habitats.

Hedges/Woodland
Species present: *Sambucus nigra* (Elderberry), *Rubus fruticosus* (Bramble), *Corylus avellana* (Hazel), *Torilis japonica* (Upright Hedge Parsley), *Stellaria nemorum* (Wood Stitchwort). Although possibly representing woodland, these species are also likely to have been growing on nearby waste ground or hedges.

Pasture/Meadow
Species present: *Taraxacum officinale* (Dandelion), *Rumex acetosa* (Sorrel), *Rumex acetosella* (Sheeps sorrel), *Silene otites* (Spanish Catchfly). Bearing in mind the absence of other species that might be expected if these environments were strongly represented, it seems likely that these too were growing in a suitable locality nearby.

Weeds of Crops
Species present: *Anthemis cotula* (Stinking Mayweed), *Centurea cyanus* (Cornflower), *Ranunculus arvensis* (Corn buttercup), *Scandix pecten-veneris* (Shepherds Needle), *Chrysanthemum leucanthemum* (Ox-eye Daisy), *Vallerianella dentata* (Narrow Fruited Cornsalad), *Anagallis arvensis* (Shepherds Purse), *Papaver rhoeas* (Field Poppy), *Lithospermum arvense* (Corn Gromwell). These species are more specifically associated with arable agriculture. Since they were generally not preserved by charring, and were not found in association with cereal chaff fragments, it is unlikely they represent the residue from sieving grain to remove impurities. The relatively large size of some of the seeds may suggest that individual weed seeds were hand picked from the grain before it was processed further. Alternatively, they may have been associated with straw used for fodder, flooring, or roofing.

Assemblages by Period and Building

Period 1: 13th to mid 14th century

Building 2, Phase 2.3
Samples 23 (119) and 24 (123)
Both these samples were taken from the fills of a hearth or oven sealed directly below layer (114). Sample 23 appears to be a mixed backfill deposit, while Sample 24 is an undisturbed primary use deposit. Despite the intensity of the occupation, there is still sufficient evidence from the weed assemblage to suggest that local conditions were consistently or periodically wet, with pondweed and water flea eggs indicating the presence of standing water.

These samples are by far the richest in quality of preservation and range of species represented of all the samples from the site. While this is in part due to their association with the only hearth encountered during the excavation, the fact that the same density and range of plant material is not encountered in other samples may suggest that in later phases similar domestic activities were either not being undertaken, or were carried out elsewhere beyond the limits of the excavation. This may be due to changes in the status, function or layout of the buildings as a whole, in response to the impact of flooding.

Building 2, Phase 2.4
Sample 22 (114)
This deposit was a compacted silty organic rich floor layer. In addition to fish bones and marine mollusc fragments the sample contains a significant quantity of charred cereals, chaff and straw fragments. Other food plants include field bean and hazel nut. The sample also contains a wide range of non-charred weed seeds, likely to derive from a variety of sources. This deposit appeared to seal a backfilled oven (120) immediately below (Samples 23 and 24). The range and quantity of crops and weeds represented in all these samples appears very similar. This suggests that, if not derived from the same hearth, the Sample 22 assemblage is derived from another hearth beyond the area of excavation, indicating continuity in an almost identical domestic activity (probably based on the same resources) between the deposition of the two floors. It can therefore be assumed that there is no great temporal gap between these deposition events.

Building 3, Phase 3.1
Sample 20 (48)
This was a soft silty layer interpreted during excavation as occupation debris, or possibly sub-floor make-up. In addition to a small quantity of charred cereals and pulses, hazelnut and cherry stone fragments, a few fly pupae were recovered.

Period 2: mid 14th to mid 15th century

Building 4, Phase 4.1
Sample 17 (92)
This sample was taken from a compact and laminated occupation surface. Although the yield of identifiable charred and waterlogged plant material was not great, a sample of this floor was taken for more careful excavation and peroxide flotation to check whether significant data was being lost. This revealed compact laminated layers of probable cereal straw and rush stems which was presumably used as flooring (or possibly roofing) material. These were interleaved with laminations of fish bone and egg shell. The bulk of the rest of the material recovered by peroxide flotation proved to be compacted unidentifiable decomposed organic material. The traces of straw and rushes were themselves sufficiently decomposed not to survive further processing.

Building 4, Phase 4.2
Sample 14 (46)
This sample was taken from an occupation layer. Numerous fish bones were recovered along with low quantities of charred cereals and fly pupae. The weed flora represents generally dry conditions, but also with some wetland indicated.

Buildings 6 and 7, Phase 6.1
Samples 2 (44), 11 (85), 12 (44), 13 (44) and 21 (111)
This group of samples was taken from an occupation surface and the fill of an associated drain/trough. Sample 2 was taken during the evaluation excavation, while Samples 12 and 13 came from the floor deposit to the north and south-west of the drain. Sample 11 was taken from the drain fill. Although Samples 2 and 11 are virtually sterile, Samples 12 and 13 contain a variety of weed seeds in addition to a low presence of charred cereals and chaff fragments along with fish bones, egg shell and fly pupae suggesting a domestic context. Sample 21 was taken from a layer of metalworking and occupation debris forming a working surface. This contains low quantities of bone, mussel shell fragments and egg shell associated with domestic occupation, along with non-charred specimens of pea and hulled oats.

Building 7, Phase 6.3
Samples 16 (97), 19 (97)
These samples were taken from the backfills of the drain/trough. Sample 16 was taken from a deposit consisting largely of metalworking debris dumped into the drain, while Sample 19 was the contents of a large pot found within it. In addition to metalworking debris, Sample 19 again contains low quantities of bone, mussel shell fragments and egg shell associated with domestic occupation. Sample 16 does not contain occupation debris, and may therefore have been dumped directly into the feature. Non-charred specimens of a pea and hulled oats came from Sample 19 and Sample 21 from the adjacent surface (see above). These are the only such specimens surviving on the site, possibly preserved by their proximity to the metalworking debris.

Period 3: mid 15th century to c.1500

Building 8, Phase 7.1
Sample 8 (73)
Very little at all was recovered from this sample. This suggests either that it was a very short-lived surface, or perhaps that the room or area it represents was not an intensive occupation surface. Alternatively, it may not represent a surface at all, or the original surface may have been eroded away by a subsequent flooding event. The limited weed flora represented in this sample is not particularly indicative of wet conditions.

Building 8, Phases 7.3 and 7.2
Samples 10 (83) and 15 (93)
These samples were taken from deposits derived from flooding. Both, however, contain inclusions derived from domestic or industrial activity. Sample 10 produced a small quantity of charred cereals and a small quantity of weeds consistent with other domestic surfaces. Sample 15 contains virtually nothing other than small quantities of fish bone and mussel shell fragments and large quantities of slag and coal. It seems likely that this material was washed in during the flood event, though it is

also possible that the material in Sample 10 derives from a short lived occupation surface within the silts.

Building 9, Phase 8.1
Sample 1 (31)
This sample came from an earlier floor deposit below Sample 7. A low presence of charred cereals suggests a domestic environment. The majority of the weed flora does not suggest a wet environment. Although not identical to Sample 7, both share a lack of the inclusions found in Sample 6, suggesting a continuity in the different activities carried out in each room from one phase to the other.

Building 10, Phase 9.1
Samples 6 (15) and 7 (23)
These samples were taken from two contemporary surfaces separated by a partition. They may represent front and back rooms. Sample 6 came from a thicker floor deposit possibly indicating more intensive use at the front of the building, while Sample 7 was from a less substantial floor. Both samples produced the same range of charred cereals and pulses in low quantities. In addition, Sample 6 contains small quantities of bone and egg shell suggesting a domestic context and a difference in use to Sample 7. Although fragments of coal and slag were recovered, there were not sufficient quantities to suggest industrial activity in the immediate vicinity. They may, however, suggest that industrial activity similar to the metalworking present in Samples 16 and 21 was being practised somewhere nearby in this phase. The very limited weed flora is not indicative of wet conditions.

Period 4: 16th century

Building 12: Phase 11.2
Samples 4 (17) and 5 (50)
These two pit fills contained low quantities of cereal grains and rachis fragments. A charred fragment of possible dung or bread was recovered from Sample 4, along with a charred fragment of a probable cherry stone. During excavation it was suggested Sample 4 might contain cessy material. The presence of fly pupae may support this idea, though no other evidence suggesting cess (typically mineralised seeds) was recovered. Sample 5 yielded a wider variety of charred cereals, chaff and pulses than Sample 4, perhaps suggesting that this sample contained more general domestic cooking debris (including eggshell) than did Sample 4 with its possible cess pit function.

Discussion and Interpretation
The range of wild and cultivated plants recovered from the samples reflects the species represented on many similar sites. Evidence of the range of foodstuffs available to the inhabitants appears to be essentially consistent throughout the excavated sequence. There is a basic range of cereals, with wheat and oats being more prevalent than rye and barley. Other staples are field beans and peas. With the exception of a few fruit pips, there is no evidence for other plant foods, and nothing that might suggest access to dietary resources from elsewhere, or any high status or exotic foods.

Although in some cases relatively good, the organic preservation of non-charred items appears to be limited to plants that were growing in the immediate vicinity or are likely to have been washed in during floods. These were divided (see above) more or less into the environments that they favour, to suggest possible habitats from which resources may have come onto the site. Many plants will grow under a range of conditions and may not have originated from the proposed habitats. While these plants supply environmental background data, they do not add to the range of dietary or economic plant resources available. The shortcomings of the organic preservation are illustrated by the range of plants identified from pollen in floor 92 (Phase 4.1, Period 2; see Wiltshire, below). While it is possible that some of this pollen has been washed in during floods, the cereals, grasses, bracken and heather are highly likely to indicate imported floor or roofing material. Although traces of this material were observed during excavation, the plant material had essentially decomposed, leaving nothing but impressions in the floor laminations. Samples from less well preserved floors only produced very small quantities of seeds. In many cases the species represented were not particularly representative of wetland environments. This may be a result of differential seed preservation (the wetland component has not survived in the less well preserved floors), or may indicate dryer conditions when the surfaces were actually in use.

There is little available environmental material from similar sites elsewhere in Cambridgeshire with which to compare this assemblage. Excavations at Ely Forehill (Alexander 1998) revealed urban occupation stratigraphy covering a wider range of dates than it was possible to excavate at Wisbech, but including deposits of the same date range. Deposition and preservation conditions at Ely differ greatly from those encountered at Wisbech, and this is reflected in the range and quantity of weed seeds represented. Although partly due to differences in taphonomy, the weed assemblage is also likely to reflect differences in access to and economic importance of different agricultural and natural environments. Thus, at Ely the wetland component is narrower, but arable, waste ground, pasture and meadow land is more strongly represented. Plants such as rushes and sedges are present in both assemblages, reflecting their shared availability, but also their use as a resource in domestic contexts.

Although there are similarities in the basic range and emphasis of cultivated and wild food and economic plants, the Ely samples contain a wider range of dietary resources. The presence of walnut, grape and fig, for example, suggests both access to imported foods and possibly a higher economic status than would appear to be the case at Wisbech. While this may be due to the socio-economic conditions pertaining to the specific properties that were excavated at the two sites, it may also reflect more generalised differences between the socio-economic status of the two urban centres.

V. Palynological Analysis
by Patricia E.J. Wiltshire
(Table 11)

Introduction
A monolith sample was taken through a floor deposit associated with Building 4 (92, Phase 4.1, Period 2; the same sample as Thin Section 4, Fig. 4) which consisted of layers of occupation horizons intercalated by clays and flood silts. Sampling was restricted to the upper 15cm of the monolith simply to assess the potential for the deposits for palynological analysis.

Methods
Samples were taken in each distinct horizon within the sediments and subjected to standard processing for concentration of palynomorphs. In each case 2.0 cu^3 of sediment were used. Samples were scanned under phase contrast at x 400, and examined at x 1000 magnification where necessary. A minimum of 10 scans per slide were made and all palynomorphs encountered were recorded. A

Depth (cm)	0.5	1	3	4	6.5	11	13.5	14.5	English Names
Relative Palynomorph Abundance	2	5	2	3	2	0	1	1	
Wood Debris								+	
Microscopic Charcoal	+	+	+	+	+	+	+	++	
Trees / Shrubs									**Trees / Shrubs**
Alnus sp.		+				N	+		Alder
Betula sp.	+	+				O	+		Birch
Corylus-type	+	+	++	++	++		++	+	Hazel
Pinus sp.						P	+		Pine
Quercus sp.						O		+	Oak
Dwarf Shrub						L			**Dwarf Shrub**
Calluna sp.		++	+	+	+	L	+++	++	Heather
Crops						E			**Crops**
Cereal-type	+++	+++	++	++		N		++	Cereals
Herbs									**Herbs**
Anthemis-type	+	++	+				+		e.g. stinking mayweed/yarrow
Apiaceae-type							+		e.g. hogweed
Aster-type									e.g. daisy
Brassicaceae (Sinapis-type)	+	++	+				+		e.g. bitter cress/cabbage family
Chenopdiiaceae sp.			+						goosefoots
Cirsium sp.							+		thistles
Fabaceae (Trifolium-type)		+							e.g. clover
Lactuceae							+		e.g. dandelion/hawkbits
Plantago lanceolata							+		ribwort plantain
Plantago major		+							greater plantain
Poaceae	+++	+++	+++	+++	+++		++	++	grasses
Polygonum bistorta		+	+					+	common bistort
Rhinathus-type		+							e.g. yellow rattle
Plants of wet places									**Plants of wet places**
Cyperaceae							++	+	sedges
Sphagnum sp.					++		++		sphagnum moss
Typha angustifolia-type		+							e.g. bur-reed
Ferns									**Ferns**
Pteridium aquilinum		+	+		+		+		bracken
Pteropsida monolete indet.							+		undifferentiated ferns

Table 11 Relative palynomorph abundance

subjective estimation was made for palynomorph abundance (Table 11) and recorded on a fivepoint scale with five being the most abundant. Relative abundance of individual taxa was recorded with '+' representing presence or moderately low abundance and '+++' very abundant.

Results

The most abundant palynomorphs were found at 1.0cm and 4.0cm. None were found at 11.0cm and they were sparse at 13.5 and 14.5cm. Microscopic charcoal was present in every sample and was particularly abundant at 14.5cm along with wood debris and burnt wood vessels. The dominant taxa were those of Poaceae (grasses), cereal-type, and Calluna (heather). The lower layers appeared to have more heather and other taxa which might have been derived from heathland and possibly damper soils. These include *Cyperaceae* (sedges), *Sphagnum* moss, *Pteridium* (bracken), and *Pteropsida monolete* indet. (other ferns). The upper layers appear to contain more cereal type, grasses, and herbs characteristic of weedy grassland or meadow. The most abundant woody taxon was *Corylus-type* (*c.f.* hazel) although *Alnus* (alder), *Betula* (birch), *Pinus* (pine) and *Quercus* (oak) were recorded.

Discussion

Although palynomorphs were rather sparse in most of the samples, it is obvious that some of the laminations within the sequence contain sufficient palynomorphs to allow a fuller analysis than that presented here. Since these deposits are known to have been floor layers, it is likely that palynomorphs will reflect plant material which was collected elsewhere and laid onto the floor surface for purposes of hygiene and convenience. Thus the taphonomic processes affecting the pollen assemblages here must have been very variable and, because of mixing, the pollen spectra cannot be taken as indicative of specific habitats around the site. However, these data do give some idea of plant communities which might have been available in the vicinity. All the tree and shrub taxa recorded in the deposits are wind pollinated and could have been growing some distance away from where the floor material was collected. However, hazel seems to have been moderately frequent and alder, birch, pine and oak were probably growing in the catchment. Of the layers examined here, the lower ones seem to have had heather and heathland plants incorporated into them. The presence of weeds and cereal type pollen suggests that cereal straw was also being used. The sample at 13.5cm had relatively large amounts of heather, sedges, *Sphagnum* moss and bracken. It is likely that heather was being collected from heathy areas to cover the floors. In the upper layers, grasses, grassland/meadow weeds, and particularly cereal straw seem to have been important although heather was still being used.

Conclusion

While palynological analysis of domestic floors cannot give detailed information about surrounding landscape or precise information on specific habitats it is possible to show variation in use of flooring materials and this may provide useful information. The data presented here suggests that emphasis varied in the use of flooring materials associated with the particular building investigated. Heather and heathland plants were dominant in the lower layer and probably cereal straw was more important in the upper one.

Chapter 5. Sediment Micromorphology
by Karen Milek and Charly French

I. Summary

Micromorphological analysis was conducted on the sediments of presumed floor and flood deposits dating from the 13th to the 16th century. As a result of the finely laminated nature and the variable texture and composition of these sediments, high resolution thin section analysis was used to increase the level of stratigraphic detail and to enhance the interpretation of natural and human activity on the site. Major differences in the composition of the 13th- to 14th- and 16th-century floors indicate changes in the methods of building construction and the use of the area over time, while sediments from the intervening period show evidence for local activity in the region of the site, but an absence of recognisable floor surfaces. Occupation layers are interspersed with overbank flood deposits, reworked river-derived very fine sand and silt, and a thick channel infill (roddon) deposit. This indicates that the site was probably located on the bank of a small river channel which flooded periodically, and which at one point shifted its bed directly over the site.

II. Introduction

During the excavation at Market Mews a sequence of clearly stratified medieval deposits was excavated to a depth of 4.1m. In the field, this sequence was observed to consist of finely laminated organic material and occupation debris separated by layers of virtually sterile very fine sand and silt, which occasionally reached depths of several tens of centimetres. On this basis, the site was interpreted to consist of a series of construction/occupation phases interrupted by episodes of flooding. However, due to the restricted area of the excavation, structural features were few and incomplete, making it difficult to evaluate the nature of the structures or the type or extent of human activity. Thin section micromorphology was employed in order to investigate the microscopic composition and structure (the size, shape and arrangement of particles and voids) of key contexts, in order to enhance ability to interpret the activities that occurred on the site and to evaluate the hypothesis that the site was periodically affected by flooding.

III. Methods

Five undisturbed sediment blocks for micromorphological analysis were taken from four locations in the ready-made section faces (located in Fig. 5), following the procedure outlined by Courty *et al.* (1989). From the north-facing section of Area 1, levelling layer 21 (Building 12) was sampled during a site visit (French 1996a) in order to target the finely laminated organic and sand/silt lenses thought to be floor levels of 16th century date (Thin Section 1). Further samples were taken from the north-facing section of Area 2, including the bottom of context 22, a presumed flood layer, and context 15, which

was thought to consist of successive floor deposits (Thin Sections 2 and 3). Another sample came from context 46 in the north-facing section of Area 3 (Thin Section 4), which was thought to be a well-preserved floor layer due to its finely laminated sediments, and has been dated to the mid 14th to mid 15th century. Thin Section 5 was taken by the excavators from the west-facing section of Area 3, through contexts 48, 114, 119 and 134 (dating to the 13th to mid 14th century). These were also thought to represent floor layers, and context 134 was of special interest due to its thick deposit of carbonised organic material and its association with an oven (120) immediately to the west of the section.

All sample blocks were taken to the geo-archaeology laboratory at the Department of Archaeology, University of Cambridge, where they were air-dried, impregnated with a crystic polyester resin, and thin sectioned following Murphy (1986). Thin sections were analysed at magnifications ranging from x5 to x250 on petrological microscopes using transmitted light (plane polarised and crossed polarised light), oblique incident light and UV autofluorescence. When microstratigraphic layers within a single context were visible under the microscope, they were designated as sub-layers within that context by the use of a number after a decimal point (*e.g.* context 21.5 is a fine layer within context 21).

Micromorphology descriptions were made using the internationally accepted terminology of Bullock *et al.* (1985) to facilitate the comparison of these results with similar work conducted at other sites (*e.g.* Ely Forehill (Milek and French 1996); Peterborough Long Causeway (French 1996b) and London Jubilee Hall (Macphail 1986)). Time did not permit a full mineralogical analysis. The thin sections are currently stored as part of a reference collection in the McBurney Geoarchaeology Laboratory at the University of Cambridge.

IV. Results and Discussion

Period 1 (13th to mid 14th century)

Buildings 2 and 3, Phases 3.1, 2.4 and 2.3
Thin Section 5 (contexts 48, 114, 119 and 134)
(Plates 11, 13 and 14)
Two occupation surfaces with accumulations of organic debris were identified in Thin Section 5 (Tables App.2.1–2.2). The lower surface (context 134.2) is situated on reworked/redeposited river sand, and is characterised by compacted fine silty sand, horizontally bedded, decomposed organic remains, a range of phytolith types, and food preparation debris such as fragments of bone and egg shell, ash and charcoal. Above floor 134.2 is a black, 3.2cm thick, horizontally bedded deposit of charred and partially charred wood and plant remains (context 134.1; Plate 14). Material that could be identified due to a good cross-section included oak, alder and birch (including twigs), and herbaceous (grass/sedge/rush)

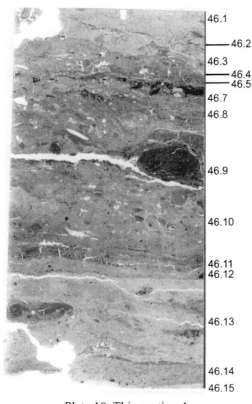

46.1
46.2
46.3
46.4
46.5
46.7
46.8

46.9

46.10

46.11
46.12

46.13

46.14
46.15

Plate 10 Thin section 4

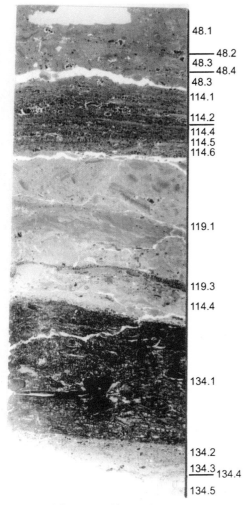

48.1
48.2
48.3
48.4
48.3
114.1
114.2
114.4
114.5
114.6

119.1

119.3

114.4

134.1

134.2
134.3 134.4
134.5

Plate 11 Thin section 5

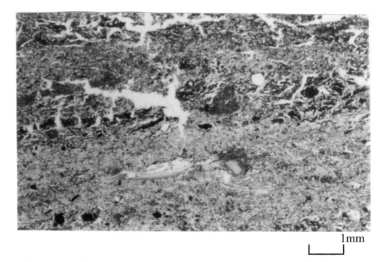

1mm

Plate 12 Thin section 4: context 46.12, which has been interpreted as a floor

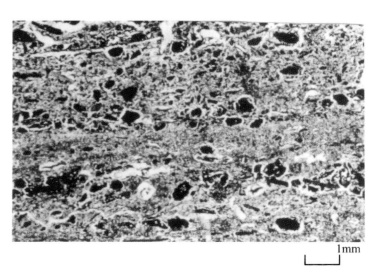

1mm

Plate 13 Thin section 5: contexts 114.2 and 114.4 from Sample 5

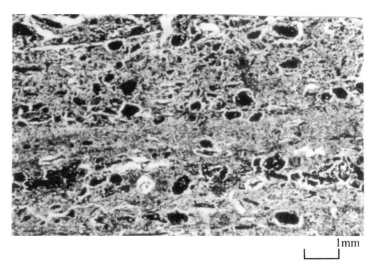

1mm

Plate 14 Thin section 5: context 134.1

stems and leaves (Alan Clapham, pers. comm.). The mixture of woody and herbaceous materials suggests that context 134.1 was produced by the raking out of a domestic hearth or oven. The twigs and herbaceous remains could be kindling and/or food-processing waste that was added to the fire.

Above the layer of charred organic remains is an horizon of redeposited river sand containing randomly oriented, rectangular aggregates of laminated levee material (contexts 119.1–119.3). The size of the aggregates in context 119.1 (up to 4cm in length), their random orientation, and the lack of disturbance of a fine organic lens (context 119.2), all suggest that the deposit is the result of a rapid dumping event.

This dumping event was succeeded by a sequence of alternating layers of decomposing organic matter and compacted sandy silt loam, each between 1 and 5 mm thick (contexts 114.1–114.6; see Table App.2.1 and Plates 11 and 13). The tight, horizontal bedding of these layers, their heterogeneity, the compaction of the mineral component, the small amount of anthropogenic material (bone and shell fragments) and the variety of clay and marl inclusions all suggest that these layers represent a trampled floor that had fresh plant material strewn on its surface. This floor level is significantly different from all of the other floors in Thin Sections 1, 4 and 5 (below), both in the type and quantity of accumulated debris (*e.g.* less bone, no ash or egg shell, more herbaceous material). This may indicate a change in the use of space and/or the methods of maintaining the floor.

Period 2 (mid 14th to mid 15th century)

Building 4, Phase 4.2
Thin Section 4 (context 46)
(Plates 10 and 12)
Thin Section 4 is composed of a series of 15 finely laminated deposits of variable composition. Four floor surfaces were interpreted (contexts 46.7, 46.9, 46.12, 46.14) on the basis of the compaction of the underlying sediments, the significantly higher concentration of organic and anthropogenic inclusions (see Tables App.2.3–2.4), and the horizontal bedding of the anthropogenic and organic component, particularly the amorphous organic fine material, which is the result of *in-situ* decay of plant material. Unlike the 16th-century floor in Thin Section 1, which contained gravel-sized inclusions of pottery and lime plaster, the floors in Thin Section 4 are characterised by much finer material (with the exception of the gravel-sized clay aggregate in context 46.9), much higher organic contents, and a broader suite of domestic debris such as different types of bone (including fish), egg shell, charcoal and ash. Neither pottery nor lime plaster (see below) are present in the floors of Thin Section 4. However, context 46.7 contains a gravel-sized aggregate of what appears to be burnt clay, which may represent daubing or hearth-lining material. The floors in context 46 therefore seem to be more indicative of domestic kitchen activities than the floor in context 21.

The sediments separating the floor deposits have variable origins. Situated between floors 46.12 and 46.14, context 46.13 is composed of very well sorted very fine sandy silt, with gravel-sized, horizontally-oriented aggregates of clay making up approximately 15% of the observable area (see Table App.2.3 and Plate 10). The sediment in this layer appears to be redeposited, although it is not possible to determine whether it accumulated gradually during a hiatus in the life of the structure, or whether it represents a single phase of dumping, in which case it may have been intentionally laid as a smooth, clean floor surface on top of which the debris in floor 46.12 accumulated. Due to the horizontal orientation of the clay aggregates and the fact they have horizontally flattened upper surfaces, it seems more likely that they accumulated gradually and were occasionally trampled.

In contrast, the sediment between floors 46.9 and 46.12 (contexts 46.10–46.11), between floors 46.7 and 46.9 (context 46.8), and above floor 46.7 (contexts 46.4–46.6) consists of laminated silt and silty clay. These layers resemble levee or floodplain deposits, where fine material suspended in overbank floodwater settles in sorted bands of silt and clay when the speed and turbulence of the water has dropped (Reading 1996). In addition, context 46.5 contains and is surrounded by iron-impregnated clay and plant remains (iron pans 46.4 and 46.6), indicating that the sediment was deposited while wet. These layers are best interpreted as natural overbank flooding events. Context 46.10, which is above the undisturbed, horizontally laminated context 46.11, and below floor 46.9, appears to have been substantially affected by post-depositional bioturbation. Besides being substantially reworked, faunal burrowing and *in-situ* organic decay left vughs (irregularly shaped voids) and channels within 20% of the observable area. There is also a large worm channel (10% of the observable area), that has been infilled with loose sand and anthropogenic debris from the layer above. It would appear, therefore, that following the flood event that deposited contexts 46.10 and 46.11, and prior to the reoccupation of the site, there was a period of time in which context 46.10 dried out, and soil fauna were permitted to move in and disturb the upper portion of the flood deposit.

Period 3 (mid 15th century to *c.*1500)

Building 10, Phases 9.3 and 9.1,
Thin Sections 2 and 3 (Contexts 22 and 15)
(Plates 15–18)
Two thin sections were taken adjacent to one another in the north-facing section of Area 2. They were staggered so that the lowest horizon in Thin Section 2 (contexts 15.3–15.5) overlapped with the uppermost horizon in Thin Section 3 (contexts 15.6–15.7), thereby producing a continuous profile over a depth of 24cm.

Context 22, the uppermost horizon in Thin Section 2 (see Tables App.2.5–2.6 and Plates 15 and 17), consists of very well sorted very fine sand. Like all of the fine sand and coarse silt in the sediments of this site, it is composed predominantly of quartz (*c.*75%), with lower concentrations of carbonate (15%), feldspar (including plagioclase; 4%), biotite (2%), muscovite (2%) and glauconite (1%). In the field, context 22 was originally interpreted as a flooding event due to its depth, homogeneity, and lack of anthropogenic inclusions. However, it is the current authors' view that the homogeneity of the layer, which is visible both in thin section and in section photographs, and the near perfect sorting of its mineral component (*i.e.* the absence of clay) provide evidence against its interpretation as a

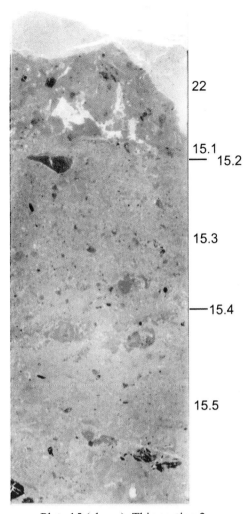

22

15.1
15.2

15.3

15.4

15.5

Plate 15 (above) Thin section 2
Plate 16 (below) Thin section 3

100mm

Plate 17 Thin section 2: boundary between contexts 22 and 15.1

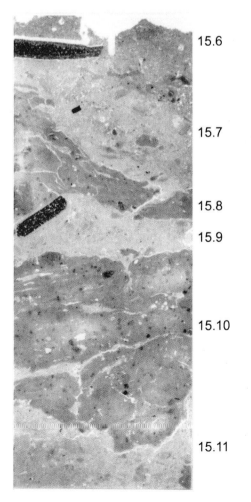

15.6

15.7

15.8

15.9

15.10

15.11

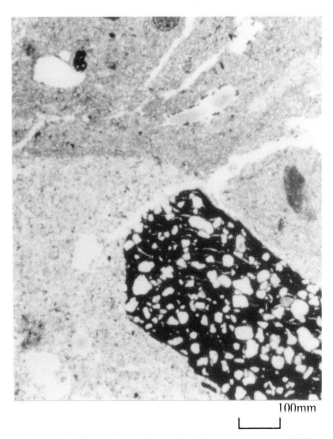

100mm

Plate 18 Thin section 3: boundary between contexts 15.8
and 15.9

catastrophic flood deposit. The high degree of size-sorting could be due to one of two physical processes: i) sorting by wind, which would suggest that the material was originally derived from coastal sand dunes; or ii) sorting by a fairly slow river of uniform velocity that had carried its bedload of sand over a long distance, a characteristic that is typical of many fenland rivers (Reading 1996).

The deposition of this well-sorted material on the site could therefore be due to one of two processes. It could have been intentionally selected and deposited by humans in order to elevate and level the ground surface, an action that has been observed at other low-lying urban sites (*e.g.* Jensen 1993). It should be noted, however, that the depth and quantity of sand involved would have made this a very labour intensive project. The alternate scenario is that context 22 is an entirely natural deposit, and represents a river channel infilled with a fine, sandy bedload. Context 22 does in fact look identical to the roddon deposits so common in the fens, which consist of fine sand and silt infilling tidal (salt marsh) creeks (Zalaciewicz 1985/86). This interpretation will be explored further below, under the discussion of context 15. It is extremely unlikely, however, that context 22 represents a catastrophic flooding event washing over the floors of a standing structure, since the lowest horizon of such a deposit is more likely to be mixed, coarse and contain both organic and anthropogenic inclusions. Flood deposits typically contain a 'fining up' sequence, with coarser material at the bottom of the deposit (material that was the first to settle out of suspension when a river overflows its banks), and finer silts and clays at the top, as the flood subsides and the rate of flow decreases (Reading 1996). In the case of context 22, no such 'fining up' sequence is visible in thin section, nor was it visible at the macroscopic scale in the field.

Below context 22, context 15 is represented by a series of alternating layers of clay (contexts 15.1, 15.8 and 15.10) and very fine sandy silt loam (contexts 15.3 to 15.7, 15.9 and 15.11; Thin Sections 2 and 3; see Tables App.2.5–2.8 and Plates 15–18) which were respectively interpreted as clay floors and flood events. The clay layers are nearly identical in composition, consisting of 60% clay and 40% very fine sand and silt, typical of mud that accumulates in very low energy environments or standing water, where fine mineral material is permitted to settle out of suspension (Reading 1996). The clay layers in Thin Sections 2 and 3 are massive in structure, with the exception of the channels that were burrowed into them post-depositionally by soil fauna. This structure, along with the high frequency of iron impregnation of the fine mineral material, indicates that these layers were deposited while wet. There is no evidence that these layers were intentionally constructed mud floors, since there are no anthropogenic inclusions embedded within them, and there is no occupation debris accumulated above them. In addition, they do not possess a horizontal crack structure, or any surface disaggregation or compaction, characteristics which are normally thought to be typical of trampled surfaces (Gé *et al.* 1993; Courty *et al.* 1994; Matthews *et al.* 1997). On the contrary, these layers seem to have an entirely natural origin. The relevant section (Fig. 5) shows dark, clay-rich layers (context 23) interdigitating with the 'roddon' silts at the western edge of context 22 and occasionally intercalating with these channel silts at the base of the deposit, features which could only be a result of natural processes.

The layers of very fine sandy silt loam (contexts 15.3 to 15.7, 15.9 and 15.11), which occur between the clay layers in context 15, are characterised by a high porosity and complex microstructure, including packing voids between sand grains, irregularly shaped vughs and elongated channels. They contain very few anthropogenic inclusions, all of which are randomly distributed and orientated. These layers appear to be composed of reworked roddon silts, while the presence of anthropogenic inclusions indicates nearby domestic activity. It is difficult to interpret the agency of deposition and the source of these deposits on the basis of thin section analysis alone, but a close inspection of photographs of the relevant section shows them to be intercalated with the layers of mud described above. For this reason, context 15 is thought to have originated as a pool adjacent to a tidal creek, which occasionally received an inwash of fine sand, silt and fragments of any anthropogenic material that happened to be in the vicinity. At some point the bed of the tidal creek shifted, and context 22 developed as the channel became infilled with very fine sand and silt, forming a typical roddon deposit.

Further discussion over the interpretation of context 15 and the apparent differences between archaeological and micromorphological interpretation is given in Chapter 2.

Period 4 (16th century)

Building 12, Phase 11.1
Thin Section 1 (context 21)
(Plates 19–22)
In Thin Section 1, it was possible to see that context 21 was in fact composed of seven distinct layers (contexts 21.1–21.7; see Tables App.2.9–2.10 and Plate 19). On the basis of sedimentary composition, these layers can be grouped into three main horizons. The lowest of these horizons, which contains contexts 21.4–21.7, is a heterogeneous clay loam containing trace amounts (up to 1% only) of anthropogenic material such as small fragments of bone, egg shell and lime plaster, as well as gravel-sized clay aggregates, which should also be viewed as anthropogenic inclusions. All inclusions were deposited randomly throughout the layer rather than being concentrated on an occupation surface, which suggests that they are merely the result of local domestic and building activity in an area close to the sampling location. This horizon also has a significantly higher organic component than the sterile horizon above it (contexts 21.2–21.3), and includes two fine horizontal layers composed of articulated phytoliths and plant matter that had decayed *in situ* (21.4 and 21.6; see Plates 19, 21 and 22). The phytoliths are of two types: smooth rods, which are most typical of grass stems, and dendritic rods, which are most common in the suite associated with husks (Arlene Rosen, pers. comm.). It can therefore be assumed that they represent the deposition of entire herbaceous plants, rather than selective parts of them. In addition, the remarkable preservation of the dendritic rods, which are very fragile and prone to breakage by mechanical disturbance, indicates that they had been left undisturbed *in situ* since the time of the deposition of the fresh plant material (Alex Powers-Jones, pers. comm.). It seems likely, therefore, that they were rapidly sealed after deposition. The particle size distribution of the mineral

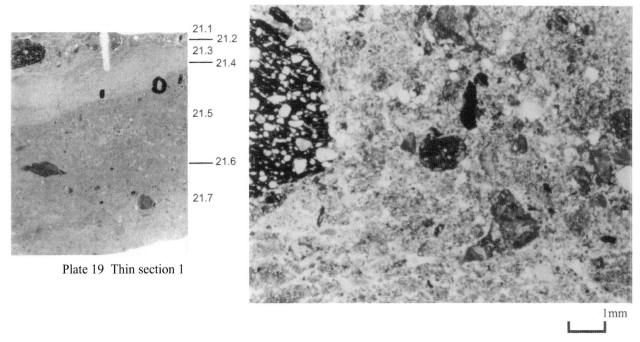

Plate 19 Thin section 1

Plate 20 Thin section 1: context 21.1 which has been interpreted as a floor

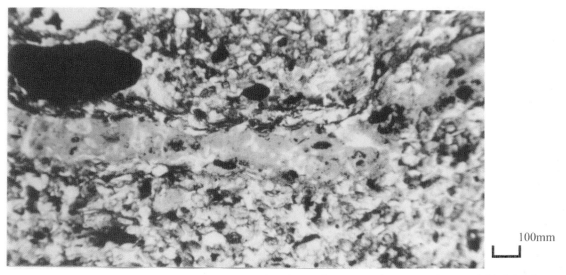

100mm

Plate 21 (above) Thin section 1: context 21.6, showing yellow amorphous organic material left by the *in-situ* decomposition of plant tissues
Plate 22 (below) Thin section 1: context 21.6, showing *in-situ* articulated phytoliths left by the decomposition of plant tissues

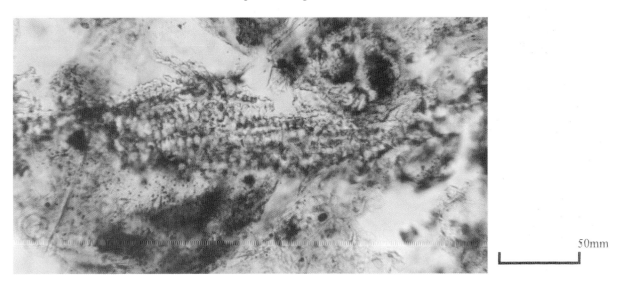

50mm

component suggests that it originated as river mud, and it is therefore interpreted as river derived, redeposited sediment, which accrued fairly rapidly during the course of nearby human domestic and building activity.

The horizon above (contexts 21.2–21.3) is just over 1cm in thickness and consists of a homogeneous, virtually sterile fine sandy silt loam. It is lighter in colour than the layer below due to significantly lower clay and organic contents (see Tables App.2.9–2.10). In the uppermost 2mm of this horizon, the sediment has been compacted and shows the horizontal crack structure that is characteristic of trampled surfaces (Gé *et al*. 1993). Above this floor surface, context 21.1 contains a mixed accumulation of domestic debris, such as fragments of pottery, bone, and a coarse lime plaster or mortar, all of which accumulated on top of and were trampled into the underlying sediment while the floor was in use. The presence of mortar gives some indication of the materials used in the construction of the 16th-century house. Due to the trampling of the upper boundary of context 21.3, and the accumulation of occupation debris above it, it is possible that this deposit was intentionally laid down as flooring material. Such a rapid depositional event would also explain the *in-situ* preservation of the herbaceous plant material and phytoliths in context 21.4, which is immediately below.

V. Conclusions

Micromorphological analysis of finely stratified deposits was able to increase the level of stratigraphic detail available to the archaeologist, and to contribute to the interpretation of natural and human activities at the site. This is especially true of the fine floor levels, which were only 4 to 15mm thick, making it very difficult to distinguish them in the field and making it virtually impossible to sample them discretely for macrofossil analysis. The microscopic composition of these floors, as seen in thin section, was therefore the only available source of information about the intensity and type of occupation taking place on the site.

At this site, the preferred flooring material was redeposited very fine river sand, which would probably have been soft, well drained and clean. Activities that produced the earliest of the sampled contexts, context 134 (Phase 2.3, Period 1), caused food processing debris to accumulate in the floor, as well as a thick deposit of charred and partially charred fuel (both wood and herbaceous plants) that had been raked out of the nearby oven. Floor 114 (Phase 2.4) is very different in character. It is difficult to interpret the activities that occurred on this floor due to the lack of inclusions, but it is possible to propose that either the activities occurring in the room resulted in the deposition and trampling of fresh organic matter, or that plant material was intentionally strewn on the floor as a covering. Context 46 (Phase 4.2, Period 2) contained four separate floor layers, all of which contained food processing debris. The two lowest ones were situated on redeposited river sand, but the two highest floors were situated on and separated by natural flood events that left clayey levee-like deposits. Increased flooding seems to have changed the pattern of occupation on the site, since the thin sections taken from contexts 22 and 15 (Phase 9, Period 3) do not contain any floor layers at all. Instead, they contain layers of river mud and reworked very fine sand and silt, and are sealed by a thick deposit that probably represents an infilled tidal creek channel (see earlier discussion in Chapter 2). Highest in the sampled sequence, in context 21 (Phase 11.1, Period 4), the debris that accumulated in the floor layer was significantly coarser, and consisted of relatively large fragments of pottery and plaster rather than microscopic food preparation residues. This suggests that a different range of activities were occurring in context 21 than in the earlier occupation levels.

Chapter 6. Discussion and Conclusions
by Elizabeth Popescu, with Mark Hinman

'It is impossible, except by conjecture, to form the slightest idea of the actual state of the society and appearance of the town at a period so remote as this is from our times; but if we conceive a personage with hat steepling high above the head, his cloak hanging loosely from his shoulders, the toes of his shoes turned up and brought to a point; and could we associate with him irregular streets of houses and hostels, built perhaps of mud, clay, or wood, and thatched with reed or straw, we should probably have a tolerable idea of the appearance of the inhabitants and town of Wisbech'

T.S. Watson, *The History of Wisbech*, 1833, 111

I. The Regional Context

During the medieval period, the coast of the Wash lay about 16km inland from its current position, with Wisbech initially forming its major port (Fig. 33). The town supported the transportation of goods across the eastern region, both from local sources and across the North Sea from at least the time of the Norman Conquest (Hall and Coles 1994, 4). In the 13th century, the River Ouse flowed into the Wash at Wisbech, rather than at King's Lynn as it does today (Clarke and Carter 1977, 413 and fig. 187). Around the middle of the 13th century 'the Wisbech estuary silted up, and at least some of the waters of the Ouse and the Nene began to flow along Well Creek' (Clarke and Carter 1977, 413 and fig. 188), until 'by the fourteenth century it had become part of the great water highway between Lynn and the midland counties' (Darby 1983, 34 and figs 24 and 25). Other contemporary changes in the fenland river system included the diversion of the Great Ouse closer to Ely and the construction of the Ten Mile river, that took the eastern Ouse/Cam waters into the Norfolk river system and thence towards King's Lynn (see further comments in Chapter 1.IV). These changes had a considerable impact on the economy and topography of the fenland, as well as on Wisbech. The cutting of Morton's Leam in 1478 improved the flow of the Nene, with beneficial environmental and economic effects for Wisbech, but this was of minor consequence in comparison with the earlier changes that had seen the major outfalls and trade potential migrate to Lynn. 'After its diversion during the 13th century the Great Ouse seems not to have changed its course through the fenland to any significant degree until the post-medieval period … and it was not until late in the 17th century that the Dutch engineer Vermuyden revolutionized the fenland system by his great drainage scheme' (Clarke and Carter 1977, 415 and fig. 190).

At Domesday, Cambridgeshire demonstrated a clear distinction between the northern area of generally undrained fen with no villages other than those on islands, and the well-populated upland further south (Darby 1987, 27 and fig. 1). Wisbech, however, was an exception to this trend: it lay in the only part of Cambridgeshire that, like Marshland in Norfolk and the Lincolnshire coastline in siltland, was sufficiently raised during the late 11th century to offer island-like, permanent settlement (Paul Spoerry, pers. comm.). A general overview of the history and topography of the area surrounding Wisbech is given

by Hall (1996, 164–191), supplementing earlier work by Silvester, who studied the siltlands between Wisbech and King's Lynn (1988). As noted in Chapter 1, a key factor in the development of Wisbech during the medieval period was its relationship to and rivalry with King's Lynn. Although earlier settlement appears to have existed in the vicinity from at least the Middle Saxon period, the latter town was founded by Herbert de Losinga, Bishop of Thetford, in 1090 and formalised in 1096. It developed diverse trading links, including those with the Hanseatic League of north-west Europe. Indeed, its 'versatility and prosperity, coupled with the many overseas contacts, meant that for a time King's Lynn was one of the richest towns in the land', reaching the peak of its wealth in the late 14th century (Brown and Hardy 2011). It has been suggested that, had not the forces of nature intervened, it would have been Wisbech (rather than King's Lynn) that functioned as the primary seaport of the late medieval period for eastern England (Spoerry 2005, 102).

Recent excavations at King's Lynn by Oxford Archaeology South took place in the area known as Newlands, between the original southern core (South Lynn) and a later northern settlement which developed around a secondary market site (Brown and Hardy 2011, 4). At least part of Newlands itself appears to date to the mid 12th century although whether this area was deliberately 'planned' remains open to question. The excavations were positioned on both the north and south sides of the Purfleet, now also being divided by the course of New Conduit Street. They provide useful comparisons and contrasts with the Wisbech excavation which are noted in subsequent text.

The estuarine primary ports of Boston and Spalding provide comparable evidence in the Lincolnshire fenland: floods are known to have occurred across southern Lincolnshire throughout the relevant period, with notable examples in 1287, 1439, 1467, 1571, 1603 and 1625 (Wheeler 1990). While documentary evidence attests to flooding at Boston and the surrounding fenland during the medieval period, focused in the 13th century, there has been little substantial excavation in the town to date. At Spalding, numerous excavations have recorded flooding although here, as at King's Lynn, these have proved difficult to correlate across the town due to the variability of the evidence from one site to another. At Double Street, a flood horizon separated the late medieval and earliest post-medieval phases, but this site lay next to the river in an area particularly prone to flooding (Tom Lane, pers. comm.).

II. Fenland Flooding
(Fig. 33)

Flooding along the eastern coast of England has a long history. In November 1099, 100,000 lost their lives in severe storms along the coast here and in the Netherlands when, as the Anglo-Saxon Chronicle records, 'the tide rose so strongly and did so much damage that no-one remembered it ever before' (Swanton trans and ed 2000, 235). It has long been known that a succession of previous landscapes survive below the current surface of the fens. Sir William Dugdale records a series of early observations of this phenomenon. He relates, for example, that in digging a moat at Whittlesea, the labourers came to a perfect soil eight feet below the surface of the land with swaths of grass on it, lying as they were first mown (Dugdale 1662, 171; quoted in Walker and Craddock 1849, 10).

While the Roman fenland drainage system had been based on natural features, this changed during the medieval period when drainage channels were cut and banks constructed (Silvester 1988, 185). The region as a whole was defended by the Sea Bank (a marine flood defence; known locally as the Roman Bank but thought to be of post-Roman origin; SAM51) and the Fen Bank (which retained fresh water). Wisbech is one of many settlements protected by the Sea Bank, stretches of which survive to up to 3m high. This bank marks the seaward limit of land reclamation during the medieval period (Fig. 33) and was constructed to protect villages and farmland from the ravages of high tides and sea floods. Excavations have indicated the complexity of its construction. In the 1970s, a culvert beneath the bank was examined (Taylor 1977) and proved to have been built from massive interlocking timbers, radiocarbon dating of which indicates a date of c.1250. This culvert, which is held at the Wisbech and Fenland Museum, suggests the original presence of a series of similar features, probably functioning with simple hand-operated sluice gates to drain excess water from the fens (Taylor 1977, 65). The bank and culvert system was evidently supplemented by a sequence of ramparts placed at right angles on the seaward side of the Sea Bank and serving as breakwaters; fifteen such ramparts (up to 30m wide and 50–300m long) have been recorded in the 5km stretch between Newton and Leverington, to the north-west of Wisbech (Hall 1977, 67). It has been suggested that climate change, which began during the 13th century, led to a rise in sea level which engendered the construction of such massive flood defences (Hall 1977, 68).

To the west and south of Wisbech, areas of dry land were protected from freshwater floods by the Fen Bank (cf Hall 1996, fig. 98), with a complex subsidiary network of smaller banks protecting medieval field systems (Hall 1996, fig. 99; Hallam 1965). The land was divided into strip fields, interspersed with droves and other routeways (Hall 1996, figs 98–99). An inner flood bank faced towards the west and another lay around Elm. These may represent two constructional phases, the date of the earliest perhaps being pre-Conquest and the later outer bank apparently built before c.1200 (Hall 1996, 186). At least some of these drainage activities were the result of large scale planning to improve the siltlands on the part of manorial owners, which included Ely's monastery and cathedral (Hall 1996, 186). On the western side of the

Wisbech estuary, a sequence of flood banks was gradually constructed, one in front of the other (Fig. 33). Evidence for the wapentake of Elloe (Lincolnshire) indicates the presence of a sequence of banks aligned east to west, beginning at the River Welland to the west and turning southwards to the east as they approached the estuary (Darby 1983, 13–15 and fig. 13). The earliest defence is probably pre-Conquest and the latest dates to 1241. Although records exist for catastrophic flood events on the Lincolnshire coast of the Wash during the medieval and post-medieval periods, these may be under-represented in the published evidence for the fenland coastal villages due to lack of recognition (James Rackham, pers. comm.).

Three issues have been highlighted as of particular relevance to coastal wetland communities by the 14th and 15th centuries: 'declining population, climatic deterioration, and falling prices' (Rippon 2000, 18). Attention must be directed towards the reasons why flood-prone settlements such as Wisbech continued to be occupied. It has been suggested that life in medieval coastal wetlands was high cost (i.e. the need to maintain flood defences) and high risk (i.e. threat of flooding), but also high return (i.e. agricultural productivity) (Rippon 2000, 18). Examples of complete abandonment of wetlands at this time appear to have been surprisingly rare, with schemes of managed retreat, maintenance and investment evidently being devised. In the late 13th century, for example, the town of Old Winchelsea on Romney Marsh was washed away, initiating a major period of investment which included the provision of dams (Rippon 2000, 22–26). This is by no means an isolated example. In many wetland areas, land not completely lost to flooding generally continued in agricultural production, with a shift towards pastoralism: grain prices fell while wool prices rose — coastal marshes were particularly suited to pasture with high grass yields and rich meadows (Rippon 2000, 27). Large numbers of sheep were grazed in the area between Wisbech and King's Lynn, such as those recorded in the Domesday Survey: 2,100 at West Walton and 515 at Terrington (Darby 1987, 30 and fig. 7). A complex system of droves developed providing access to summer grazing at West Fen (to the south-east of Wisbech) and, from the 13th century, attracted settlement (Silvester 1988, 163 and fig. 115).

Alterations in the flood pattern, and in particular the depth of material deposited during flooding episodes, appear to relate directly to a deterioration in the climate which, when combined with the silting up of the Wellstream (Ouse) and the Nene, resulted in the increased frequency of overbank flooding. Despite such difficult living conditions, however, the continuing cycle of post-flood rebuilding provides clear evidence of determined occupation. A chronological list of severe weather events is included in Appendix 1; further excavation may well permit linkage between historical flood events and particular deposits, although caution should be exercised in linking specific deposits to known historical incidents until a tighter dating sequence can be established. A particularly severe series of storms and floods is known to have occurred in the mid-14th century. In January 1362, one of the worst storms on record swept across south-eastern England. Only two years later in 1364 sea floods along the east coast destroyed the port of Ravensburgh on Humber and several other towns in Holderness were also lost (see Chapter 1.III). These events undoubtedly took

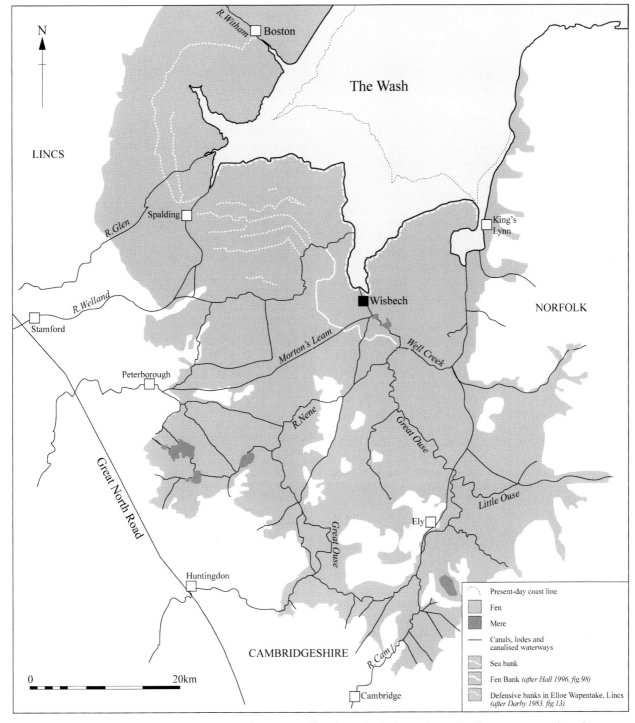

Figure 33 Wisbech in its fenland context, showing medieval canals, lodes and canalised water courses in existence and/or created AD1100–1500

their toll on Wisbech, although the low lying position of the town within the fens and its proximity to the Ouse and Nene meant that prolonged periods of wet weather could pose a similar threat. The archaeological record amply demonstrates the frequency with which the New Market area was prone to inundation. The major flood event recorded at Market Mews appears to have occurred during the mid to late 15th century, when over a metre of silt was deposited in a single flood (Phase 7.3; Fig. 6). At least part of the contemporary building (Building 8) was swept away and the flooding waters deposited debris including riverine vegetation across the site. The documentary record notes twenty severe or wet weather events in the

period 1421–1500 (Appendix 1), many of which affected East Anglia and the Midlands. In 1437, for example, the decay of Wisbech Fen Dyke caused a freshwater breach in which it is recorded that 4,400 acres of land in Wisbech were drowned (Watson 1827, 369), followed in 1438 by a particularly wet summer.

By the 16th century (Period 4) at Market Mews, there appears to have been a reduced expectation of flooding: the weather may have been improving or the perceived threat of flooding may have been reduced through the implementation of new drainage schemes, possibly allied to the redeposition of Crab Mersh Bank in the first half of the 16th century. The substantial construction cut of mid-15th- to mid-16th-century date (Phase 12) may have been a brick-built culvert: this example adds to those already known to run beneath the town.

III. Formation Processes
(Fig. 34)

The distinctive formation processes recorded at Wisbech have previously been explored, along with the difficulties in recording and interpreting such fluid sequences (Hinman forthcoming). The probable sequence of events leading to the destruction of timber-framed buildings by flooding at Market Mews is summarised in Fig. 34, detritus such as aquatic weeds and fish being left in its wake. The character of the flood-borne material, being composed of extremely fine sand grains encased in a thin covering of clay, enabled it to be carried in suspension. As the water level dropped these silts were deposited within and around the buildings (Fig. 34, Stage 2/3). It appears that wooden structures, such as those excavated at Market Mews would have suffered from the pressures of water and silt against their walls. The buildings appear to have acted as silt traps, with new floors being laid over newly deposited silts within surviving, but partially buried buildings.

In some instances, the lower interface of flooding preserved evidence of erosion caused at the onset of flooding, during flooding and as the floodwaters receded. Initial damage seems to have been exacerbated by the presence of extant or disused drainage channels, including gaps between buildings, which forced the rising waters to back up. The localised currents generated could remove walls and cut through earlier deposits within the stratigraphic sequence (Fig. 34, Stage 4/5) and eventually lead to the collapse of a building (Stage 6). Material disturbed in this manner was subsequently redeposited as horizontally laid strata as the waters rose (Fig. 34, Stage 7).

Disproportionate erosion was also recorded when the flood waters receded: it appears that the retreating waters followed the path of least resistance represented by extant or disused drainage channels, gaps between buildings and roadways. Scouring and cutting caused by receding floodwaters seems to have been exacerbated by the presence of barriers such as surviving buildings or walls. Once the flooding had ceased, it appears that accessible building materials might be salvaged, with the next building sequence initiated (Fig. 34, Stages 8–10).

The deposits left as a result of gradual accumulation through the process of many cycles of 'tidal' deposition were quite different in character to those that appear to have resulted from sudden flooding. In the latter instances, the flood waters evidently separated into their constituent components in a fining upward sequence, with the coarser material at the base of the deposit: these were clearly recognisable during excavation as thick, sterile deposits (note that none of these sudden flooding sequences were sampled by micromorphology at Market Mews, which targeted the finely laminated sequences associated with floors). Similar deposition processes have recently been recorded below the foundations of Thurloe's Mansion at the Wisbech Castle site (Fletcher in prep.). In contrast, the deposits at Market Mews identified as the result of slow accumulation of flood silts and sands, separated by occupation surfaces, are reminiscent of some of the opportunistic roddon bank prehistoric and Roman settlements elsewhere in the region. The residues left by the flood waters reflect both marine and riverine flooding, the latter linking both to the shifting outfalls of the Nene and Ouse and to a small river channel which appears to have run close to the site.

Similar flood events have been archaeologically recorded elsewhere. At King's Lynn probable flood deposits dating to c.1250–1350 were recorded at Baker Lane in 1968–9, such deposits being recorded at more than twenty sites across the town at a level of 3.65–4.26m OD (12 to 14 ft OD; Clarke and Carter 1977, 63 and fn 87). As at Market Mews, timber buildings were subsequently constructed immediately above the flood silts at Baker Lane, although at least one building was deliberately demolished *prior* to flooding, with timber uprights being cut off close to the ground and then burnt flush with it (Clarke and Carter 1977, 63). Reclamation of the King's Lynn area from the sea 'was driven by the exaggeration of naturally formed sand banks through saltern works and later midden dumping' (Brown and Hardy 2011, p.2). Of particular note here are the ridges which remain in many of the modern streets, apparently the result of underlying sand banks. Recent excavations revealed deposits spanning the 13th to 16th centuries, the earliest of which indicate land reclamation in an intertidal environment, including possible saltern mounds or sand banks, as well as fills of tidal creeks. Interleaved with some of these were occupation deposits similar to those found at Wisbech, including boat timbers perhaps used as revetments. In some parts of the excavation, linear cuts may have functioned as drains and property boundaries, as well as providing access for small craft to the town's larger water channels (or 'fleets').

Another useful comparator to the Wisbech sequences is provided by the twelve phases of activity recorded at Fuller's Hill, Great Yarmouth in 1974 (Rogerson 1976). Here, deposits dating to the 11th and 12th centuries were interspersed with layers of wind-blown sand. This area of the town is traditionally believed to be the earliest and its height above sea level (8m OD) suggests that it 'might have been the first part of the spit to emerge from the sea' (Rogerson 1976, 133). The successive layers of flooring, minor timber structures and associated features are remarkably similar to those found at Wisbech (*cf* Fig. 4, this volume with Rogerson 1976, fig. 45 and plate XVIII), representing a population largely engaged in fishing. As at Wisbech, rushes appear to have been used for both flooring and roofing. At Fuller's Hill, however, the occupation sequences were interleaved with thick deposits of wind-blown material, rather than flood deposits, leading to questions of possible seasonal activity (Rogerson 1976, 159). Destruction and replacement of buildings was similar to that at Wisbech: 'when the inhabitants returned after a storm they may have removed quantities of debris and re-established themselves close to their original floor level .... in other cases they seem to have levelled off the surface of the newly arrived sand and then built a new structure' (Rogerson 1976, 159).

The medieval inhabitants of Monmouth, Monmouthshire, evidently used domestic rubbish and metalworking debris to raise the floors of their buildings above flood levels (Clarke 1995). Further afield, in eastern Scotland, Perth — which is linked to the flood regime of the River Tay — has suffered thirty-four floods since

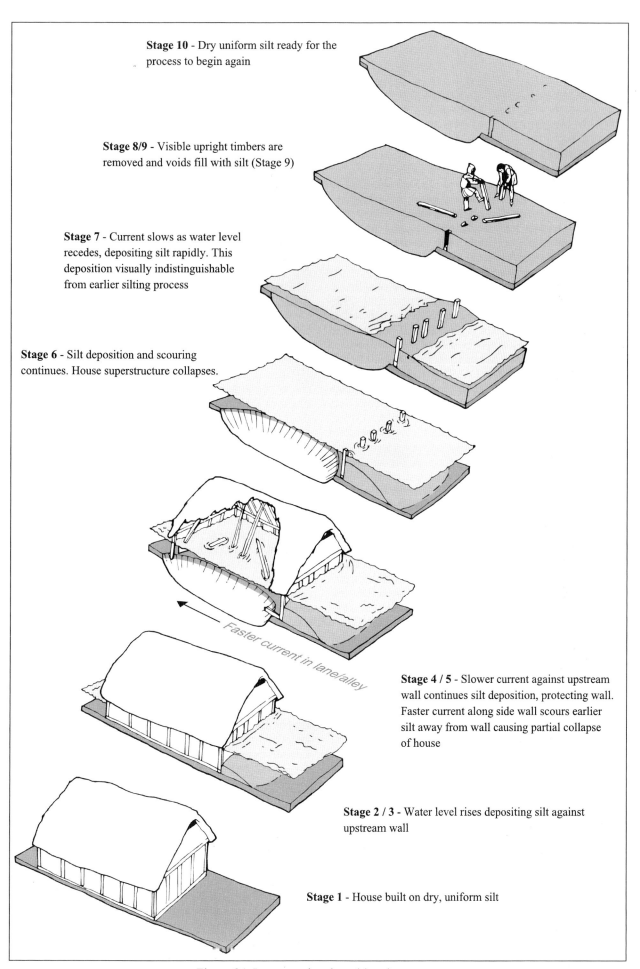

Stage 10 - Dry uniform silt ready for the process to begin again

Stage 8/9 - Visible upright timbers are removed and voids fill with silt (Stage 9)

Stage 7 - Current slows as water level recedes, depositing silt rapidly. This deposition visually indistinguishable from earlier silting process

Stage 6 - Silt deposition and scouring continues. House superstructure collapses.

Faster current in lane/alley

Stage 4 / 5 - Slower current against upstream wall continues silt deposition, protecting wall. Faster current along side wall scours earlier silt away from wall causing partial collapse of house

Stage 2 / 3 - Water level rises depositing silt against upstream wall

Stage 1 - House built on dry, uniform silt

Figure 34 Interpretative depositional sequence

1209, the effects of which have been modelled (Bowler 2004, 12–20). The excavated remains of the medieval period are very similar to those found at Wisbech, including clay and timber structures, with associated yards.

IV. The Topography of Medieval Wisbech

That the earliest references to the Market and its tenants in 1236 (Chapter 1.IV) record the destruction of their property by the sea is significant: at Market Mews the first recorded inundation — apparently highly destructive — duly occurred in the 13th century (Phase 2.2, Period 1). There is, however, some evidence to indicate the earlier post-depositional movement of deposits, perhaps associated with the presence of a drainage gully or erosion channel running along Market Mews (Phase 1.1). At Sandyland Street undated flood levels were recorded at between 1.50 and 2.50m OD, while truncated 12–13th-century flood levels at Wisbech Castle were recorded within the probable moat at 3.50m OD. At New Inn Yard just to the west of Market Mews, flood deposits perhaps dating to the 13th to 14th century were recorded at levels of between 4.40 and 5.05m OD. This evidence is broadly contemporary with Period 1 at Market Mews, although deposits here lay slightly lower (with an upper level of *c.* 3.80m OD). Further flood deposits at New Inn Yard of possible mid-14th- to 15th-century date had an upper level of 6.00m OD, with an associated possible terrace cut. This broadly equates to Periods 2 and 3 at Market Mews, although again the upper levels here were lower at *c.*4.40m OD. Interestingly, the implied medieval groundslopes are a reversal of the modern topography. The New Inn Yard site appears to have lain on the edge of slightly higher ground in the medieval period. The deposition of flood silts further east (as at Market Mews) appears to have gradually raised the ground level here. The eventual renaming of the road just to the north of Market Mews from Ship Lane to Hill Street in 1825 may reflect this physical alteration in the topography of the town, while earlier references to Market Hill and the presence of a windmill serve to emphasise such changes (Hoyland, Chapter 1.IV).

The account of the redeposition of Crab Mersh Bank in the early to mid 16th century (see Hoyland, Chapter 1.IV) has important archaeological implications since the material potentially seals earlier archaeological remains within the Market Place. As noted above, it is possible that the reordering evident at the Market Mews site in Phase 11 (Period 4) took place at the time of the landscaping, implying a reduced expectation of flooding.

Although the recent excavations provide no direct evidence for street pattern, they do provide indirect evidence for the character of local streets, suggesting that they served as drainage channels at times of flood. The erosion gully and 'swamp' deposits associated with Building 10 during the 15th century, for example, appear to indicate that buildings within the town were constructed on islands or banks which rose over time above the flood-prone thoroughfares of the town. At the excavation site an adjacent river channel, apparently running along the course of Market Mews, shifted its bed over the site on at least one occasion. At the All Saints Street/Bridge Street site, King's Lynn, an 11th-century watercourse (possibly the River Nar) evidently ran adjacent to the

excavated area, and flooded in the early 12th century, depositing a thick layer of blue silt (Clarke and Carter 1977, 137 and 139). A subsequent drainage channel (Clarke and Carter 1977, 139 and fig. 53) was dug across the site, followed by further flooding and attempts at drainage: the land here may only have become habitable as a result of drainage. Immediately following the second drainage phase, occupation in the form of four timber buildings was recorded across the site (Clarke and Carter 1977, 143). No further evidence of flooding was evident in later phases and it appears that the earlier drainage channels had proved effective in providing dry ground, the possibility of flooding perhaps being reduced by a westward movement of the River Nar (Clarke and Carter 1977, 147).

V. Building Types and Construction Materials
(Table 12)

In terms of its vernacular architectural heritage, Wisbech lies securely within the Lowland Zone. The predominant building method of this area was box frame construction (Clifton-Taylor 1972, 306–309). The relative absence of oak as a building material combined with the common use of thatch for roofing would have ensured the adoption of the relatively light frame characteristic of many East Anglian buildings. This shortage of wood, particularly in the fens, may go some way to explaining the lengths to which the residents of Wisbech apparently went in reclaiming such material following major floods, and also places the early adoption of brick as the primary building material in the town (noted below) more fully in context.

No complete building plans were exposed at Market Mews and it is possible that some of the earliest buildings were not fully roofed or fully enclosed, but were open-sided shelters, wind-breaks, booths or stalls. The changing constructional character of the buildings is indicated in Table 12, demonstrating a range of timber and clay constructions which culminated in the use of brick. Across the country, the 13th century saw a major change in vernacular architecture, from earthfast to dwarf-wall construction when 'the sill beam was made to run uninterrupted around the whole building and the posts were mortised into it: in order to preserve the sill beam it was placed above ground level on a low wall, often referred to … as a dwarf wall. This is the moment at which the building becomes fully framed and dependent entirely on its jointing for stability' (Grenville 1997, 35). In many London examples, this change in technique occurred by the early 13th century. Construction of the earliest building at Market Mews (Building 1, 13th century) included what was recorded as a timber-lined foundation trench, although it is possible that this building was in fact a free-standing timber framed construction without foundations. Three of the recorded buildings utilised clay sills (Buildings 2, 5 and 9, spanning the 13th to 15th centuries), Building 9 providing clear evidence for surface-laid timbers serving as internal partitions. Prior to the laying of a timber beam or 'sill', the ground may first have been levelled and compacted, in a process known as 'groundsilling' (Salzman 1952, 202).

Information about clay/earth walled construction techniques from this period in the region was previously somewhat limited, although recent excavations in urban centres such as Norwich, Boston and King's Lynn have greatly increased the corpus. At Boston, similar clay and wattle buildings have been found sealed beneath thick flood deposits (James Rackham, pers. comm.). Recent excavations at King's Lynn have located similar buildings with at least one major episode of flooding. At the Norfolk Street site, eight medieval structures were found, including clay-walled, stone- and brick-built examples (HER 31393; Cope-Faulkner 2005). One building of clay and timber construction dating to the mid 13th to mid 14th century appears to have been a smithy (see below), whilst other crafts represented at the site include copper alloy working, wood-working and possibly brewing. Excavations in the western part of the town close to the Purfleet found 12th- to 13th-century tenements housing wattle-walled buildings (Clarke and Carter 1977, fig. 35) and similar timber buildings were found during the recent work by Oxford Archaeology, although these were soon replaced (starting perhaps in the mid 13th century), by stone-footed buildings (Brown and Hardy 2011, p.105). Brick was introduced to King's Lynn during the late 13th century (Brown and Hardy 2011, 10) and its first documented use in Norwich occurred at the castle in 1268–70 (Shepherd Popescu 2009, 463). At the Wisbech site, the first use of brick occurred during the second half of the 15th century (Period 3, Phase 9.2). Documentary evidence, however, indicates that peat turves were being used as fuel to produce bricks at Wisbech as early as 1333, in what appears to be the earliest reference to the methods of medieval brick manufacture in England (Sherlock 1999, 59). This reference occurs amongst the manorial account roles of Wisbech Castle, spanning c.1332–1522, when it was a property of the bishops of Ely 'and the administrative and fiscal centre of their valuable Fenland estates' (Sherlock 1999, 59).

The excavated remains at Market Mews provide direct evidence for the use of the stems and leaves of grasses, rushes and sedge for flooring in several phases, with evidence from micromorphology indicating that the preferred flooring matrix was fine sand. In particular the floor recorded within Building 4, dating to the mid 14th to mid 15th century, highlights the use of wetland plant species and whole reed-mace (bullrush) stems and heads were visible within it. Pollen analysis found the remains of cereal grasses and heather, with sedges, sphagnum moss, bracken and other ferns present. This spongy floor still provided a soft and comfortable surface, centuries after its original deposition. Similar evidence for flooring using straw, moss and plant stems has recently been found at King's Lynn (Rackham in Cope-Faulkner 2005, appendix 10). The evidence supplements medieval account rolls which refer to such flooring materials. The use of fenland resources such as reeds, rush and sedge was carefully controlled and subject to regulation. The court rolls of 1285–1327 for the Bishop of Ely's manor at Littleport, for example, contain many references to the 'cutting, binding and carriage of 'lesch [a now obsolete word for all species of sedge] and rushes'' (Darby 1983, 24–25). The value of such commodities is indicated by the occasions on which they appear to have been stolen: in 1307 the Abbot of Bury St Edmunds made a complaint that his meadows and marshes at *Suthreye by Helgeye* had been entered, the grass cut and carried away (Hall and Coles 1994, 138).

It is notable that several of the buildings found at Market Mews occupied the same ground plan, indicating that no opportunity was taken to modify the layout. This may suggest that the buildings in the area were so tightly spaced that there was no option but to follow the previous layout. Possibly the clearest illustration that the Wisbech excavation encountered separate rooms within the same building comes from the excavation of Building 10 (mid to late 15th century). Here, the rooms measured between 2.70m and 2.80m from east to west. If the building is assumed to have faced onto a precursor of Little Church Street then the total width of this building would be less than 6m which is reasonable for a structure within a long, narrow tenement. Work by the Norwich Survey has demonstrated that, as anticipated in an urban setting, tenements towards the centre of the city might be as little as 4m wide; considerably narrower than those on the outskirts where pressure for land was not so great (Atkin and Evans 2002, 241). At the Norwich Castle site, the few surviving medieval tenements demonstrate similar widths of c.6m (c.19.5ft; Shepherd Popescu 2009, 1066), while properties dating to the late 12th to late 13th century recorded at Westwick Street were of very similar width (Atkin and Evans 2002, 120, fig. 24). Here, boundaries were effectively preserved into the 17th century, a fact which confirms the stability of the ground-plans of such tenements. Recent work in Southampton which examined a series of high and late medieval tenements recorded average property widths of 6.85m (22.5ft) (Brown and Hardy forthcoming).

It is highly probable that the plot boundary apparent at Market Mews in Period 4 (16th century) existed earlier, perhaps forming the basis of the markedly different

Period	Phase	Date	Building	Construction type
Period 1	Phase 1	c.1200>	1	timber-lined foundation, earthfast timbers
	Phase 2		2	?earthfast timber with stake uprights, upstanding clay sill (floor only)
	Phase 3	c.1250–1350	3	
Period 2	Phase 4	c.1350–1450	4	post-built (limited observation)
	Phase 5	-	5	?clay sill, earthfast posts
	Phase 6	c.1350–1450	6	internal drain/trough
			7	internal drain/?trough
Period 3	Phase 7	mid 15th	8	earthfast timber with posts
	Phase 8	c.1450–1500	9	clay sill
	Phase 9	c.1450–1500	10	surface laid timbers, posts, clay and brick foundation post-built
			11	
Period 4	Phase 11	c.1500–1600	12	earthfast timber
	Phase 12	c.1500–1600	13	brick wall footings and post pads

Table 12 Building types by period

character of the remains present within Areas 2 and 3. The apparent absence of a building on the western part of the site during the 16th century may indicate that the owners of Building 12 had acquired the adjacent plot formerly occupied by Building 11. Equally, both plots of land could have been held by a single owner although the provision of what appears to have been a yard at the western end (back?) of Building 12 would indicate a change in status for the area.

VI. Craft and Economy

The history of Wisbech's markets has been outlined in Chapter 1.IV and, despite their modest scale, the excavations at Market Mews have to some extent characterised the medieval buildings, activities and environment specifically within the New Market. Excavated remains suggest that the majority of activities conducted at Market Mews were domestic in character, despite their commercial setting, the exception being the evidence for late medieval metalworking (see below). As noted in earlier text, it has been suggested that the New Market was initially somewhat larger than its current size (Taylor 1973). Excavation indicates that infilling of the Market Square as defined by Taylor was clearly well established by the 13th century, with domestic encroachment of the area perhaps resulting from the shortage of habitable land as a result of flooding or reflecting the familiar pressure for space within an urban setting. Recent excavations in the Norman Market Place at Norwich (founded before 1096) indicate similarly early settlement within the commercial space, with two stone buildings of possible 12th-century origin constructed along a road frontage (Percival and Hutcheson, in prep.). The clearest archaeological evidence for activity in the vicinity directly relating to the later market at Wisbech comes from excavations within the Market Place in 1991, where traces of market stalls and associated features pre-dating 1811 were located (see Chapter 1.V).

One of the major discoveries at the Market Mews site was a mid 14th- to mid 15th-century metalworker's workshop (Building 7; Phase 6, Period 2), containing a working 'trough' or drain and associated water storage within ceramic vessels. Pots set actually within floors have been found in post-medieval domestic and ecclesiastical buildings in London, where various functions have been suggested: as sumps, foundation offerings, spells, storage, food preparation or vermin traps — in several instances, two pots were utilised, one draining into the other (Blair and Sankey, in prep.). At Chepstow, a medieval pot had been used as a sump with a rusty internal deposit being attributed to the high iron content of the water rather than an association with metalworking (Alan Vince, pers. comm.). A Thetford-type ware pot set into a pit at Fullers Hill, Great Yarmouth was interpreted as a possible cistern (Rogerson 1976, 160). At Market Mews, however, a direct association with metalworking seems fairly secure and smiths would certainly have needed a ready supply of water to quench tools or during plating or brazing processes when small items might have been dipped directly into the pottery vessels (Quita Mould, pers. comm.). Both ferrous (probably smithing) and non-ferrous working are indicated and it is possible that padlocks and bells were

being manufactured, although this material may simply have been gathered as scrap (Crummy, Chapter 3.II; Mortimer, Chapter 3.III). Although the full character of the building at Market Mews remains uncertain, for many metalworking tasks shelter is required not only to provide cover from the elements, a potential hazard when working with metals at high temperature, but also to control lighting levels. Low lighting is essential for the effective estimation of temperature when working with iron and other materials.

By the 14th century, the requirement for ironwork had increased to such an extent that the craft sub-divided into specialist trades (Tylecote 1981, 42). Zoning of urban industries is common in many medieval towns and the archaeological evidence for such metalworking is increasing: at Norwich, many sites attest to the presence of such activity during the medieval and later periods and considerable evidence has been found for the extraction and preparation of raw materials, as well as the necessary tools and equipment for processing and manufacture (Goodall 1993, 174–177). Evidence for copper smelting and working has recently been recorded within the former French Borough to the west of Norwich Castle (Percival and Hutcheson, in prep.), in an area of the city noted for its wide range of metal trades (Kelly 1983, 31). Further evidence for a wide range of related trades comes from the castle's former baileys, notably including a significant mid to late 15th-century assemblage from a castle well (Shepherd Popescu 2009, 654–745). Excavations to the north of the medieval market place at Nos 31–51 Pottergate (149N) indicated the presence of a number of workshops, one of which may have been associated with the production of bronze vessels during the 15th century (Atkin et al 1985, 83). A blacksmith was apparently operating there at the time of a major fire in 1507, although it has been suggested that smithing would not necessarily have been carried out on the premises, but rather on the outskirts of the city (Margeson 1993, 174).

Dugdale records that upon digging the foundation of Skirbeck sluice, near Boston, a smith's forge was discovered with all the tools belonging to it, embedded in silt sixteen feet deep (Watson 1827, 16). Recent excavations at Norfolk Street in King's Lynn have provided important evidence for a medieval smithy, within a clay and timber building similar to those encountered at Market Mews (Cope-Faulkner 2005, fig. 6). Products included drawn wire and fish-hooks, providing a significant assemblage which is as yet unparalleled in Western Europe (Cowgill in Cope-Faulkner 2005, appendix 5). Amongst the similar buildings found at Perth were workshops for metalworking, including one with hearths surrounded by wattle screens, with an associated drain and sluice for water provision (Bowler and Perry 2004, 31).

The most obvious evidence for the fuels utilised at Market Mews is coal, which was found in the flood deposit above Building 5 and within Buildings 6 and 7, the latter being a putative metalworker's workshop. Coal may have been traded, along with iron ore, down trade routes along the east coast of England although the exact source remains uncertain. It was evidently imported to Norwich from the Durham area to fuel a range of metalworking processes until the end of the 14th century (Atkin et al 1985). At Wisbech, coal was certainly imported by boat from the 16th century, when along with cereals, it formed one of the town's major imports (Taylor 1973, 253).

Archaeological evidence for locally sourced fuels and tinder includes straw, chaff, sedges, rushes, twigs and other herbaceous material.

Amongst the metalwork from the Market Mews site there is a general scarcity of personalia, which is not usual in a domestic assemblage and may indicate craft activity although no associated tools were found. The most notable personal item is a seal matrix of 13th-century type, its manufacture in jet placing it in an unusual class (Rogerson and Ashley, Chapter 3.VI). The recovery of two spindlewhorls from the floor of Building 4 offers information about Wisbech's cloth trade (Crummy, Chapter 3.II) and it is possible that fine yarn was being produced from wool or flax. Waste from shoe repairs was found associated with Phase 1 and 2 deposits, most notably in the floor of Building 3.

The faunal remains indicate a meat-based economy, with the lack of neonatal and juvenile elements suggesting that animals were bred elsewhere, probably on surrounding pasture. Both cattle and sheep appear to have reached young adulthood before slaughter. Mutton was the most frequently consumed meat during all periods, with cattle of secondary importance and relatively little pig. The prevalence of mutton links to the marshland economy, which saw sheep reared in large numbers. Evidence of carcase preparation is similar for all species, indicating heavy butchery with large knives or cleavers. The bones apparently represent waste products from preparation and consumption, with some of the larger meat-bearing elements being deposited elsewhere. Much of the meat was probably locally sourced via the Market Place, the Shambles having been constructed in 1591, possibly just to the south of the excavation site (Chapter 1.IV and Fig. 3B). As is common in urban domestic contexts, horse remains were rare at Market Mews, while small mammal species include cat, rabbit, house mouse and pygmy shrew.

Although a wide range of wildfowl is known to have been available locally, evidence for the exploitation of fenland bird species was surprisingly rare at the Market Mews site, although the assemblage is admittedly very small as a result of the limited scale of the investigation. The domesticates include chicken and goose, whilst wild species comprise (?goose), duck, kittiwake and grey heron. Such wild species were hunted in extremely large numbers and their eggs collected. Towards the end of the 12th century, for example, *Liber Eliensis* records that birds such as goose, fig-birds (possibly chiff-chaff or other small species), coots, divers, cormorants, herons and ducks were netted, trapped or caught with bird-lime up to three hundred at a time (Fairweather trans 2005, ii, 105).

Many of the samples taken from deposits at Market Mews contained eggshell, often trampled into floors alongside other debris. Eggs were another key resource collected from the surrounding fens and demand was so great that in the early 16th century an act was passed to restrict the taking of both wild birds and their eggs (Hall and Coles 1994, 138).

Fisheries were valuable commodities during the medieval period and at Domesday, Wisbech was amongst Cambridgeshire's most important fisheries (Darby 1940, 23), being well placed to access both freshwater and marine resources. The vast numbers of fish, particularly eel, caught locally have been noted in Chapter 1.IV. The fish bone assemblage from Market Mews, which spans the 13th to 16th centuries, shows the consistent consumption of herring and eel, the latter abundant in the local freshwater systems, together with pike, perch, salmonids and some cyprinids (Curl and Locker, Chapter 4.II). Marine exploitation appears to have been restricted to shoreline and inshore waters as represented by rays, flatfishes and winter cod. There is no definitive evidence for consumption of fish from deep water fisheries, such as those available at King's Lynn. The bones show little evidence of butchery, while many of the herring bones were burnt. The large bone needle found in Building 1 may have been used in the manufacture/repair of nets or sails.

The plant species recovered indicate a range of local environments indicating exploitation of various resources. These environments include cultivated ground and wasteland, hedges, woodland, pasture and meadow. Localised wet conditions at the site itself are clearly evident including standing water in buildings. While a range of dietary sources is evident, there is no evidence for importation of exotic material in contrast to Ely sites which have shown a more extensive species range (Schlee, Chapter 4.IV). Leguminous crops were grown locally, their preference for heavy soils and relatively salt-tolerant character making them ideal for coastal wetlands (Rippon 2000, 30): at the Market Mews site, peas and beans appear to have been dietary staples.

Taken as a whole, the material recovered from the site generally indicates relatively low status occupation. The ceramic assemblage demonstrates 'conservatism' with a general lack of imports and dominance of local products. Such trends have been noted at other Cambridgeshire sites (Spoerry, Chapter 3.IV).

VII. Towards a Research Framework

Whilst a vast amount of data has now been collated about the development and management of the East Anglian fens by the Fenland Survey project and other analysts, the information contained in this volume provides crucial new evidence for the impact of local environmental conditions — in particular repeated flooding — on life in the medieval urban environment of the fens. This can be set within the framework established for the surrounding area and objectives for future research in both Wisbech and the fen islands can be formulated, building on the work of the Extensive Urban Survey for Wisbech (Cambridgeshire County Council 2002) and feeding into other relevant initiatives. For example, at a regional level it has been suggested that 'the impact of climate change in the medieval period should be further studied; including the development and application of techniques for recording flooded contexts, and identifying the impact of the onset of the Little Ice Age on the economy and settlement of the region' (Medlycott 2011). The fenland towns such as Wisbech will clearly have a significant part to play in such future research.

Although the Market Mews excavation had many limitations, the quantity and quality of environmental data recovered from this small site indicates that there is extremely high potential for obtaining useful information on the past economies and environments of Wisbech. The detailed results from the micromorphological and thin section analysis demonstrate the potential for similar recording at other sites. Both the character of the deposits and the degree of preservation suggest the likelihood that equally significant deposits survive elsewhere within the town. The Market Mews excavation was unable to reach the base of the archaeological sequence — a direct result of its extreme depth and the limited timescale available — and it is likely that preservation will be equally as good or better in earlier deposits. It is to be hoped that there will be future opportunities to excavate larger areas within the centre of Wisbech, and environmental sampling will clearly form an important component of any future work. This will permit the information recovered thus far to be placed more firmly into its local setting, and the development of Wisbech as a whole to be placed more firmly into its regional and historical context, while emphasising its wider links beyond the North Sea to the lowlands of Europe.

Appendix 1: Historic Rains and Floods in England, AD 1300–1550

by John Kington

Chronology

1307: *c.*2 February: wind storm and sea floods affected 'all the English coast'.

1309: floods (January) following a sudden thaw.

1314: wet spell and floods (harvest).

1315: rains and floods (summer and autumn).

1316: rains and floods.

1326: wind storm (winter); port of Dunwich, Suffolk destroyed. However, Lamb (1977) has suggested that this storm had more to do with cliff erosion than with any widespread sea flooding.

1327: rains and floods (northern England).

1330: rains (summer and autumn). There is a complaint from the Bishop of Ely that in this year certain purloiners have made away with the great part of a Whale which had been cast on shore near Wisbech, at a spot where he claims all *ureccum maris* as his sole property.

1334: 23 November: sea floods (Thames).

1335: wet year; sea floods (the Fens).

1338: rains (autumn).

1339: floods (northern England).

1348: wet year with flood; rains (mid-summer to Christmas).

1350: wet summer.

1351: wet summer.

1355: wet summer.

1356: wet summer with floods. A survey of the manor of Wisbech mentions damage from flooding, in some cases from upland waters. The castle and manor house are valued at only £2 and there are many ruinous houses that would cost more to repair than they were worth.

1357: sea floods (Sussex).

1358: rains and floods (northern England).

1362: 24 January; wind storm and floods. This appears to have been one of the most severe storms on record in south-eastern England, comparable to the great storms of November 1703 and October 1987; wet summer.

1364: sea floods (port of Ravensburgh or Ravenspur on Humber mostly destroyed and several other towns lost in Holderness).

1366: wet mid-summer.

1370: wet summer.

1377: floods, (northern England).

1381: floods (southern England).

1382: floods.

1386: floods (West Country).

1389: wet autumn with floods.

1393: floods (September and October).

1395: wet summer.

1396: wet summer.

1398: wet autumn.

1400: wet year; sea floods (Humberside).

1404: 19 November: sea floods (Kent).

1408: floods (northern England).

1409: wet summer.

1413: floods.

1418: north-easterly wind storm; wet summer.

1421: 19 November: sea floods.

1427: rains (Easter to Michaelmas) and floods (southern England).

1428: wet year.

1429: wet summer.

1438: wet summer.

1439: floods (East Anglia); south-westerly wind storm in January; another wind storm in November.

1447: floods on Thames, April.

1450: sea and land floods.

1461: rains and floods (February).

1470: 1 November: sea floods (North sea coasts).

1475: sea floods (towns lost about the Humber).

1477: wet summer.

1481: wet summer and floods.

1482: wet summer.

1483: floods (Wales).

1484: rains (October), with floods on Severn.

1485: floods (Midlands).

1488: floods (Midlands).

1499: wind storm (December).

1500: floods (winter and spring).

Sources and References

Climatic Research Unit Collection of historical weather data

Lamb, H.H., 1977, *Climate: Present, Past and Future*, Volume 2, Climatic History and the Future (Methuen: London)

Notes

1. Calendar dates have been adjusted to the New Style calendar.
2. If river flooding (*e.g.* Thames, 1447) or sea flooding (*e.g.* 1334) cannot be determined, only the term 'floods' is used.

Appendix 2: Micromorphological Data
by Karen Milek and Charly French

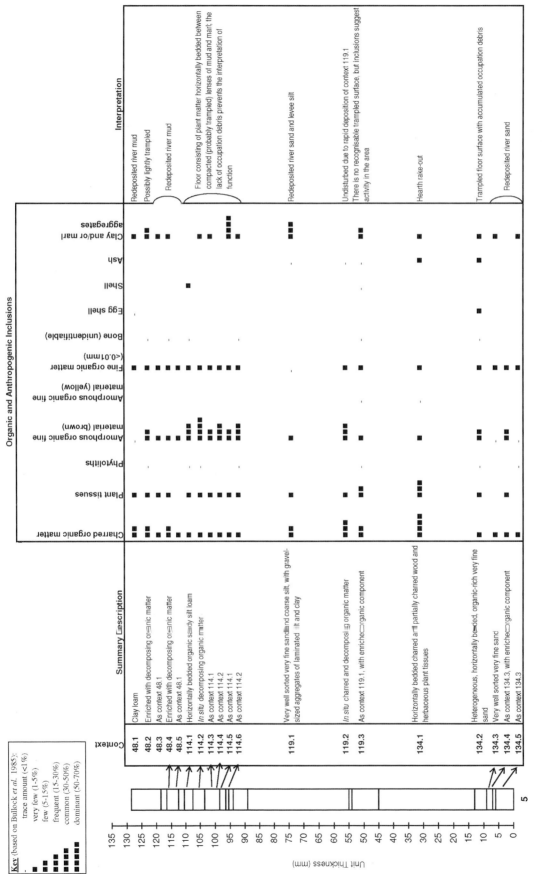

Table App.2.1 Thin Section 5: Summary micromorphology descriptions of contexts 48, 114, 119, 134, including organic and anthropogenic inclusions

88

Table App.2.2 Thin Section 5: Detailed micromorphology description of the mineral component

Thin section	Context	Microstructure	Packing voids	Horizontal planar voids	Channels and vughs	c/f (0.01mm) ratio	c/f related distribution	Medium sand (0.25-0.5mm)	Fine sand (0.1-0.25mm)	Very fine sand (0.05-0.1mm)	Silt (0.002-0.05mm)	Clay (<0.002mm)	Nature of fine mineral material (PPL)	Birefringence fabric (XPL)	Non-laminated dusty clay coatings around grains	Iron staining of fine mineral material	Iron pseudomorphs of plant tissues
5	48.1	vughy			■■	65/35	porphyric	-	■	■■■	■■■	■■■	brown, reddish brown, speckled	mosaic speckled		■	-
	48.2	spongy	■		■■■	65/35	porphyric		■	■■■	■■■	■■■	brown, reddish brown, speckled	mosaic speckled		-	■
	48.3	vughy			■■	65/35	porphyric		■	■■■	■■■	■■■	brown, reddish brown, speckled	mosaic speckled		■	■
	48.4	spongy			■■■	65/35	porphyric		■	■■■	■■■	■■■	brown, reddish brown, speckled	mosaic speckled		-	■
	48.5	vughy			■■	65/35	porphyric		■	■■■	■■■	■■■	brown, reddish brown, speckled	mosaic speckled		-	■
	114.1	complex			■■■	80/20	porphyric	■	■	■■■	■■■	■■	brown, dotted	undifferentiated			
	114.2	spongy			■■■	90/10	porphyric		■	■■■	■■■	■■	brown, dotted	undifferentiated			
	114.3	massive			■■	80/20	porphyric		■	■■■	■■■	■■	brown, dotted	undifferentiated			
	114.4	spongy			■■	90/10	porphyric		■	■■■	■■■	■■	brown, dotted	undifferentiated			
	114.5	massive				80/20	porphyric		■	■■	■■■	■■	brown, dotted	undifferentiated			
	114.6	complex	■		■■	90/10	porphyric		■	■■	■■■	■■	brown, dotted	undifferentiated			
	119.1	intergrain channel	■	■		99/1	chitonic		■	■■■	■■■	■	n/a	n/a	■		
	119.2	spongy			■■	98/2	chitonic	■	■	■■■	■■■	■	n/a	n/a	■		
	119.3	intergrain channel	■■		■■	98/2	chitonic		■	■■■	■■■	■	n/a	n/a	■		
	134.1	spongy	■		■■	95/5	chit; porph	■	■	■■■	■■■	■	n/a	n/a	■		
	134.2	spongy	■	■	■■	95/5	chit; porph	■	■	■■■	■■■	■	n/a	n/a	■		
	134.3	single grain	■■■			98/2	chitonic		■	■■■	■■■	■	n/a	n/a	■		
	134.4	spongy	■■■		■■	98/2	chitonic		■	■■■	■■■	■	n/a	n/a	■		
	134.5	single grain	■■■			98/2	chitonic		■	■■■	■■■	■	n/a	n/a	■		

Frequency class refers to appropriate area of thin section (based on Bullock et al. 1985): - :trace (<1%); ■:very few (<5%); ■■:few (5-15%); ■■■:frequent (15-30%); ■■■■:common (30-50%); ■■■■■:dominant (50-70%); n/a:negligible/not applicable

Frequency class for pedofeatures (based on Bullock et al. 1985): - :trace (<1%); ■:rare(1-2%); ■■:occasional (2-5%); ■■■:many (5-10%)

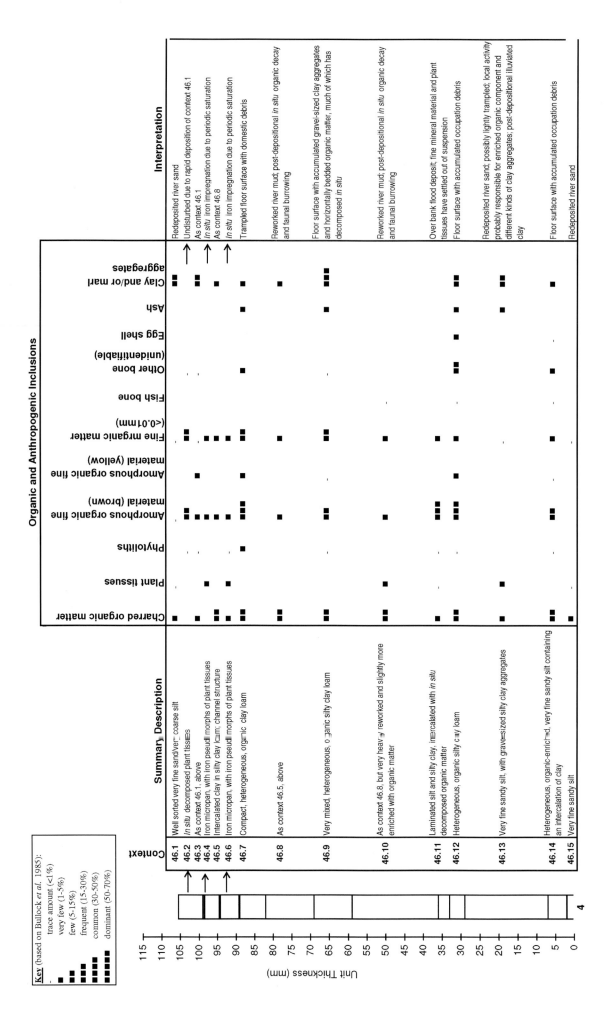

Table App.2.3 Thin Section 4: Summary micromorphology descriptions of layers within context 46, including organic and anthropogenic inclusions

Table App.2.4 Thin Section 4: Detailed micromorphology description of the mineral component

Context	Microstructure	c/f (0.01mm) ratio	c/f related distribution	Nature of fine mineral material (PPL)	Birefringence fabric (XPL)
46.1	single grain	97/3	chitonic	n/a	n/a
46.2	complex	97/3	chitonic	n/a	n/a
46.3	intergrain channel	97/3	chitonic	n/a	n/a
46.4	complex	60/40	close porphyric	reddish brown, speckled	undifferentiated
46.5	channel	60/40; intercalations 10/90	close porphyric; intercalations open porphyric	brown, reddish brown, speckled	granostriated
46.6	complex	60/40	close porphyric	reddish brown, speckled	undifferentiated
46.7	complex	80/20	close porphyric	brown, reddish brown, grey, dotted	undifferentiated; crystallitic
46.8	channel	70/30; intercalations 5/95	close porphyric; intercalations open porphyric	brown, dotted	mosaic speckled
46.9	complex	70/30	close porphyric	brown, reddish brown, dotted	undifferentiated; mosaic speckled
46.10	vughy	70/30; intercalations 5/95	close porphyric; intercalations open porphyric	brown, reddish brown, speckled	mosaic speckled
46.11	complex	30/70	close to single spaced porphyric	brown, yellowish brown, speckled	mosaic speckled
46.12	complex	70/30	close porphyric	brown, reddish brown, speckled	undifferentiated; mosaic speckled
46.13	intergrain channel	97/3	chitonic	n/a	n/a
46.14	intergrain channel	97/3; intercalation 20/80	chitonic; intercalation close porphyric	n/a	n/a
46.15	intergrain channel	98/2	chitonic	n/a	n/a

Frequency class refers to appropriate area of thin section (based on Bullock et al. 1985): -:trace (<1%); ■:very few (<5%); ■■:few (5-15%); ■■■:frequent (15-30%); ■■■■:common (30-50%); ■■■■■:dominant (50-70%); n/a: negligible/not applicable

Frequency class for pedofeatures (based on Bullock et al. 1985): -:trace (<1%); ■:rare(1-2%); ■■:occasional (2-5%); ■■■:many (5-10%)

91

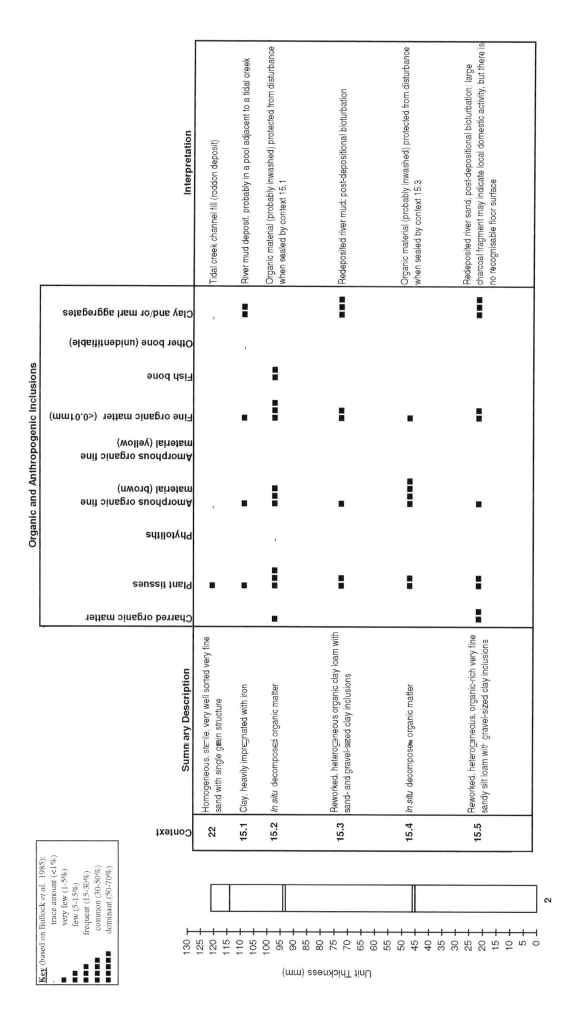

Key (based on Bullock *et al.* 1985):
- trace amount (<1%)
- very few (1-5%)
- few (5-15%)
- frequent (15-30%)
- common (30-50%)
- dominant (50-70%)

Organic and Anthropogenic Inclusions

Context	Summary Description	Charred organic matter	Plant tissues	Phytoliths	Amorphous organic fine material (brown)	Amorphous organic fine material (yellow)	Fine organic matter (<0.01mm)	Fish bone	Other bone (unidentifiable)	Clay and/or marl aggregates	Interpretation
22	Homogeneous, sterile, very well sorted very fine sand with single grain structure		■		-				-	-	Tidal creek channel fill (roddon deposit)
15.1	Clay, heavily impregnated with iron		■		■		■			■■	River mud deposit, probably in a pool adjacent to a tidal creek
15.2	*In situ* decomposed organic matter	■	■■	-	■■		■■	■■			Organic material (probably inwashed) protected from disturbance when sealed by context 15.1
15.3	Reworked, heterogeneous organic clay loam with sand- and gravel-sized clay inclusions		■■		■		■			■■	Redeposited river mud; post-depositional bioturbation
15.4	*In situ* decomposed organic matter		■		■■■		■				Organic material (probably inwashed) protected from disturbance when sealed by context 15.3
15.5	Reworked, heterogeneous, organic-rich very fine sandy silt loam with gravel-sized clay inclusions	■■	■■		■		■			■■	Redeposited river sand; post-depositional bioturbation; large charcoal fragment may indicate local domestic activity, but there is no recognisable floor surface

Unit Thickness (mm)

130 125 120 115 110 105 100 95 90 85 80 75 70 65 60 55 50 45 40 35 30 25 20 15 10 5 0

2

Table App.2.5 Thin Section 2: Summary micromorphology descriptions of layers within contexts 22 and 15, including organic and anthropogenic inclusions

92

Table App.2.6 Thin Section 2: Detailed micromorphology description of the mineral component

Context		Microstructure						Texture								Pedofeatures		
Thin Section	Context	Microstructure	Packing voids	Horizontal planar voids	Channels and vughs	c/f (0.01mm) ratio	c/f related distribution	Coarse sand (0.5-2 mm)	Medium sand (0.25-0.5mm)	Fine sand (0.1-0.25mm)	Very fine sand (0.05-0.1 mm)	Silt (0.002-0.05mm)	Clay (<0.002mm)	Nature of fine mineral material (PPL)	Birefringence fabric (XPL)	Non-laminated dusty clay coatings	Iron impregnation of fine mineral material	Soil fauna excrement (mammilated)
2	22	single grain	■■■		■	95/2	chitonic			■■■	■■■	■	■	n/a	n/a	-		
	15.1	channel	■■■		■■■	40/60	close porphyric			■	■■■	■■■	■■■■	brown, reddish brown, dotted	granostriated		■	■
	15.2	spongy		■	■■■■	70/30	chitonic, close porphyric			■	■■■	■■■	■■■■	brown, dotted	undifferentiated, granostriated			
	15.3	complex	■■■		■■■	60/40	chitonic, close porphyric			■	■■■	■■■	■■■■	brown, dotted	granostriated			
	15.4	spongy	■■■		■■■	90/10	chitonic, gefuric, close porphyric			■	■■■	■■■	■■■■	brown, dotted	undifferentiated, granostriated			
	15.5	complex	■■■		■■■	90/10	chitonic, gefuric, close porphyric			■	■■■	■■■	■■■■	brown, dotted	granostriated	■		■

Frequency class refers to appropriate area of thin section (based on Bullock et al. 1985): -:trace (<1%); ■:very few (<5%); ■■:few (5-15%); ■■■:frequent (15-30%); ■■■■:common (30-50%); ■■■■■:dominant (50-70%); n/a:negligible/not applicable
Frequency class for pedofeatures (based on Bullock et al. 1985): -:trace (<1%); ■:rare(1-2%); ■■:occasional (2-5%); ■■■:many (5-10%)

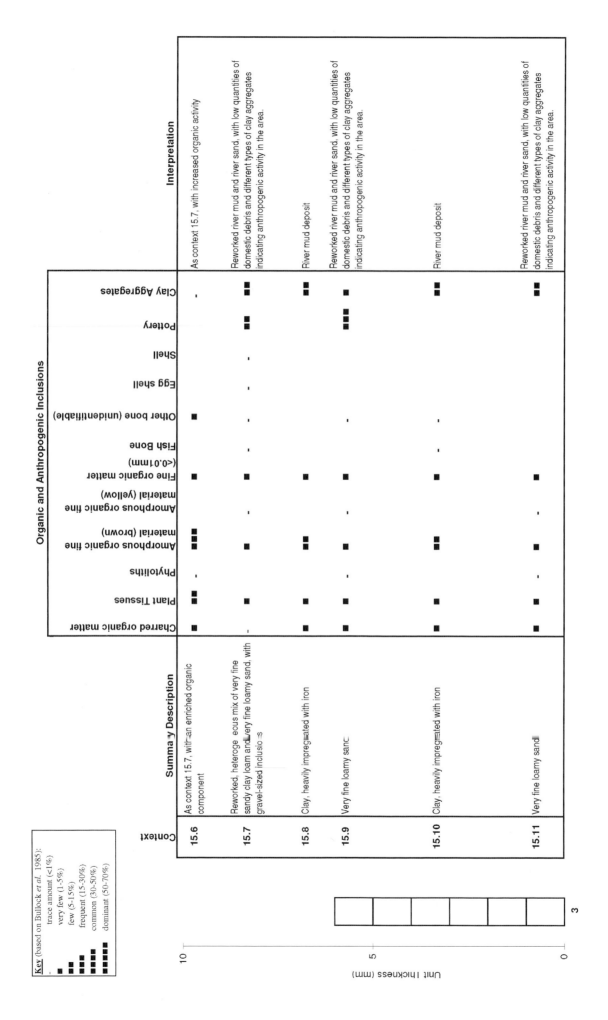

Table App.2.7 Thin Section 3: Summary micromorphology descriptions of layers within context 15, including organic and anthropogenic inclusions

94

Thin section	Context	Microstructure	Packing voids	Horizontal planar voids	Channels and vughs	c/f (0.01mm) ratio	c/f related distribution	Coarse sand (0.5-2 mm)	Medium sand (0.25-0.5mm)	Fine sand (0.1-0.25mm)	Very fine sand (0.05-0.1mm)	Silt (0.002-0.05mm)	Clay (<0.002mm)	Nature of fine mineral material (PPL)	Birefringence fabric (XPL)	Non-laminated dusty clay coatings	Iron impregnation of fine mineral material	Soil fauna excrement (mammilated)	Biogenic calcium carbonate granules
3	15.6	complex	■■	■	■■	80/20	chitonic		■	■	■■■	■■■	■■	brown, dotted	granostriated			■	
	15.7	complex	■■		■■	80/20	chitonic		■	■	■■■	■■■	■■	brown, speckled	granostriated			■■	
	15.8	channel	■■■		■■■	40/60	porphyric	-	■	■	■	■■	■■■	brown, reddish brown, dotted	granostriated	■	■■	■	
	15.9	complex	■■■		■	95/5	chitonic			■■	■■	■	■	brown, speckled	n/a				■
	15.10	channel	■■■		■■■	40/60	porphyric	-	■		■	■■	■■■	brown, reddish brown, dotted	granostriated	■	■■	■	
	15.11	complex	■■■		■■	95/5	chitonic	-	■	■	■■	■■	■	brown, speckled	n/a	■		■	

Frequency class refers to appropriate area of thin section (based on Bullock et al. 1985): -:trace (<1%); ■:very few (<5%); ■■:few (5-15%); ■■■:frequent (15-30%); ■■■■:common (30-50%); ■■■■■:dominant (50-70%); n/a:negligible/not applicable

Frequency class for pedofeatures (based on Bullock et al. 1985): -:trace (<1%); ■:rare(1-2%); ■■:occasional (2-5%); ■■■:many (5-10%)

Table App.2.8 Thin Section 3: Detailed micromorphology description of the mineral component

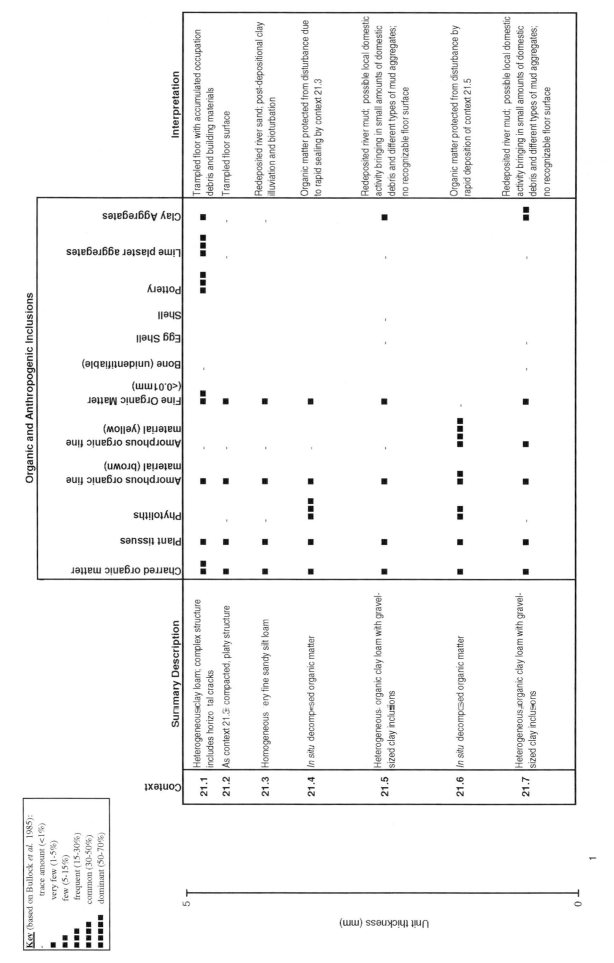

Table App.2.9 Thin Section 1: Summary micromorphology descriptions of layers within context 21, including organic and anthropogenic inclusions

Context		Microstructure						Texture								Pedofeatures		
Thin section	Context	Microstructure	Packing voids	Horizontal planar voids	Channels and vughs	c/f (0.01mm) ratio	c/f related distribution	Coarse sand (0.5-2 mm)	Medium sand (0.25-0.5mm)	Fine sand (0.1-0.25mm)	Very fine sand (0.05-0.1mm)	Silt (0.002-0.05mm)	Clay (<0.002mm)	Nature of fine mineral material (PPL)	Birefringence fabric (XPL)	Non-laminated dusty clay coatings	Iron pseudomorphs of plant tissues	Biogenic calcium carbonate granules
1	21.1	complex	■	■	■■■	75/25	close porphyric, chitonic	■	■	■	■■■■	■■	■■	brown, dotted	granostriated	■		
	21.2	platy		■■	■	90/10	close porphyric, chitonic	-	-	■	■■■	■■■	■■■	brown, speckled	granostriated	■		
	21.3	complex	■		■	90/10	close porphyric, chitonic	-	-	■	■■	■■	■■	brown, speckled	granostriated	■		
	21.4	complex	■		■■■	70/30	close porphyric	-	-	■	■■	■■	■■	brown, dotted	granostriated		-	
	21.5	complex	■		■■■	70/30	close porphyric	-	-	■	■■■	■■	■■	brown, dotted	granostriated	■		
	21.6	spongy	■		■■■	98/2	chitonic	■	■	■	■■■■	■■	■	brown, yellowish brown, dotted	undifferentiated			-
	21.7	complex	■		■■■	70/30	close porphyric	-	-	■	■■■■	■■	■■	brown, dotted	granostriated	■	-	

Table App.2.10 Thin Section 1: Detailed micromorphology description of the mineral component

Bibliography

A. Manuscript and Pictorial Sources

Manuscripts

Accessions Book of Wisbech and Fenland Museum. Photographs and illustrations held in the Wisbech and Fenland Museum collection.

Wisbech Corporation Records: Transcripts and indexes to the Minutes (WTC/31–34). Details as follows:

WTC/31 *Index to the Records of the Burgesses of Wisbech, Compiled and Presented to the Corporation by Revd. Jeremiah Jackson A.M., AD 1819.* Volume 1, 1599–1827. [Jackson compiled the entries for 1599 to 1818 and these were continued by William Watson until 1827. The book is not an index and actually contains extracts from the original minutes]

WTC/32 *Index to the Records of the Burgesses of Wisbech*, compiled by William Watson. Volume 2, 1827–1834. [Again, this book is not an index and actually contains extracts from the original minutes]

WTC/33 *Substance of the Records of the Guild of the Holy Trinity in Wisbech from 1379 to 1540 with extracts of the Proceedings of the Corporate Body from that period to the year 1599.* Translated and Presented to the Corporation by Wm. Watson, Esq., AD 1822. [Guild minutes 1379–1540; Corporation minutes 1564–1599, with additional memoranda]

WTC/34 *Alphabetical Index to the Substance of the Ancient Records of the Guild of the Holy Trinity in Wisbech. And also to the index to the Records made by the Rev. J. Jackson A.M. comprising altogether a Period of 444 years by Wm. Watson, Esq., AD 1823.* [This is the index to books WTC/31–33]

Maps

Plan of Castle estates, detailing southern edge of the Market Place. Untitled and undated, but probably late 18th to early 19th century. Wisbech and Fenland Museum: MIS/612

Plan of Castle estates and premises, surveyed by J. Watte in 1792 at a scale of approximately 80 inches to the mile. Probably drawn up prior to sale of estate. Cambridgeshire Archives: 408/E6

First survey of the whole town of Wisbech by John Wood in 1830. Wisbech and Fenland Museum

Plan of Wisbech by F. Utting in 1850. Wisbech and Fenland Museum

Detailed Plan of the Town Part of the District of Wisbech made for the purposes of the Public Health Act of 1848, surveyed in 1853 by R.W. Dobson and C. Weekes, under the Public Health Act of 1848. Shows the Market Place in detail. Wisbech and Fenland Museum: TMN.650

Map of the Town of Wisbech with New Walsoken reduced from the 1853 Board of Health Map and revised by Charles Mumford, 1867. Cambridgeshire Archives: 1040/P1

Miscellaneous

Wisbech 1820–1920, Manpower Services Commission project in conjunction with Cambridgeshire Libraries

B. Printed Primary Sources

Fairweather, J., (trans) 2005 — *Liber Eliensis* (Woodbridge: Boydell)

Luard, H.R., 1890 — *Flores Historiarum* (London: HMSO)

Luard, H.R, 1872–83 — *Matthaei Parisiensis, Monachi Sancti Albani Chronica majora,* Vol.3, AD 1216 to 1239 (London: Longman)

Swanton, M., (trans. and ed.), 2000 — *The Anglo-Saxon Chronicles* (London: Phoenix)

C. Printed Secondary Sources

Albarella, U., Beech, M., Locker, A., Moreno-Garcia, M., Mulville, J. and Curl, J., 2009 — *Norwich Castle: Excavations and Survey 1987–98. Part III: A Zooarchaeological Study*, E. Anglian Archaeol. Occas. Pap. 22

Alexander, M., 1998 — *Excavation at Forehill, Ely, Post-Excavation Assessment and Updated Project design*, Cambridge Archaeol. Unit Report No. 282 (unpublished)

Allin, C. E., 1981 — *The Medieval Leather Industry in Leicester*, Leicester Museums, Art Galleries and Records Service Archaeological Report No. 3 (Leicester: Leicestershire County Council)

Anniss, G., 1977 — *A History of Wisbech Castle* (Ely: EARO)

Atkin, M. and Evans, D.H., 2002 — *Excavations in Norwich 1971–1978 part III*, E. Anglian Archaeol. 100

Atkin, M., Carter, A. and Evans, D.H., 1985 — *Excavations in Norwich 1971–1978 part II,* E. Anglian Archaeol. 26

Austin, L., 1996 — *Design brief for archaeological evaluation at Market Mews, 1996* (unpublished)

Beresford, G., 1987 — *Goltho: the development of an early medieval manor c. 850–1150,* English Heritage Archaeological Report 4 (London: Historic Buildings and Monuments Commission for England)

Blair, I. and Sankey, D., in prep. — *Roman occupation and drainage, medieval tenements and the Great Fire: excavations at 30–35 Botolph Lane and 13–21 Eastcheap, City of London* (MoLAS Archaeology Study Series)

Bowler, D.P., 2004 — *Perth: the archaeology and development of a Scottish Burgh*, Tayside and Fife Archaeological Committee 4 (Historic Scotland)

Bowler, D.P. and Perry, D., 2004 — 'The medieval and early modern town', in Bowler, D.P., *Perth: the archaeology and development of a Scottish Burgh*, Tayside and Fife Archaeological Committee 4 (Historic Scotland), 21–34

Bradbury, C.W., 1990 — 'Sword pieces', in Biddle, M., *Object and economy in medieval Winchester*, Winchester Studies 7.ii (Oxford: Clarendon), 1080–2

British Geological Survey 1995 — *Wisbech. England and Wales Sheet 159. Solid and Drift Geology*

Brown, P.D.C., 1972 — 'The ironwork' in Brodribb, A.C.C., Hands, A.R. and Walker, D.R., *Excavations at Shakenoak Farm, near Wilcote, Oxfordshire 3* (Oxford: A.C.C. Brodribb), 86–117

Brown, R. and Hardy, A., 2011 — *Archaeology of the Newland: Excavations in King's Lynn, Norfolk 2003–05*, E. Anglian Archaeol. 140

Brown, R. and Hardy, A., forthcoming — *Trade and Prosperity, War and Poverty: an archaeological investigation into Southampton's French Quarter*, Oxford Archaeology

Bullock, P., Fedoroff, N., Jongerius, A., Stoops, G., Tursina, T. and Babel, U., 1985
Handbook for Soil Thin Section Description (Wolverhampton: Waine Research Publications)

Cambridgeshire County Council, 2002
Cambridgeshire Extensive Urban Survey: Wisbech. Draft report 10/05/2002

Cherry, J., 1991
'Seal matrices' in Saunders, P. and Saunders, E. (eds.) *Salisbury Museum Medieval Catalogue Part I*, 29–39 (Salisbury: Salisbury and South Wiltshire Museum)

Clarke, H. and Carter, A., 1977
Excavations in King's Lynn 1963–1970, Society Medieval Archaeol. Monogr. Ser. 7 (London: Society for Medieval Archaeology)

Clarke, S., 1995
'Rubbish in the Floods', *British Archaeology 4*. Accessed 19.11.08

Clifton-Taylor, A., 1972
The Pattern of English Building (London: Faber)

Coles, J.M., and Hall, D., 1998
Changing Landscapes: the ancient fenlands, Wetland Archaeology Research Project Occas. Pap. 13

Cope-Faulkner, P., 2005
Assessment of the Archaeological Remains from Excavations at Norfolk Street, King's Lynn, Norfolk, Archaeological Project Services Report 182/04

Courty, M.A., Goldberg, P. and Macphail, R., 1989
Soils and Micromorphology in Archaeology, (Cambridge: Cambridge University Press)

Courty, M.A., Goldberg, P. and Macphail, R., 1994
'Ancient people – lifestyles and cultural patterns', in Wilding, L. and Oleshko, K. (eds.), *Micromorphological indicators of anthropogenic affects on soils*, Transactions of the 15th World Congress of Soil Science, Vol. 6a, 250–269

Crabbe. G., 1783
The Village, Book 1 (London: J. Dodsley)

Creighton, O.H., 2002
Castles and Landscapes (London/New York: Continuum)

Crummy, N., 1988
The post-Roman small finds from excavations in Colchester 1971–85, Colchester Archaeological Report 5 (Colchester: Colchester Archaeological Trust)

Crummy, N., 2002
'From self-sufficiency to commerce: structural and artefactual evidence for textile manufacture in Eastern England in the pre-conquest period' in Koslin, D.G. and Snyder, J.E., *Encountering medieval textiles and dress: objects, texts, images* (New York/Basingstoke: Palgrave)

Cunningham, C.M., 1985
'A Typology for Post-Roman Pottery in Essex' in C.M. Cunningham and P.J. Drury, *Post-Medieval Sites and Their Pottery: Moulsham Street, Chelmsford*, Counc. Brit Archaeol. Res. Rep. 54, Chelmsford Archaeol. Trust Rep. 5

Darby, H.C., 1940
The Draining of the Fens (Cambridge Studies in Economic History)

Darby, H.C., 1983
The Changing Fenland (Cambridge: Cambridge University Press)

Darby, H.C., 1987
'The Geography of Domesday England', Williams, A., and Erskine, R.W.H. (eds), *Domesday Book Studies* (London: Alecto Historical Editions), 23–36

Dobney, K. and Reilly, K., 1988
'A method for recording archaeological animal bones: the use of diagnostic zones', *Circaea* 5(2), 79–96

Driesch, A. von den, 1976
A guide to the measurement of animal bones from archaeological sites, Harvard: Peabody Museum of Archaeology and Ethnology Bulletin 1

Dugdale, W., 1662
The History of Imbanking and drayning of divers Fenns and Marshes, both in foreign parts and in this Kingdom; and of the improvements thereby (London), 2nd edition edited by Cole, C.N., 1772

Edwards, D. and Hall, D., 1997
'Medieval Pottery from Cambridge: Sites in the Bene't Street — Market area', *Proc. Cambridge Antiq. Soc.* 86, 153–168

Egan, G., 1998
The medieval household, daily living c. 1150–1450, Medieval finds from excavations in London 6 (London: HMSO)

Egan, G. and Pritchard, F., 1991
Dress accessories, c. 1150–1450, Medieval finds from excavations in London 3 (London: HMSO)

Fletcher, T., 2009
Wisbech Castle Defences and Georgian Cellars: Archaeological Investigations at Wisbech Library 2008–2009, Oxford Archaeology East Rep. 1091 (unpublished)

Fletcher, T., in prep.
Archaeological Excavations at Wisbech Castle: a community archaeology project, Oxford Archaeology East Rep. 1137 (unpublished)

French, C.A.I., 1996a
Wisbech, 1996: Micromorphological Assessment of Medieval and Post-Medieval Floor Levels, Cambridgeshire County Council Archaeol. Field Unit (unpublished)

French, C.A.I., 1996b
25–6 Long Causeway, Peterborough: Micromorphological Analysis of Floor Levels in Structure 4, Birmingham University Field Archaeol. Unit (unpublished)

Gardiner, F.J., 1898
History of Wisbech and Neighbourhood during the last 50 Years (1848–1898), (Wisbech: Wisbech Advertiser Office)

Garrard, I.P., 1995
'Other objects of copper alloy and silver' in Blockley, K., Blockley, M., Blockley P., Frere S.S. and Stow, S., *Excavations in the Marlowe car park and surrounding areas*, The Archaeology of Canterbury 5 (Canterbury: Canterbury Archaeological Trust), 1005–62

Gé, T., Courty, M.A., Matthews, W. and Wattez, J., 1993
'Sedimentary Formation Processes of Occupation Surfaces', in P. Goldberg, D.T. Nash and M.D. Petraglia (eds.), *Formation Processes in Archaeological Context*, Monographs in World Archaeology 17

Geddes, J. and Carter, A., 1977
'Objects of non-ferrous metal, amber and paste' in Clarke, H. and Carter, A., *Excavations in King's Lynn 1963–1970*, Society Medieval Archaeol. Monogr. Ser. 7 (London: Society for Medieval Archaeology), 287–91

Geddes, J. and Dunning, G.C., 1977
'Stone objects' in Clarke, H. and Carter, A., *Excavations in King's Lynn 1963–1970*, Society Medieval Archaeol. Monogr. Ser. 7 (London: Society for Medieval Archaeology), 315–47

Getty, R. (ed.), 1975
Sisson, S. and Grossman, J.D., *The Anatomy of the Domestic Animals* (Philadelphia/London: Saunders)

Goodall, A.R., 1984
'Objects of non-ferrous metal' in Allan, J.P., *Medieval and post-medieval finds from Exeter, 1971 1980*, Exeter Archaeological Report 3 (Exeter: Exeter City Council), 337–48

Goodall, A.R., 1992 'Objects of copper alloy' in Evans, D.H. and Tomlinson, D.G., *Excavations at 33–35 Eastgate, Beverley*, Sheffield Excavation Report 3 (Sheffield: J.R. Collis Publications), 138–42

Goodall, I.H., 1990a 'Locks and keys' in Biddle, M., *Object and economy in medieval Winchester*, Winchester Studies 7.ii (Oxford: Clarendon), 1001–36

Goodall, I.H., 1990b 'Iron buckles and belt-fittings' in Biddle, M., *Object and economy in medieval Winchester*, Winchester Studies 7.ii (Oxford: Clarendon), 526–36

Goodall, I.H., 1992 'The iron objects' in Evans, D.H. and Tomlinson, D.G., *Excavations at 33–35 Eastgate, Beverley*, Sheffield Excavation Report 3 (Sheffield: J.R. Collis Publications), 151–61

Goodall, I.H. 1993 'Metalworking' in Margeson, S., *Norwich Households: the Medieval and Post-Medieval Finds from Norwich Survey Excavations 1971–78*, E. Anglian Archaeol. 58

Goodall, I.H. and Carter, A., 1977 'Iron objects' in Clarke, H. and Carter, A., *Excavations in King's Lynn 1963–1970*, Society Medieval Archaeol. Monogr. Ser. 7 (London: Society for Medieval Archaeology), 291–8

Grant, A., 1982 'The use of tooth wear as a guide to the age of domestic ungulates', in Wilson, B., Grigson, C. and Payne, S., (eds.) *Ageing and sexing animal bones from archaeological sites*, Oxford: Brit. Archaeol. Rep. Brit. Ser. 199, 91–108

Grenville, J., 1997 *Medieval Housing* (London/Washington: Leicester University Press)

Hall, D., 1977 '"Roman Bank": A Medieval Sea-Wall, II. The sea bank in Cambridgeshire', *Proc. Cambridge Antiq. Soc.* 67, 66–68

Hall, D., 1996 *The Fenland Project, Number 10: Cambridgeshire Survey, The Isle of Ely and Wisbech*, E. Anglian Archaeol. 79

Hall, D., 2001 'Medieval pottery from Forehilll, Ely, Cambridgeshire', *Med. Ceram.* 25, 2–21

Hall, D. and Coles, J.M., 1994 *Fenland Survey: an essay in landscape and persistence*, English Heritage Archaeological Report 1 (English Heritage)

Hallam, H.E., 1965 *Settlement and Society: A Study of the Early Agrarian History of South Lincolnshire*

Hambelton, E., 2000 'A method for converting Grant mandible wear stages to Payne style wear stages in sheep, cow and pig', in Millard, A (ed.) *Archaeological Sciences 1997. Proceedings of the conference held at the University of Durham*. Brit. Archaeol. Rep. Int. Ser. 939

Harvey, P.D.A. and McGuinness, A., 1996 *A Guide to British Medieval Seals* (London: British Library and Public Records Office)

Hatton, A., 2004 *Archaeological Investigation at Church Terrace, Wisbech*, Cambridgeshire County Council Archaeol. Field Unit Rep. 770 (unpublished)

Healey, R.H., 1975 *Medieval and Sub-Medieval Pottery in Lincolnshire*, Mphil thesis, University of Nottingham (unpublished)

Heslop, T.A., 1987 'Techniques for making seal matrices and impressions' in Alexander, J. and Binski, P. (eds.) *Age of Chivalry*, 396–7 (London: Royal Academy of Arts in association with Weidenfeld and Nicholson)

Hinman, M., 1997 *Medieval and Early Post-Medieval Structural Remains at Market Mews, Wisbech: An Assessment and Post-Excavation Project Design*, Cambridgeshire County Council Archaeol. Field Unit Rep. C001

Hinman, M., forthcoming 'Time and Tide in the Medieval Town', *Proceedings of Interpreting Stratigraphy Conference 11, 2000*, Brit. Archaeol. Rep. Brit. Ser.

Hinton, D.A., 1990 'Belt-hasps and other belt-fittings' in *Object and economy in medieval Winchester*, Winchester Studies 7.ii (Oxford: Clarendon), 3539–42

Holinshed, R., 1577 *Chronicles of England, Scotlande and Irelande.* Vol. III (London)

Hoyland, L., 1992 *Wisbech Market Place, An Archaeological Assessment and Historical Survey*, Cambridgeshire County Council Archaeol. Field Unit Rep. 47

Hurst, J.G., Neal, D.S. and Van Beuningen, H.J.E., 1986 *Pottery Produced and Traded in North-West Europe 1350–1650*, Rotterdam Papers VI (Rotterdam: Gepubliceerd door)

Jennings, S., 1981 *Eighteen Centuries of Pottery from Norwich*, E. Anglian Archaeol. 13

Jensen, S., 1993 *The Vikings of Ribe* (Ribe: Viking Museum)

Kelly, S., 1983 'The economic topography and structure of Norwich c.1300', in Kelly, S., Rutledge, E. and Tillyard, M., *Men of Property: an analysis of the Norwich enrolled deeds 1285–1311*, (CEAS, University of East Anglia), 13–32

King, D.J.C., 1983 *Castellarium Anglicanum*, 2 vols (London: Klaus)

Lamb, H.H., 1977 *Climate: Present, Past and Future*, Volume 2, Climatic History and the Future (London: Methuen)

Little, A., 1994 'The Pottery from Sites 22954 and 24054' in Leah, M., *Grimston, Norfolk The Late Saxon and Medieval Pottery Industry: Excavations 1962–92*, E. Anglian Archaeol. 64, 84–91

Locker, A., 1998 *The Fish Bones from South Street, Boston*, unpublished report for James Rackham, The Environmental Archaeology Consultancy

Locker, A., 2000 'The Fish Remains', in *Austin Street, King's Lynn, 5530 KLY. The Environmental Archaeology Report*, unpublished report for James Rackham, The Environmental Archaeology Consultancy 22–26

Locker, A., 2003 *The Fish Bones from Boston (BSS03)*, unpublished report for James Rackham, The Environmental Archaeology Consultancy

Locker, A., 2004a *The Fish Bones from Holbeach Road Spalding HOLS04*, unpublished report for James Rackham, The Environmental Archaeology Consultancy

Locker, A., 2004b *The Fish Bones from Springfield Road Spalding SSFG03*, unpublished report for James Rackham, The Environmental Archaeology Consultancy

Locker, A., 2009a 'Fish Bones' in Shepherd Popescu, E., *Norwich Castle: Excavations and Historical Survey 1987–98*, 2 vols, E. Anglian Archaeol. 132, *passim*

Locker, A., 2009b 'Fish Bone from Castle Mall', in Albarella, U., Beech, M., Locker, A., Moreno-Garcia, M.,

Mulville, J. and Curl, J., *Norwich Castle: Excavations and Survey 1987–98, Part III: A Zooarchaeological Study*, E. Anglian Archaeol. Occas. Pap. 22, 131–146

Lucas, R., 1993 — 'Ely bricks and roof-tiles and their distribution in Norfolk and elsewhere in the sixteenth to eighteenth centuries', *Proc. Cambridge Antiq. Soc.* 82, 157–162

Luff, R.M. and Moreno-García, M., 1995 — 'Killing cats in the medieval period: an unusual episode in the history of Cambridge', *Archaeofauna* 4

Lysons, D., 1806 — *Magna Britannia* Vol. II, part 1 (London: T. Cadwell and W. Davies)

Macphail, R.I., 1986 — *Soil Report on the Mid-Saxon Floor and Dark Earth at London, Jubilee Hall, Covent Garden, London*, Ancient Monuments Laboratory Report 39/87, Historic Buildings and Monuments Commission for England

Maitland, P. and Campbell, R., 1992 — *Freshwater Fishes* (London: Harper Collins)

Margeson, S., 1993 — *Norwich Households: The Medieval and Post-Medieval Finds from Norwich Survey Excavations 1971–1978*, E. Anglian Archaeol. 58

Matthews, W., French, C.A.I., Lawrence, T., Cutler, D.F. and Jones, M.K., 1997 — 'Microstratigraphic traces of site formation processes and human activities', *World Archaeology* 29(2), 281–308

McCarthy, M.R. and Brooks, C.M., 1988 — *Medieval Pottery in Britain AD900–1600* (Leicester: Leicester University Press)

Medlycott, M., 2011 — *Research and Archaeology Revisited: A Revised Framework for the East of England*, E. Anglian Archaeol. Occ. Pap. 24

Milek, K.B. and French, C.A.I., 1996 — *The Micromorphological Analysis of a Medieval Occupation Sequence and Buried Soils at Forehill, Ely, Cambridgeshire*, Cambridge Archaeol. Unit (unpublished)

Milligan, W., 1982 — 'The Pottery' in Coad, J.G. and Streeten, A.D.F., 'Excavations at Castle Acre Castle, Norfolk, 1972–77', *Archaeol. J.* 139, 138–301

Mortimer, R., forthcoming — *New Inn Yard, Wisbech, Cambridgeshire*, Oxford Archaeology East Rep. 992 (unpublished)

Murphy, C.P., 1986 — *Thin Section Preparation of Soils and Sediments* (Berkhamsted: AB Academic)

Oakley, G.E. and Hall, A.D., 1979 — 'The spindlewhorls' in J.H. Williams, *St Peter's Street, Northampton, excavations 1973–6* (Northampton: Northampton Development Corporation), 286–9

Ottaway, P., 1992 — *Anglo-Scandinavian ironwork from Coppergate*, The Archaeology of York 17/6 (London: Counc. Brit. Archaeol. for York Archaeological Trust)

Ottaway, P. and Rogers, N., 2002 — *Craft, industry and everyday life: finds from medieval York*, The Archaeology of York 17/15 (York)

Payne, S., 1973 — 'Kill-off patterns in sheep and goats, the mandibles from Asvan Kale', *Anatolian Studies* 23, 281–303

Percival, J.W. and Hutcheson, A.R.J., in prep. — *Excavations within the French Borough (between Theatre Street and Bethel Street), Norwich 1998–9*

Pestell, T., 2001 — 'Monastic Foundation Strategies in the Early Norman Diocese of Norwich', *Anglo-Norman Studies* 23, 199–229

Phillips, T., 2008 — *Wisbech Library, Wisbech, Cambridgeshire*, Oxford Archaeology East Rep. 1048 (unpublished)

Pugh, R.B., 1967 — *A History of the County of Cambridgeshire and the Isle of Ely*, Victoria Hist. Co. Engl., Vol. IV (Oxford University Press)

Reading, H.G., (ed.), 1996 — *Sedimentary Environments: Processes, Facies and Stratigraphy*, 3rd edition (London: Blackwell)

Reaney, P.H., 1943 — *The Place-Names of Cambridgeshire and the Isle of Ely*, Vol. 19 (Cambridge: Cambridge University Press)

Rippon, S., 2000 — *The Transformation of Coastal Wetlands* (Oxford: Oxford University Press)

Rogerson, A., 1976 — 'Excavations at Fuller's Hill, Great Yarmouth', in Wade-Martins, P., (ed.), *Norfolk*, E. Anglian Archaeol. 2, 131–246

Rogerson, A. and Ashley, S.J., 1985 — 'A medieval pottery production site at Blackborough End, Middleton', *Norfolk Archaeol.* 39, 181–9

Salzman, L.F., 1952 — *Building in England Down to 1540, A Documentary History* (Oxford: Oxford University Press)

Shepherd Popescu, E., 2009 — *Norwich Castle: Excavations and Historical Survey 1987–98*, 2 vols, E. Anglian Archaeol. 132

Sherlock, D., 1999 — 'Brickmaking Accounts for Wisbech, 1333–1356', *Proc. Cambridge Antiq. Soc.* 87, 59–69

Silvester, R.J., 1988 — *The Fenland Project Number 3: Marshland and the Nar Valley, Norfolk*, E. Anglian Archaeol. 45

Spoerry, P., 1998 — 'The Pottery', in Hinman, M., and Spoerry, P.S., *The Still, Peterborough: Medieval Remains between Westgate and Cumbergate*, Cambridgeshire County Council Archaeol. Field Unit Monogr. 1

Spoerry, P., 2005 — 'Town and Country in the Medieval Fenland', in Giles, K. and Dyer, C., *Town and Country in the Middle Ages*, Soc. Medieval Archaeol. Monogr. 22, 85–110

Spoerry, P., 2008 — *Ely Wares*, E. Anglian Archaeol. 122

Taylor, A., 1977 — '"Roman Bank": A Medieval Sea-Wall, I. A culvert beneath the sea bank at Newton, near Wisbech', *Proc. Cambridge Antiq. Soc.* 67, 63–65

Taylor, C., 1973 — *The Cambridgeshire Landscape: Cambridgeshire and the southern fens*, (London: Hodder and Stoughton)

The Wisbech Society, 1964 — *Annual Report* 25

Thorton, J.H., 1973 — 'A Glossary of Shoe Terms', *Transactions of the Museum Assistants' Group for 1973*, 12, 44–48

Tonnochy, A.B., 1952 — *Catalogue of British Seal-dies in the British Museum* (London: British Museum)

Tylecote, R.F., 1981 — 'The medieval smith and his methods', in Crossley, D.W. (ed.), *Medieval Industry*, Counc. Brit. Archaeol. Res. Rep. 40

Virgoe, R., (ed.), 1989 — *Private Life in the Fifteenth Century: Illustrated Letters of the Paston Family* (London: Macmillan)

Wade, K., 1980 — 'The Pottery' in Wade-Martins, P., *Excavations in North Elmham Park 1967–72*, E. Anglian Archaeol. 9, 413–478

Waller, M., 1994 — *Flandrian Environmental Change in Fenland*, E. Anglian Archaeol. 70

Walker, N. and Craddock, T., 1849 — *The History of Wisbech and the Fens* (Wisbech: Walker)

Walton, P., 1991 — 'Textiles' in Blair, S.J. and Ramsay, N., *English medieval industries* (London: Hambledon), 319–54

Walton Rogers, P., 1997 — *Textile production at 16–22 Coppergate*, The Archaeology of York 17/11 (York: Counc. Brit. Archaeol. for York Archaeological Trust)

Watson, W., 1827 — *An Historical Account of the Ancient Town and Port of Wisbech* (Wisbech: Leach)

Watson, T.S., 1833 — *The History of Wisbech with an Historical Sketch of the Fens and their former and present aspect* (Wisbech)

Wheeler, A., 1977 — 'Fish Bone', in Clarke, H. and Carter, A., *Excavation in King's Lynn 1963–1970*, Society for Medieval Archaeology Monograph Series 7, 403–474

Wheeler, A., 1978 — *Key to the Fishes of Northern Europe* (London: Warne)

Wheeler, W.H., 1990 — *A History of the Fens of South Lincolnshire* (Stamford: Paul Watkins)

Williams, M., 2005 — *Archaeological Evaluation and Watching Brief at Sandyland Street, Wisbech, Cambridgeshire*, Archaeological Project Services Report 118/04 (unpublished)

Woodland, M., 1990 — 'Spindlewhorls' in Biddle, M., *Object and economy in medieval Winchester*, Winchester Studies 7.ii (Oxford: Clarendon), 216–25

Zalaciewicz, J.A., 1985/86 — 'Sedimentological evolution of the Fenland during the Flandrian: problems and prospects', *Fenland Research* 3, 45–49

D. Web sites

http://the-orb.net/encyclop/culture/towns/biography/biolynn.html

http://www.fishbase.org

Fishing in Early Medieval Times: http://www.regia.org/fishing.htm

Index

Illustrations are denoted by page numbers in *italics*. Streets and locations are in Wisbech unless indicated otherwise.

East Anglian Archaeology

is a serial publication sponsored by ALGAO EE and English Heritage. It is the main vehicle for publishing final reports on archaeological excavations and surveys in the region. For information about titles in the series, visit **www.eaareports.org.uk**. Reports can be obtained from:

Oxbow Books, 10 Hythe Bridge Street, Oxford OX1 2EW

or directly from the organisation publishing a particular volume.

Reports available so far:

No.1, 1975 Suffolk: various papers
No.2, 1976 Norfolk: various papers
No.3, 1977 Suffolk: various papers
No.4, 1976 Norfolk: Late Saxon town of Thetford
No.5, 1977 Norfolk: various papers on Roman sites
No.6, 1977 Norfolk: Spong Hill Anglo-Saxon cemetery, Part I
No.7, 1978 Norfolk: Bergh Apton Anglo-Saxon cemetery
No.8, 1978 Norfolk: various papers
No.9, 1980 Norfolk: North Elmham Park
No.10, 1980 Norfolk: village sites in Launditch Hundred
No.11, 1981 Norfolk: Spong Hill, Part II: Catalogue of Cremations
No.12, 1981 The barrows of East Anglia
No.13, 1981 Norwich: Eighteen centuries of pottery from Norwich
No.14, 1982 Norfolk: various papers
No.15, 1982 Norwich: Excavations in Norwich 1971–1978; Part I
No.16, 1982 Norfolk: Beaker domestic sites in the Fen-edge and East Anglia
No.17, 1983 Norfolk: Waterfront excavations and Thetford-type Ware production, Norwich
No.18, 1983 Norfolk: The archaeology of Witton
No.19, 1983 Norfolk: Two post-medieval earthenware pottery groups from Fulmodeston
No.20, 1983 Norfolk: Burgh Castle: excavation by Charles Green, 1958–61
No.21, 1984 Norfolk: Spong Hill, Part III: Catalogue of Inhumations
No.22, 1984 Norfolk: Excavations in Thetford, 1948–59 and 1973–80
No.23, 1985 Norfolk: Excavations at Brancaster 1974 and 1977
No.24, 1985 Suffolk: West Stow, the Anglo-Saxon village
No.25, 1985 Essex: Excavations by Mr H.P.Cooper on the Roman site at Hill Farm, Gestingthorpe, Essex
No.26, 1985 Norwich: Excavations in Norwich 1971–78; Part II
No.27, 1985 Cambridgeshire: The Fenland Project No.1: Archaeology and Environment in the Lower Welland Valley
No.28, 1985 Norfolk: Excavations within the north-east bailey of Norwich Castle, 1978
No.29, 1986 Norfolk: Barrow excavations in Norfolk, 1950–82
No.30, 1986 Norfolk: Excavations at Thornham, Warham, Wighton and Caistor St Edmund, Norfolk
No.31, 1986 Norfolk: Settlement, religion and industry on the Fen-edge; three Romano-British sites in Norfolk
No.32, 1987 Norfolk: Three Norman Churches in Norfolk
No.33, 1987 Essex: Excavation of a Cropmark Enclosure Complex at Woodham Walter, Essex, 1976 and An Assessment of Excavated Enclosures in Essex
No.34, 1987 Norfolk: Spong Hill, Part IV: Catalogue of Cremations
No.35, 1987 Cambridgeshire: The Fenland Project No.2: Fenland Landscapes and Settlement, Peterborough–March
No.36, 1987 Norfolk: The Anglo-Saxon Cemetery at Morningthorpe
No.37, 1987 Norfolk: Excavations at St Martin-at-Palace Plain, Norwich, 1981
No.38, 1987 Suffolk: The Anglo-Saxon Cemetery at Westgarth Gardens, Bury St Edmunds
No.39, 1988 Norfolk: Spong Hill, Part VI: Occupation during the 7th–2nd millennia BC
No.40, 1988 Suffolk: Burgh: The Iron Age and Roman Enclosure
No.41, 1988 Essex: Excavations at Great Dunmow, Essex: a Romano-British small town in the Trinovantian Civitas
No.42, 1988 Essex: Archaeology and Environment in South Essex, Rescue Archaeology along the Gray's By-pass 1979–80
No.43, 1988 Essex: Excavation at the North Ring, Mucking, Essex: A Late Bronze Age Enclosure
No.44, 1988 Norfolk: Six Deserted Villages in Norfolk
No.45, 1988 Norfolk: The Fenland Project No. 3: Marshland and the Nar Valley, Norfolk
No.46, 1989 Norfolk: The Deserted Medieval Village of Thuxton
No.47, 1989 Suffolk: West Stow: Early Anglo-Saxon Animal Husbandry
No.48, 1989 Suffolk: West Stow, Suffolk: The Prehistoric and Romano-British Occupations

No.49, 1990 Norfolk: The Evolution of Settlement in Three Parishes in South-East Norfolk
No.50, 1993 Proceedings of the Flatlands and Wetlands Conference
No.51, 1991 Norfolk: The Ruined and Disused Churches of Norfolk
No.52, 1991 Norfolk: The Fenland Project No. 4, The Wissey Embayment and Fen Causeway
No.53, 1992 Norfolk: Excavations in Thetford, 1980–82, Fison Way
No.54, 1992 Norfolk: The Iron Age Forts of Norfolk
No.55, 1992 Lincolnshire: The Fenland Project No.5: Lincolnshire Survey, The South-West Fens
No.56, 1992 Cambridgeshire: The Fenland Project No.6: The South-Western Cambridgeshire Fens
No.57, 1993 Norfolk and Lincolnshire: Excavations at Redgate Hill Hunstanton; and Tattershall Thorpe
No.58, 1993 Norwich: Households: The Medieval and Post-Medieval Finds from Norwich Survey Excavations 1971–1978
No.59, 1993 Fenland: The South-West Fen Dyke Survey Project 1982–86
No.60, 1993 Norfolk: Caister-on-Sea: Excavations by Charles Green, 1951–55
No.61, 1993 Fenland: The Fenland Project No.7: Excavations in Peterborough and the Lower Welland Valley 1960–1969
No.62, 1993 Norfolk: Excavations in Thetford by B.K. Davison, between 1964 and 1970
No.63, 1993 Norfolk: Illington: A Study of a Breckland Parish and its Anglo-Saxon Cemetery
No.64, 1994 Norfolk: The Late Saxon and Medieval Pottery Industry of Grimston: Excavations 1962–92
No.65, 1993 Suffolk: Settlements on Hill-tops: Seven Prehistoric Sites in Suffolk
No.66, 1993 Lincolnshire: The Fenland Project No.8: Lincolnshire Survey, the Northern Fen-Edge
No.67, 1994 Norfolk: Spong Hill, Part V: Catalogue of Cremations
No.68, 1994 Norfolk: Excavations at Fishergate, Norwich 1985
No.69, 1994 Norfolk: Spong Hill, Part VIII: The Cremations
No.70, 1994 Fenland: The Fenland Project No.9: Flandrian Environmental Change in Fenland
No.71, 1995 Essex: The Archaeology of the Essex Coast Vol.I: The Hullbridge Survey Project
No.72, 1995 Norfolk: Excavations at Redcastle Furze, Thetford, 1988–9
No.73, 1995 Norfolk: Spong Hill, Part VII: Iron Age, Roman and Early Saxon Settlement
No.74, 1995 Norfolk: A Late Neolithic, Saxon and Medieval Site at Middle Harling
No.75, 1995 Essex: North Shoebury: Settlement and Economy in South-east Essex 1500–AD1500
No.76, 1996 Nene Valley: Orton Hall Farm: A Roman and Early Anglo-Saxon Farmstead
No.77, 1996 Norfolk: Barrow Excavations in Norfolk, 1984–88
No.78, 1996 Norfolk:The Fenland Project No.11: The Wissey Embayment: Evidence for pre-Iron Age Occupation
No.79, 1996 Cambridgeshire: The Fenland Project No.10: Cambridgeshire Survey, the Isle of Ely and Wisbech
No.80, 1997 Norfolk: Barton Bendish and Caldecote: fieldwork in south-west Norfolk
No.81, 1997 Norfolk: Castle Rising Castle
No.82, 1998 Essex: Archaeology and the Landscape in the Lower Blackwater Valley
No.83, 1998 Essex: Excavations south of Chignall Roman Villa 1977–81
No.84, 1998 Suffolk: A Corpus of Anglo-Saxon Material
No.85, 1998 Suffolk: Towards a Landscape History of Walsham le Willows
No.86, 1998 Essex: Excavations at the Orsett 'Cock' Enclosure
No.87, 1999 Norfolk: Excavations in Thetford, North of the River, 1989–90
No.88, 1999 Essex: Excavations at Ivy Chimneys, Witham 1978–83
No.89, 1999 Lincolnshire: Salterns: Excavations at Helpringham, Holbeach St Johns and Bicker Haven
No.90, 1999 Essex:The Archaeology of Ardleigh, Excavations 1955–80
No.91, 2000 Norfolk: Excavations on the Norwich Southern Bypass, 1989–91 Part I Bixley, Caistor St Edmund, Trowse
No.92, 2000 Norfolk: Excavations on the Norwich Southern Bypass, 1989–91 Part II Harford Farm Anglo-Saxon Cemetery
No.93, 2001 Norfolk: Excavations on the Snettisham Bypass, 1989
No.94, 2001 Lincolnshire: Excavations at Billingborough, 1975–8
No.95, 2001 Suffolk: Snape Anglo-Saxon Cemetery: Excavations and Surveys
No.96, 2001 Norfolk: Two Medieval Churches in Norfolk
No.97, 2001 Cambridgeshire: Monument 97, Orton Longueville